EYEWITNESS IN THE CRIMEA

George Frederick Dallas

EYEWITNESS IN THE CRIMEA

The Crimean War Letters (1854–1856) of Lt. Col. George Frederick Dallas

sometime Captain, 46th Foot, and ADC to Sir Robert Garrett

Edited by

Michael Hargreave Mawson

Greenhill Books, London

Stackpole Books, Pennsylvania

Eyewitness in the Crimea first published 2001 by
Greenhill Books, Lionel Leventhal Limited, Park House,
1 Russell Gardens, London NW11 9NN
www.greenhillbooks.com
and
Stackpole Books, 5067 Ritter Road, Mechanicsburg, PA 17055, USA

British Library Cataloguing in Publication Data
Eyewitness in the Crimea: the Crimean War letters of Lt. Col. George Frederick Dallas,
1854–1856
1. Dallas, George Frederick – Correspondence   2. Crimean War, 1853–1856   3. Crimean
War, 1853–1856 – Personal narratives, British
I. Title   II. Mawson, Michael Hargreave
947′.0738′092

ISBN 1-85367-450-8

Library of Congress Cataloging-in-Publication Data

Eyewitness in the Crimea: the Crimean War Letters of Lt. Col. George Frederick Dallas,
1854–1856/edited by Michael Hargreave Mawson.
p. cm.
Includes index.
ISBN 1-85367-450-8
1. Crimean War, 1853–1856–Personal narratives, British.   2. Dallas, George Frederick,
b. 1827–Correspondence.   I. Mawson, Michael Hargreave.

DK215.97 .E95 2001
947′.0738′092–dc21

00-066099

Typeset by DP Photosetting, Aylesbury, Bucks
Printed and bound in Great Britain by CPD (Wales), Ebbw Vale

Contents

List of Illustrations

Maps

Plates

Preface

The 137 letters that George Frederick Dallas wrote to his relatives and friends whilst on active service during the Crimean War were firstly transcribed, in great haste, into exercise books, and later written up more neatly and bound into two volumes. At each transcription some errors crept in, and some light editing was carried out by the transcriber. This editing was mostly in the form of blanks being substituted for the names of officers vilified by the author. It has been a rewarding task to identify the officers concerned and reinstate their names in their proper places.

The letters herein reproduced came to me by inheritance. The responses I received to my initial enquiries about their likely historical value led me to believe that they were only of interest as family documents. In fact, the letters 'Fred' Dallas sent home provide a gripping account of the war, as well as reflecting the views, fears and hopes of a career infantry officer of the mid-nineteenth century.

I have now been able to add to the text of my great-great-grandfather's letters an amount of further information as well as introductory chapters and an afterword to provide, I hope, a fuller picture of George Frederick Dallas' life and his service in the Crimea and elsewhere.

'Fred' Dallas' written English is much more 'modern' than that of many of his contemporaries, in that he rarely uses archaic spellings or capitalises nouns; where he does, these words have been left in their original form, as they provide an authentic Victorian flavour to the text.

I should like to take this opportunity to thank the following people, without whom, as the saying goes, this book could never have been written:

John A.H. Mawson, sometime
  Captain, Royal Signals
Charles E.H. Mawson, now
  deceased, Major, Royal
  Signals

Mrs. S.S. Ripley
Mrs. H.W.J.L-R. Haywood,
  now deceased
Major Hugo White, DL, DCLI
  Museum

Major Colin Robins, OBE, MA, late RA, of the Crimean War Research Society (CWRS)

Mr. W.S. Curtis, late RA, of the CWRS

Mr. Rodney Robinson of the CWRS

Mr. Tony Margrave of the CWRS

Mr. Ken Horton of the CWRS

Ms. Megan Stevens of the CWRS

Mr. Tom Muir of the CWRS

Mr. Andrew Sewell, formerly of the CWRS

Mr. Bert Gedin of the CWRS

Mr. Glenn Fisher of the CWRS

Mr. Keith Smith of the CWRS

Mr. Mike Hinton of the CWRS

Mr. David Tibbetts of the CWRS

Mr. Bret Coulson

Mr. Mark Conrad of the CWRS

Mr. John Barham of the CWRS

Mr. Larry Crider of the CWRS

Mlle. Claude Jacir of the Musée de la Légion d'Honneur

Mr. Pete Budek

Mr. Richard Wildman

Miss Frances Dimond, of the Royal Archive, Windsor

Alice, Viscountess Boyd of Merton

Amanda Willis

Lt. Col. Patrick Mercer, MBE, of the CWRS

Mr. John Bilcliffe of the CWRS

Mr. Paul Spencer

Mr. Alasdair Hawkyard, Harrow School

Mr. Clive Morris, 1st The Queen's Dragoon Guards Museum

Major Edward Green, Staffordshire Regiment Museum

Mr. John Sly, of the CWRS and Orders and Medals Research Society (OMRS)

Mr. Alan Harrison, of the OMRS

Captain Tim Ash, MBE, of the OMRS

The Staff of Bedford Central Library

The Staff of the Public Record Office, Kew

The Staff of the National Army Museum

The Staff of the British Library, Oriental and India Office Collection

and many others.

Each and every one of these has provided information, help and guidance in my search for historical accuracy; nevertheless, the responsibility for any errors remains my own.

I must also acknowledge the patient forbearance and support of my wife, Rachel, and my son, Charles. For far too long I have been to them nothing but a figure hunched over a keyboard. As I type these final few words, I am reminded that today is not only the 147th anniversary of the British declaration of the Crimean War; but also the 5th anniversary of my son's birth. Having spent so much time on my ancestor, I shall now spend some time with my descendant. I'm coming, Charles!

Michael Hargreave Mawson. Bedford, March 2001

Of the Family of Dallas

The Dallas family was one of the ancient families of Scotland, tracing its descent from the first hereditary Laird of Dallas Michael, one William de Ripley (fl. 1165–1215). The family was prolific and successful; the branch to which the author of these letters belonged was connected with some of the greatest families in Europe. His Aunt Charlotte was the wife of Admiral Gowan Roberts; his Aunt Magdalene was Countess Blucher von Wahlstadt; his first cousin was to become Viscountess Ashbrook; his second cousin William, also born in 1827, succeeded to the title of Earl Poulett as the sixth Earl; another second cousin married the third Earl of Cottenham.

Another branch of the family had put its roots down in Jamaica and included amongst its members a Speaker of the House of Representatives, the Honourable Samuel Jackson Dallas; Robert Charles Dallas, the friend and biographer of Lord Byron, and Alexander James Dallas. This last emigrated to America shortly after the War of Independence and entered politics, becoming, under President Madison, Secretary to the Treasury and, ironically, Acting Secretary for War for the United States during the War of 1812. His son, George Mifflin Dallas, became Vice-President under President Polk, and gave his name to the Dallas-Clarendon Convention, and the city of Dallas, Texas.

As for the author's immediate family, his paternal grandfather was the Right Honourable Sir Robert Dallas, KC, PC, MP, Lord Chief Justice of the Common Pleas; his paternal grandmother, Charlotte, the daughter of Lieutenant Colonel Alexander Jardine, RA, the founder of the Royal Artillery Institution. His mother was Lucy, daughter of Henry Davidson, JP, DL, of Tulloch Castle, Chief of Clan Davidson. His father, Captain Robert William Dallas, was a veteran of the Peninsular War and of the abortive Walcheren Expedition of 1809.

It is worth examining the life of Fred Dallas' father in more detail, as his experiences, and the friends he made as a young man, were to have a considerable bearing on the careers of his sons.

Walcheren was a farce. Nearly 40,000 men under Lord Chatham

(Pitt the Younger) and Admiral Sir Richard Strachan were embarked to capture Antwerp and the Scheldt, with the twofold aim of opening a third front against Napoleon (his armies were already engaged against the Austrians and in Spain) and of breaking the Continental System, an economic blockade designed by him to starve the British into submission.

The expedition set sail far later in the year than originally intended; the fleet was still in the Channel on 21 July, well into the campaigning season, and over a fortnight after the Austrian armies had been decisively beaten at Wagram.

The port of Flushing was not taken by the British until August, and subsequent vacillations by Chatham enabled Louis Bonaparte and Marshal Bernadotte to reinforce Antwerp, with the consequence that Chatham refused to advance, and in fact withdrew the majority of his forces from Holland, leaving a garrison of 15,000 (including Dallas' regiment, the First Battalion, 9th Foot) on Walcheren Island. A third of them were to die from Walcheren Fever, a form of malarial dysentery. Of a total of approximately 35,000 officers and men who returned to England, 217 officers and 11,296 men were sick. Of these a large number died soon afterwards as a result of the Fever, and the majority of the survivors were broken in health for the rest of their lives. A contemporary medical report stated, 'Men who have suffered from this fever have their constitutions so shattered that their physical power will for the future be materially diminished.' Casualties as a result of enemy action amounted to perhaps 200.

It took the best part of a year for the Regiment to return to strength; once it had, it was immediately sent to rejoin the British Army in the Peninsula. For Ensign Dallas it must have been inspiriting to be returning to the country whence he, as part of Sir John Moore's army, had been driven in January of 1809. Curiously, his Peninsular Medal does not bear a clasp for Corunna, yet there is evidence that he was present.

It is not the function of this brief biographical chapter to describe in any detail the battles and manoeuvres of the Peninsular campaigns from 1810 to 1814; suffice it to say that Dallas took part in the battles of Busaco, Fuentes d'Onor, Salamanca, Vittoria (which marked the beginning of the end for the French in Spain), the bloody storming of San Sebastian, the passage of the Bidassoa and the march through the

Pyrenees and into France. He fought in the battles of the Nivelle and of the Nive, and was severely wounded in December 1813, south of Bayonne.

The 9th was not involved in the last two battles of the Peninsular War, Orthes and Toulouse, as it sailed for Canada. It sailed without Lieutenant Dallas; wounded, it is likely that he returned home. He exchanged later that year to a Captaincy in the York Chasseurs, and thereby hangs a mystery. W.Y. Baldry in an article for the *Journal of the Society for Army Historical Research (JSAHR)* tells us that

> this Regiment was formed in the winter of 1813–14 in the Isle of Wight, from the better class of the deserters from the Army. It was sent to the West Indies in 1814, and was shortly afterwards augmented by a draft of 540 deserters and culprits from the Isle of Wight. After four and a half years' service in the West Indies it was disbanded at Quebec on 24th August, 1819.

In other words, the York Chasseurs was one of a number of penal corps, or 'condemned battalions' in the words of Fortescue, 'to which were relegated all the worst and most desperate characters in the Army...naturally no good officer would have to do with a 'condemned battalion', if he could help it; and the off-scourings of the Army under the sweepings of its officers made up a dismal assembly.' During the three years in which Dallas served with the Regiment, the York Chasseurs took part in the last battle of the Napoleonic Wars, at Guadeloupe, suffering the heaviest casualties of any British Regiment engaged, with ten killed, nine wounded and four missing.

Clearly, in 1814, Dallas had committed some major *faux pas* and had been banished from the 9th, yet he was able to leave his 'condemned battalion' two years prior to its disbandment and by an exchange for a few weeks into the 4th West India Regiment, to rejoin the 9th in May 1817, the Regiment then forming part of the army of occupation in France.

By the Spring of 1818 he had had enough of soldiering, 'being considered incapable of much fatigue by a severe wound' and he exchanged one last time, to a half-pay Captaincy with the 14th Foot. He returned to England, married Lucy Davidson at St. George's, Bloomsbury, and settled down to raise a family.

Their first child, also Robert William, known as Bob, was born the following March, to be followed by Caroline ('Pussy' of the letters) in June of 1820, Henry in September of 1822, Duncan Davidson in August of 1823 and lastly George Frederick in 1827.

Although Robert William Senior was no longer an active soldier, he kept in touch with several friends from his time in Spain, notably Colin Campbell, who had also been a junior officer in the 9th Foot at Walcheren and in the Peninsula, later achieving fame firstly as Major-General Sir Colin Campbell, commanding the defences at Balaklava, and responsible for the 'Thin Red Line', and then in India during the Mutiny as Commander-in-Chief, being elevated to the Peerage as Lord Clyde, and attaining the rank of Field Marshal. William Napier of the 43rd (later Lieutenant General Sir William Napier, KCB, author of the definitive *History of the War in the Peninsula*) was another close friend of the family; many of the letters reproduced in this volume were originally written for his attention. A third was Robert Garrett of the 7th Royal Fusiliers, later Lieutenant General Sir Robert Garrett, KCB, KH, KLH. (A guide to all persons mentioned by Fred Dallas in his letters can be found on p.283 of this volume.) These friends were to play major roles in the lives of his children.

The eldest son had an undistinguished military career, serving with the 2nd Dragoon Guards, the Queen's Bays, for fourteen years without once having heard a shot fired in anger. He retired as a Captain, settled down and married Emily Florence Earle, the sister of Arthur Maxwell Earle of the 57th West Middlesex.

The second son, Henry, joined the 98th (Prince of Wales's) Regiment in 1842; its commander being his father's old friend, Lieutenant Colonel Colin Campbell. By June of that year the young Ensign Dallas, together with the rest of the regiment, had joined the expeditionary force in China.

On 21 July 1842, Henry Dallas took part in his first and only battle, the assault on Chin-kiang-foo, where the 98th particularly distinguished itself, capturing a Chinese dragon banner which can still be seen at the regimental museum of the Staffords. The Chinese were routed, but the Chinese were not the most formidable enemy that the soldiers of the 98th had to face. Dressed in the standard European-issue uniform, the men of the 98th suffered extremely from the heat. To quote Lieutenant General Lawrence

Shadwell, then also an Ensign in the 98th, 'Many men were struck down by the rays of that terrible sun', in fact thirteen men perished on the spot. Amongst those afflicted was Colin Campbell, who 'happily rallied under the timely influence of a little brandy administered by a brother officer, Ensign H. Dallas, who died of fever at Hong Kong in 1843, [actually, 1844] and whose memory is affectionately cherished by such of his brother officers as survive him.' Henry Dallas must have been a remarkable man for such a warm tribute to be paid him by an officer writing 37 years later. Shadwell, it should be remembered, had almost certainly never met him before he joined the regiment in 1842, two years before his death.

The third son, Duncan Davidson Dallas, was not destined for a military career; he died in infancy in 1830.

It was left to the youngest son to fulfil his father's thwarted military ambition.

Of the Author of the Letters

The author of these letters, George Frederick Dallas ('Fred') was born in 'Edgware, Hertfordshire' on 3 April 1827, the fourth son of Captain Robert William Dallas and his wife Lucy, née Davidson.

It is possible that the names of George III's two sons, George, Prince Regent, and Frederick, Duke of York, were bestowed on the child in the hope of some material advantage accruing to him from Royal patronage. As far as can be ascertained, no such benefit was ever gained.

The two names were not particularly auspicious for a boy destined to be a soldier. The Prince Regent was largely responsible for the politicking at home that so distracted and discommoded the Duke of Wellington in the Peninsula in 1810. Frederick Augustus, Duke of York, as commander of the British forces in the Dutch campaign of 1794, had presided over one of the worst debacles in British military history.

> The grand old Duke of York,
> He had ten thousand men,
> He marched them up to the top of the hill,
> And he marched them down again.

Elizabeth Longford, writing on Wellington, who was in the Duke of York's army as Lieutenant Colonel of the 33rd, summarised the campaign from Wellington's point of view, 'He saw the effects of a divided command, of a winter campaign in a bitter climate, of no properly organised food supply or winter clothing ... [he] ... "learnt what one ought not to do..."'

It is instructive to compare this description of the campaign of 1794 in Holland with the realities of Crimean campaigning sixty years later – independent commanders of the British and French armies unable to agree on tactics; British cavalry commanders divided and not talking to each other, the freezing, melting, freezing conditions in the camp before Sebastopol in the dying months of 1854, the often non-existent food supply, the winter clothing which did not arrive until the late Spring of 1855.

At least Lord Raglan did not put his troops through the fruitless marching and counter-marching that gave rise to the popular nursery-rhyme that came out of the Dutch campaign. But we anticipate; let us return to the infant Dallas.

Fred was educated firstly at Mr. Allfred's Preparatory School in Tunbridge Wells, then at Harrow from January 1842. His marks (from December 1843) show him as being slightly more than halfway down his class. He did, however, excel at cricket, playing for the Harrow XI at Lords against both Eton and Winchester, batting at No. 7 and taking a wicket in each match. Harrow won on both occasions.

Fred left Harrow in 1844 and on 16 May 1845 was gazetted Ensign, by purchase, in the 46th, South Devonshire, Regiment of Foot, commanded by Lieutenant Colonel Robert Garrett, the friend of his father since Peninsular days. When Fred bought his commission the main body of the 46th was in Halifax, Nova Scotia; consequently he was attached to the depot battalion, joining the rest of the regiment when it returned to Dover on 8 May 1848. Just over a week before his regiment came home he had been gazetted Lieutenant, by purchase. He turned 21 the same month.

During the next few years, the young Lieutenant Dallas was to serve in Liverpool, Chester, Hull, Preston and Manchester. In 1852 the regiment left Manchester for Belfast, and went from there to Dublin, and then Kilkenny – all in the space of about a year. The regiment was not even destined to remain for long at Kilkenny, and by the early part of 1854 was back in England, at Windsor. It was here that the notorious scandal over the behaviour of two of the regiment's officers, Lieutenants Perry and Greer came to light.

The following passage is taken from *The Murder of a Regiment*, by Major Colin Robins (Withycut House, 1994).

Excessive 'ragging', to the point of bullying, of one officer by his colleagues was unfortunately not unknown in the Victorian army and Perry, goaded repeatedly by Greer, eventually attacked his tormentor with a silver candlestick. His Court Martial followed, but from the first day, to the irritation of the court, there was intense public interest in the case, and *The Times* gave a full report of proceedings, and printed several very critical leading articles. The case became a *cause celebre*. A defence fund was set up for Perry, for the public view was that he was not the villain of the piece, and Greer was also then court-martialled. The Queen did not confirm the proceedings, and despite public outrage at the perceived injustice, Perry was then court-martialled on another charge. Finally both officers were required to ... leave the regiment.

Perry was cashiered but was allowed to sell his commission; Greer was 'requested' to sell out.

The Courts Martial, and the hypocrisy and snobbery of many of the officers in the regiment which became public as a result of them, ruined the reputation of the regiment almost overnight. Whilst Dallas himself was not called as a witness, and was accused of nothing, several of his closest friends in the regiment, particularly Lt. Col. Garrett and Major Colin Campbell (no relation to the future Lord Clyde), had apparently behaved appallingly badly.

Perry, having left the regiment, moved to Paris and lived a life of debauchery on the proceeds of the public appeal for his defence. The regiment was probably very glad to be rid of him.

Maxwell Earle, one of the Brigade Majors of the 4th Division in the Crimea wrote in November 1854, 'The 46th are no worse than was represented. Indeed Dallas and Garrett Jnr. are the best and only good fellows among them – they are badly disciplined and have no *ésprit de corps*.'

As war with Russia became more and more likely, the majority of regiments destined to make up the Army of the East were shipped out. Not so the 46th; the Courts Martial continued, and officers were required in England to give evidence. The 46th left for the Crimea, not as a regiment, but in three separate units; the first two companies under Captains O'Toole and Hardy left at the end of July; a second, much smaller unit, under the command of Lieutenant Dallas left on 9 August, to act as a guard of honour to the commander of the 4th Division, Lieutenant General the Honourable Sir George Cathcart, KCB, recently returned from duties at the Cape. The remainder of the regiment did not leave until 14th October. The story of the two years that followed is told in the letters that form the body of this work.

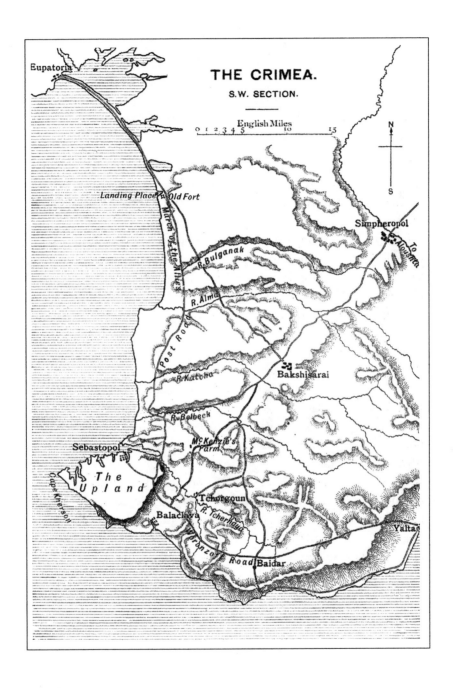

The Crimean Theatre of War. (*Wood, The Crimea in 1854 and 1894*)

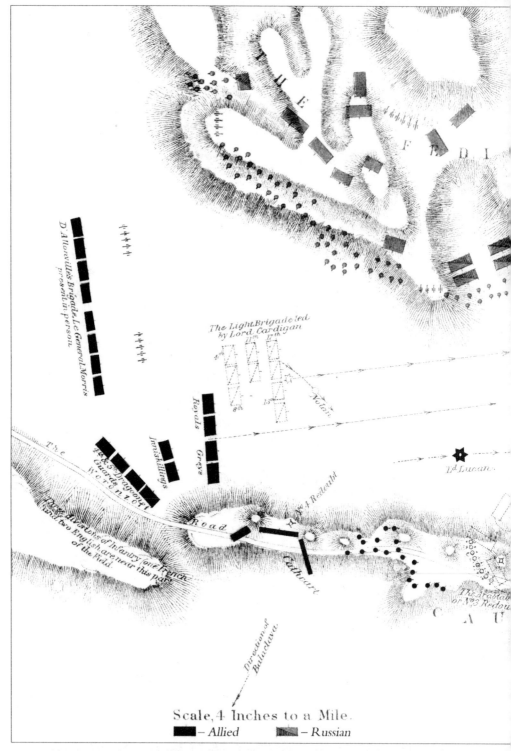

The Battle of Balaklava. Cathcart's 4th Division watches as the Light Brigade charges the Russian guns. (*Kinglake, The Invasion of the Crimea, Vol IV*)

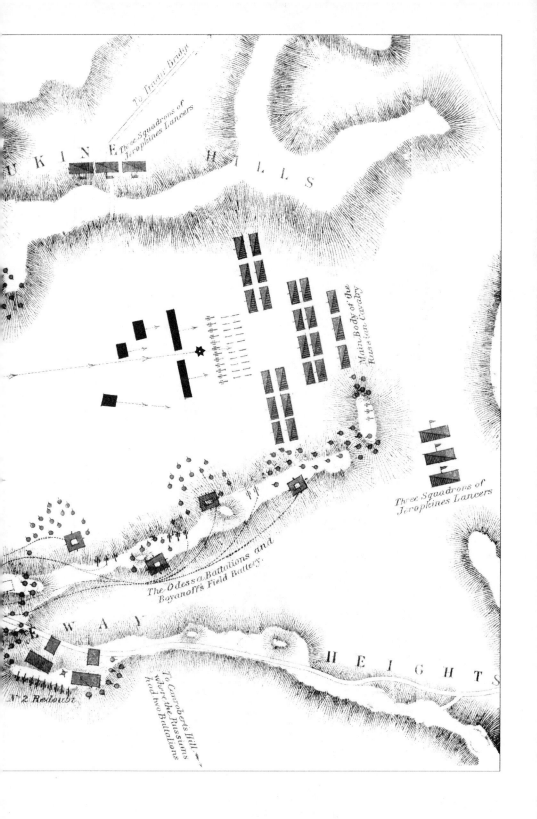

To Tractir Bridge

Three Squadrons of
Jeropkines Lancers

UKINE HILLS

Main Body of the
Russian Cavalry

Three Squadrons of
Jeropkines Lancers

The Odessa Battalions and
Boyanoff's Field Battery

No 2 Redoubt

To Canroberts Hill
where the Russians
had two Battalions

WAY HEIGHTS

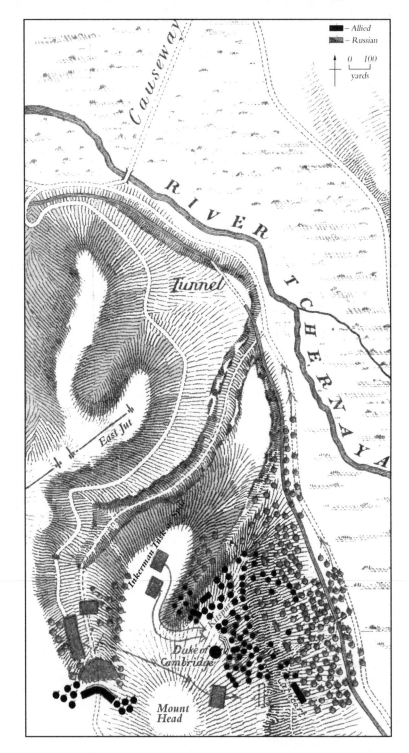

The Battle of Inkermann. Dallas accompanies Sir George Cathcart down the slope of the Kitspur. (*Kinglake, The Invasion of the Crimea, Vol V. Additions by Michael Hargreave Mawson*)

The Letters

Part One
1854

'There is one universal feeling of disgust throughout the whole Army at this murder, for it can be called nothing else.'

Letter 1

The *Harbinger*, Plymouth, 10 August

I am as comfortable on board as one can be on any ship, having a little cabin to myself, and the vessel not being at all crowded. My fellow passengers are nice and friendly. The old General [Cathcart] seems a jolly old fellow and the Staff all good fellows too. We don't know where we are going or rather what is the end of our journey, but we shall touch at Malta probably and at Constantinople & in all probability go on to Varna without delay, but nobody seems to know. This does not seem a very fast vessel, and I should say, if full of passengers a very incommodious one, but as we only half fill it, it is very nice. We take in an Admiral Stopford at Plymouth, and then the expedition will consist of an Admiral, two Generals, three Colonels, two Captains, a Lieutenant & 30 men.[1]

Letter 2

On Board the *Harbinger*, 15 August

We got to Plymouth sometime on Thursday night, at least I found myself anchored there on Friday morning. We dawdled about waiting for a crew who did not all come even at last and for an old Admiral Stopford who did, & for £100,000 in little Boxes & a Commissary [Coppinger] to take care of it, until the evening when we started with the wind in our teeth, and made very little way for 24 hours. Since then we have been travelling well and now we are just off the South coast of Oporto having lost sight of the coast of Spain which we enjoyed all yesterday.

My fellow passengers seem nice gentlemanly fellows but not jolly. The two I like best have been so dreadfully ill they can scarcely crawl. The General [Cathcart] I like best of them all and there is a very

---

[1] The other passengers were: General Torrens, Colonel Windham, Lt. Col. Seymour, Lt. Col. Maitland, Capt. A. Greville, Capt. Smith. According to the unpublished diary of Lt. Nicholas Dunscombe, 46th Regiment, the detachment commanded by Dallas was General Cathcart's Guard of Honour, and travelled from Windsor to Southampton on the morning of 9 August 'to embark on board the Harbinger for Turkey'.

pleasant Colonel Windham. On the whole I don't find it quite so cheery as I ought but I have not a single friend whom I had ever seen before I came on board and all the younger ones are just back from the Cape and are entirely wrapt up in it and their expedition there and comparing notes with one another which is not very amusing for me.

August 16th. We have been getting along very satisfactorily, wind and weather in our favour. Today we passed Cape St. Vincent at about 10 A.M. a most beautiful rugged coast: great bluff rocks right down into deep water. Last night we came along splendidly and I was up on Deck at 12 and most exhilarating it was: a very strong breeze dead in our favour, every sail out & the screw working her best, we literally tore thro' the water. Today is certainly hot, the wind gone down and the sea like glass.

I have been amusing myself drawing and have made satisfactory portraits of my fellow passengers, Sir George Cathcart at their head, as he has a very singular face. I made a very good one of him and am going to make a regular series of all the notabilities I come across. I have also done a good one of our Interpreter [Chekib] a very clean looking Turk who is great fun trying to learn English, French being his language, and who is dreadfully ill on all occasions. He was charmed with my drawing of him but said he was certain he was not a good colour. He was pea-green, I must tell you, when we picked him up at Southampton. He promised to look better in a day or two when I am to do a picture of him for, he tells me, a very beautiful woman who lives in what he calls 'La Forêt de St Jean' London.

I will continue this tomorrow; no land in sight but a most curious mirage: ships, completely topsy turvy, quite plain, apparently running about on the tips of their masts. We have seen one or two sharks, at least their horrid fins. All these things are as new to me as to you so I don't mind writing about them.

18th. I am sorry to say our Voyage has not continued so successfully. Yesterday morning we had come in sight of Africa with a very heavy wind in our teeth & we made little way all day. At night we attempted to go thro' the Straits but the wind increased to a Gale & after hours of fighting against it & making no way we were driven back into the Atlantic again. Luckily the wind is blowing dead off the shore but it is rather increased than otherwise in violence and we are drifting about at the mercy of winds and waves. The ship is behaving very well but no ship in the world could make head against such a hurricane & as she is making no way, of course the helm has no power over her. I can't see when we are to get thro' the Straits, certainly not till the wind changes. At present you could not conceive a more dreary sight than the scene on Deck; the sea one great boiling mass of foam and, what seems so odd to a Landsman, the very force of the wind prevents the waves getting much larger than they are at present and that I can assure you is large enough for me as our great ship is tossing about like a little open boat. It is rather disgusting having arrived at the mouth of the Straits yesterday close to 'Cape Spartel', a wild looking mountainous Coast of Africa, and being at least 20 miles out in the Atlantic now and quite at the mercy of the wind for the Ship will now hardly steer at all and the wind is rising if possible every minute; so different a wind too from our East Wind you cannot conceive, a very hot sticky wild wind it is in these latitudes. I got up last night at about 2 o'clock to see what was doing and really enjoyed a fine sight, a beautiful starry night, the sea one sheet of foam, the great African Hills close to our windward side and the poor ship groaning and straining every plank in her yielding only inch by inch to the gale.

19th. At last we are progressing. We had a dreadful night, the wind blowing harder than ever, but towards morning it abated and we have been able to beat up slowly from side to side of the Strait and Gibraltar is coming in view. Both the coasts are lovely, the African coast quite beautiful. There is a mountain we are now opposite I think the grandest I ever saw, rising almost straight from the sea and the top of it crowned with a heavy mass of clouds. I intend this to be posted in Gibraltar if we have time. We have been now 3 days doing about 30 miles and you may conceive the annoyances of the General, Admiral & others on board who are in an immense hurry to get to Turkey.

P.S. Malta 26th. We got here last night about 12 o'clock and start again at 10 tomorrow so I have no time to write or do anything. You have doubtless later news from Turkey than any I can give you. Varna they say is burnt down[2] and that is all the news they have here.

---

[2] A fire, believed to have been set by pro-Russian Greeks, broke out in Varna on 10 August, destroying a great deal of British and French materiel as well as devastating a large area of the town.

Letter 3

The *Harbinger*, 30 August

We are now just opposite the lovely island of Mytilene[3] having had a really most charming voyage from Malta as regards the scenery and weather but a shockingly slow one. We are now about 60 miles from the entrance of the Dardenelles. You cannot conceive anything more beautiful than the groups of islands that we have been journeying among with occasional views of the Morea.

The weather the day we were at Malta was certainly roasting, in fact the inhabitants told us it was as hot as it ever was there. It is the most charming glittering place you can conceive, the streets steep and occasionally in flights of steps and the colouring tho' perhaps painfully bright most variegated, the people's dress so picturesque, the houses so Italian and quantities of fruit stalls littering the streets. The island itself at this time of year sadly wants vegetation & looks utterly burnt up but I cannot conceive a more delightful Winter residence. We were only there a few hours and did not I am sorry to say hear very good news from the seat of war. You probably know more about it than we do.

We expect to stop in Beicos Bay about ten miles beyond Constantinople where the Division will probably be concentrated before we go on to Varna; of this we are not certain but expect to find orders for us at Constantinople, where we shall probably arrive the day after tomorrow. The weather since we left Malta has become very pleasant and cool tho' the wind is unfortunately straight in our teeth. If we were not in such a hurry to arrive we should not mind going slowly for the most beautiful islands seem to start up every time we look up. We have had no sickness on board notwithstanding the tempting variety of fruit in Malta of which we all partook more or less. We have now been 21 days from Southampton, the *Himalaya* would have taken us in 14 days to Varna! Our only consolation is that there does not seem anything done there, and the health of the troops is indifferent which will probably cause us to remain in Beicos Bay.

31st August. We entered the Dardenelles this morning at about 8 A.M. The entrance is not so striking as I expected, the land not being

---

[3] Mitilini is now a town on the Island of Lesbos in the Aegean, and was then the name of the entire island.

very pretty on either side and the 2 forts of Europe and Asia insignificant. We went close to the Europe side and could see a Turkish Village, cemetery, mosques, quantities of small vessels in the Port full of Turkish, Egyptian and other foreign soldiers. We passed a French Man of War almost touching her, so near indeed that the Officers all took off their hats. The voyage since then has been quite charming; the Asia coast now beautifully cultivated & mountainous. I have just come down from looking at the spot where Leander and Lord Byron swam across from Sertos to Abydos. Turkish forts are dotted along each coast most picturesquely and the ships all full of Grecian looking sailors and soldiers. We shall soon get to Gallipoli and then we shall have open sea again. We have passed many transports full of soldiers who shriek out the most singular cheers to us and point with their naked arms to Constantinople. The whole thing is quite Eastern: occasional camels we see on the shore and droves of cattle and all the men in Fez's with bare brown legs and arms.

Constantinople Sept 1st. Arrived this morning, but unfortunately there was a fog over the Town which much disappointed us; now that it has cleared off all looks very beautiful. However to more important matters: we go on to Varna direct from here in an hour or two. Then the whole force will embark for the Crimea, so, thank heaven, we are in time. Everyone is in great delight at this as we were afraid we should be too late – and it has been a very near thing. We have bad accounts of the health of the troops at Varna but the Crimea is healthy & the great object of occupying the men's time & minds will be effected, so much does the health depend on the spirits on these occasions. The men were getting depressed at the prolonged inaction combined with sickness. The French have suffered very much more than we have. You must not believe all you read in the papers.

Letter 4

The *Harbinger*, Varna, 3 September
We arrived here yesterday morning and a more exciting scene one cannot conceive, the place itself a pretty picturesque Bay with wooded coasts & about 500 sail in it all ready with steam up and crowded with men to embark for the Crimea. We first passed a very fine Ship

covered with some Regiment (I don't know what) who gave a cheer or rather a yell, that made our hearts leap and then we anchored, curious to relate, exactly opposite a Ship in which were my other two Companies. It is decided that we go to the Crimea to take, or rather try to take Sebastopol. As to the plan of operations, of course I, in my humble capacity, know nothing, but all the troops are embarked & half of them at the rendezvous of Baltzic Bay. The remainder sail tomorrow and I expect by Wednesday we shall all be there. A more magnificent and thrilling sight cannot be imagined than this splendid force all ready to go on such an expedition, the Bay crowded with the finest ships and the ships full of the finest troops probably in the world. This decision of attacking Sebastopol has probably been hastened by the dreadful mortality among the troops and the consequent depression both mental and physical of the survivors.

The loss by Cholera I can give you no account of, but it has been very considerable and the general appearance of the troops we find here very haggard, but full of joy & spirits at the thought of exchanging their wretched quarters where they have buried so many of their comrades for active service. The Cholera has abated now. We have only lost one man but there is a sad account of officers on the list.

We are all, as who could help being, full of enthusiasm. If the contemplated coup-de-main succeeds it will be the most brilliant affair ever heard of, but we all cannot help looking forward with somewhat more serious thoughts to the events of the next week. The Army consists of 24,000 English & 20,000 French. Whether the first struggle will take place on landing or afterwards we cannot tell. We are to land with no baggage, a blanket on our backs & 3 days food so that whatever takes place must be decided quickly. My impression is that we shall succeed but Heaven knows how many will remain to tell of it. However I cannot be too thankful for having arrived at this moment just in time for the expedition and without being obliged to land or stop at all on this deadly Coast. I will write again if I can before we attempt the landing which I believe is to take place about 10 miles from Sebastopol. I went on shore today and saw the town (Varna) where it was burnt down, at least a very considerable portion of it. The whole place was crowded with troops of all sorts, French, English, Turks, of whom, by the way, we take 10,000 I am told. I never saw so picturesque a scene. I saw a good many old friends all looking sick and thin. Jack Dallas was embarking but I shall probably meet him and many others in the Crimea.

I trust my next letter will have glorious news.

Letter 5

The middle of the Black Sea, 11 September

We started from Varna on the 5th. for Balzick Bay about 10 miles off where we again stopped for all one day and then started and sailed, we imagined, for Sebastopol. We cast anchor in the middle of the sea entirely out of sight of land the day before yesterday and here we still are just as near as when we started. I can only write our different opinions about our destination as we, & I think I may include Sir George Cathcart, know nothing. We are now under orders to sail. We are lying about 50 miles from Odessa and 100 from Sebastopol; the weather quite delightful, a cool breeze and lovely sun and sky. It is a most singular and curious sight, such an enormous fleet about 1000 sail all quietly anchored in the middle of a sea out of sight of land, that being in itself a most remarkable occurrence & in a Sea too where no force of the kind ever was. It seems as if Providence favoured our designs for we have had an almost uninterrupted calm ever since we have been here – the slightest gale would have utterly dispersed us anchored as we are in 30 fathoms of water. At night, it is a most singular beautiful and impressive scene, such an enormous armament all lighted up with the brightest full moon streaming upon us. Every side one looks one can see nothing but ships and such ships. Close to us is the *Trafalgar* that we saw launched some years ago, the *Himalaya*, the *Golden Fleece*, that we ought to have come out in, and of course hundreds of others whose names I don't know. Each division has a distinguishing flag so that we can at once see what Division each ship contains, and at night they all carry lamps. All the bands play generally in the evening; the more I look around and reflect about it the more astounding a Spectacle it appears. Including ships crews etc. etc. etc. about 100,000 men waiting in the middle of the Black Sea to be told where to go & no one appearing to know where that may be. One rumour is Odessa and to reasonable people it seems to be the best; that such a place as Sebastopol can be taken in 3 days seems hopeless, and all we know is we are to land with 3 days' provisions and 1 blanket apiece; & very cold by the way it will be as the nights are now rather biting. The health of the troops is improved. We ourselves have had no sickness, but the ship on which my other 2 Companies are have lost several since we left Balzick.

13th September. Still the *Harbinger*. We have been hanging about some time ever since the 11th waiting for each other and I think wasting time. We are now on the Coast of the Crimea, we fancy Eupatoria, and are skirting along in the direction of Sebastopol. Where we are to land we don't know and of course it will depend on circumstances. We see no soldiers as yet & no Barracks or Forts of any kind. It is blowing pretty fresh in our favour and I think we shall all be together by the Evening. Last night we anchored about 12 miles off the shore, very dark & in very deep water. Going on deck we could hardly believe we were not in the middle of some highly lighted Town. There was a long continuous line of lighted ships for I should say 2 or 3 miles. It was more like a view from one of the London bridges at night than anything else.

Letter 6

The Crimea, 16 September

We landed quite unopposed the day before yesterday on a sandy strip of land which you will find existing on the map 10 miles beyond Eupatoria between the sea and a salt lake, a most desolate place.[4] We have had one or two nights of as good (or bad) roughing it as you can well conceive. The first night it poured so we were completely wet through in about 5 minutes trying to sleep on the sand and a cold wind blowing. Last night it was very dreadfully cold and we have only a blanket each and no baggage of any description. We are now waiting for the landing of the Cavalry which presents some difficulties owing to the abrupt shore and an almost constant swell. We shall not I think be able to get on before the day after tomorrow. About the

---

[4] The landing took place on a narrow spit near to the salt lake at Kamishlu. Nearby was a disused fortification which led to the landing place becoming known as 'Old Fort'.

enemy we know nothing. The inhabitants are friendly enough in spite
of the most frightful outrages committed on every side by the French.
I have been escorting all sorts of stores, provisions &c &c all day and
am now resting myself on a comfortable stone. The weather in the day
is rather roasting. I have no time to write much more as I see a horrid
row of 'Arabas' approaching, and I know I shall have to escort them.
St. Arnaud's Body Guard have just passed by, called *Spahis* (I believe
Arabs), most picturesque looking fellows, all on little grey horses with
scarlet Bournouss & very long guns.

P.S. 18th. We are still here where we landed and our comforts not
much improved. We got tents today so that we shall have our
nights at least under cover. The nights we find very cold and the
food running short, so the sooner we move the better. Firewood is
not to be got & water miles off. The men suffer a good deal, I
fancy. As regards ourselves, I find what I always expected & knew:
that gentlemen can bear discomfort & privation better than the
lower orders. I, to whom all this is new, put up I find with it better
than most. I was certainly getting rather hungry yesterday when a
charming old soldier [Hampson] of my own Company came slyly
up with a bundle which he insisted on my taking & which contained real fresh mutton chops! He and one of his friends had met a
sheep & they had secured him which is of course against all orders.
Poor fellow! he said they would do anything for me and I don't
think he was a humbug for I always treat them as kindly as I can
and they are always pressing me to share anything they get. A cold
boiled mutton chop & biscuit does not sound nice for breakfast but
I have just been enjoying it most tremendously. I bathe in the Sea
every day which is the only way one gets a wash as fresh water is
worth gold. I am getting a little tired of my one shirt and if I look
as great a beast as my fellows (& I have no reason to doubt it) I am
rather glad there is no glass to look at myself in. We have no news
of the enemy. I met the 11th Hussars landing yesterday, looking
pretty well. They are most of them acquaintances of mine so that I
was glad to see them. Poor Jack Dallas [-Yorke] they were obliged
to leave on board ill, not Cholera, but the wretched low fever that
all have been suffering from. We have very little sickness in our
Division so far – thank God! The other Divisions are so far off I

know but little about them. You must forgive this horrid looking letter but I have neither table, chair, pen nor ink.

Letter 7

Alma River, 22 September

I have only time to write a few lines, even if I had spirits. We came here after a tremendous day's march the day before yesterday. We arrived late in the day, and even if here our Division was not engaged, a most tremendous battle had just taken place.[5] Our 1st, 2nd. & Light Divisions had taken the strongest position conceivable from about 50,000 Russians but at a fearful loss. I cannot at present tell you many particulars. It was the most desperate and splendidly done affair ever heard of. Our people marched deliberately without any cover as protection up to a position which the Enemy had been fortifying for weeks, & supposed to be utterly impregnable, except for regular operations. The 23rd. suffered perhaps most. They came out of action commanded by a junior Captain! [Bell] I am not in spirits to write you a long account of anything, for a more dreadful position you cannot conceive than where our camp is placed, close to the field of Battle, dead and dying on every side. We leave, I hope, soon. The Russians will, I think, never make such a resistance again, & they say Sebastopol itself is not nearly so strong as the position our people have taken from them here. The Cholera has abated somewhat tho' we are all losing a few.

Letter 8

The Heights over Sebastopol, 12 October

The enemy keep on firing shot and shell at us constantly, but our Camps now are out of range, as we have retired 100 yds or so. We

---

[5] The Second Brigade of the 4th Division was under-strength on landing – the 57th Regiment did not arrive until 23 September. As a result this brigade, under the command of Brigadier-General Torrens, together with a troop of 4th Light Dragoons, was detailed to clear up the landing site, and to follow after the rest of the Army. Due to the brigade getting lost, it arrived too late to participate in the battle of the Alma. Nevertheless, all members of the brigade received Alma clasps to their Crimea Medals.

were well within their range, & for a day or two had constantly to be dodging their shells, & no one luckily was hit so that our bright Authorities seemed to think that they were very clever, & courageous in keeping our position; but one day, as might have been expected, a shell rolled into a tent of the Regiment next to us, & killed one & frightfully wounded others who were near, so that we were withdrawn about 200 yds.

These last few days we have been having really desperate hard work & though one is utterly exhausted it is infinitely better than the stupid inaction we have been suffering from for nearly a fortnight. We are all hard at work preparing the Trenches & the position for our guns. The ground is as hard as iron & full of stones so that the work is most laborious. One party works in the Trenches & another armed Party protects them. We are quite close to the Town when at work, & the enemy keeps up a constant cannonade on us, but does little harm as we all 'duck' behind the Trenches when a shot is seen coming. This goes on constantly night & day.

This morning 100 of us came home from a most harassing 24 hours work. We formed, with two Companies of the 68th., a big advanced Picquet to protect the diggers in the Trenches. We were posted under cover from the guns of the city, about 800 yds from the Gates, on a magnificent road that leads to Sebastopol, winding most abruptly through rocky grand mountains straight up on each side. We were there for 24 hours. Of course no one could attempt to shut his eyes. We could see from our position the trenches, by peeping through rocks, or rather over rocks, the batteries of the Town close to us, & a most constant cannonade was kept up on us, & on the trenches about 300 yds to our rear & left. Hardly anyone is hit by this, as we are always placed under cover, but it is most exciting, for upon any one showing his head above the trenches 10 guns at least immediately opened upon him, & the extraordinary echoes among the mountains we were placed in, added to the beautiful horror of the scene. At night we were ordered to send out a Patrol, 400 yds further on the road, bringing it to about 500 yds of the City gates. We went for 2 hours each & a most extra-ordinary situation it was to be placed in. I went out first with 12 men, with orders to place them in as safe a position as circum-stances would permit. We all lay down behind a small rock we found, about the distance we were ordered to advance & lay perfectly still. We heard all the usual noises one habitually does when close to a large city – the church clocks striking, the murmur of men talking & rattling of carts and carriages. The constant cannonade that they had kept up all day had somewhat ceased about this time – the attention, the strain of eyesight & one's ears on an occasion of this kind is quite painful. We were certain that some party of theirs would come out some time in the night along this road to intercept our works. When my 2 hours were nearly over, an old soldier near me told me he was certain he heard a Party approaching; our orders were to fire on any one approaching as no friend could come from that side. There was a sharp turn of the road where I had placed my men & we could see (by day at least) 100 yds of the road. When the steps came decidedly nearer & we could distinguish a small body of men cautiously coming up the road, I ordered half my men to fire, which they did from our snug place & evidently disconcerted our approaching friends. They returned our fire irregularly, hit no one, & then according to orders I retired to our main body. I suppose they were sent out to provoke our fire & so point out our position, for a minute or two after I had rejoined our main body (under the cover we had been posted in) & reported what I had done, the most tremendous cannonade opened upon us, or rather the rocks we were quite covered by – I think it was the most beautiful and horrid sight I ever witnessed. The romantic situation we were in, lighted up by the constant bursting of shells, the awful noise and reverberation through the hills, & the knowledge of the very important position we were in charge of, all combined to make it a most exciting position to be placed in. We fully expected our position to be attacked, but after waiting all night in our places we were not further molested. All this tremendous and comparatively useless fire that the Russians keep up is just done I think to make a good report to the Emperor [Nicholas], as to the obstinate defence, that of course they will write to say they are making. We all the time are merely preparing, & have not fired a shot yet. How ominous it must seem to them, seeing us quietly sitting down round their City. Our batteries when up (& they say they will be in a day or two) will all open at once, & then Heaven help the poor city, for we have I am told 3 times as large a battery as has ever brought against any City or fortress, & the most commanding position to place them in. 70 guns we have brought up from the ships, & 1500 Sailors to work them. I expect that in a few days the whole town will be a heap of ruins, & that then we shall be sent to wherever we are intended to winter.

Letter 9

Before Sebastopol, 21 October

Thank dear Mum a thousand times for a letter I got from her (my first) a few days ago in which she told me about my promotion, the first announcement of which by the way, I heard by the Gazette.[6]

This is now the 4th. day of the regular Siege or bombardment of the Town & I can only tell you what I see myself as the camp is as full as usual of stories of all sorts on which no dependence can be placed. We have been now in the midst of the most horrid din for 4 days, all our guns constantly playing on the Town & all their guns returning on us. Our Authorities are I am told quite satisfied with our progress, tho' after Alma I think we have been underrating our enemy somewhat; today for the first time, the Russian fire was certainly slackened, they are not firing above one gun to our two or three & until now they have been firing two to our one. I & my Division are in a very commanding place to see the whole thing. Our loss has been wonderfully trifling, tho' our labors have been tremendous. We are 24 hours all of us in the Trenches to protect the guns & repair the Works, & then only 12 hours rest, then 24 hours again, trenches. So you may fancy how completely fagged we all are, & tho' there is not much actual labor in the Trenches, the entire want of rest (as one can never shut one's eyes for a minute) & the constant attention & look out which must be kept up, is most harassing. The regular routine is constant firing all day from 5 until sunset & then as by mutual understanding, a cessation of big guns during the night, but hard work at the Trenches & constant alarms & occasional skirmishes with the enemy all night. They are afraid to make any regular sorties, but our outposts are constantly engaged.

---

[6] Dallas was promoted Captain with effect from 22 September 1854.

The French had a slight engagement last night with a party of the enemy & I am told utterly destroyed them. They came out to try & take a very advanced Battery of the French supposing that there were only a few French. There happened to be a strong force of *Zouaves* (a splendid but rather irregular force the French have here from Africa). The *Zouaves* waited till they were almost touching them in the dark & I am told utterly annihilated them. They never dare come near us, however. The French have been rather unlucky with their powder, having had 4 magazines blown up, tho' not large ones; it interrupted their work, tho'. Today however they are firing well & have silenced a most annoying Battery in front of them. We have had no loss of guns or powder yet & have blown up one or two of their magazines. We are now I believe firing red-hot shell to burn the town, I don't think they can succeed as it is all built of stone. Odd to say, the town through a glass looks not much injured, but we have destroyed several of their batteries. The Fleet went in at them 3 days ago & I am told met with frightful loss and had no success.[7] I hope this account is exaggerated, we could not see what they were doing from here on account of the dense smoke from our guns between us & them. They have not since fired a shot so that I am afraid they did not do much good. Today is the first in my opinion (who, you must recollect, know nothing about guns) that we have done any good & the fire from the enemy is actually diminished by half since yesterday.

P.S. I am writing on the ground with a considerable wind, with black paint, not encouraging circumstances for a poor Scribe.

Letter 10

Before Sebastopol, 27 October
The Siege is still going on tho' rather languidly. I can tell you no news about when we are likely to take the place tho' of course we

---

[7] The assault on the entrance to Sebastopol harbour by the combined forces of the French and Royal Navies on 17 October was indeed less than successful. The British alone lost 44 killed and 266 wounded, and very little damage was done to the defences of the port.

have no doubt about the result of our operations. We keep on firing away constantly, & the enemy at us, & if we do them no more harm than they do us, I don't see when it is going to end. However, it is natural to conclude that our shot must do them great injury, for every shot fired at a Town must hit something... We have not battered down the place at all in the way that our Engineers & Artillery led us to expect we should, & tho' I hear that the Authorities are quite satisfied with our progress, we who have hard work in the Trenches, & don't see much visible result, are getting rather tired of it. We are now too firing our guns sparingly as we are afraid of running short of ammunition. You may fancy our disgust at reading the false news of the taking of Sebastopol in the *Times*.

A great gloom is cast over the Army from a most dreadful disaster that happened to our Light Cavalry. I will tell the story as I saw it. There has been an Army of (it is supposed) about 15 or 20,000 Russians in our rear for some time & Sir Colin Campbell has had the command of our rear position which consists of Balaklava our port and the adjacent heights. He had the 93rd. with him, 4,000 Marines occupying the Heights & I don't know how many Turks also occupying 'Redoubts' we had made above Balaklava, & the whole of our Cavalry. The day before yesterday the Russians came down with their 15 or 20,000 men, and attacked the Redoubts where the Turks were, drove them out, & took our guns that we had lent them. There are many rumours about their conduct. I believe they bolted immediately.[8]

The Cossacks of whom there were a large force, then charged down on the Highlanders in their Camp, & the Celts has just time to 'form

---

[8] The Turkish militia in the hastily-constructed redoubts along the Causeway Heights put up a spirited defence against ten times their numbers for the best part of three hours. On the redoubts being overrun, they fled back across the valley, where, for the most part, they formed up on either side of Sir Colin Campbell's Highlanders. It was the sight of their undisciplined rout, and the fact that some, more demoralised than the rest, continued to flee towards Balaklava Harbour, that coloured the general British view of the value of their services.

square' & utterly disperse them.[9] Then the 'Scots Greys' & some other 'Heavies' made two or three most splendid Charges amongst them, doing great execution. So far so well.[10]

The main body of the Russians all this time were halted close to Balaklava in line of battle with lots of Artillery. There is great doubt as to whom to attribute the Catastrophe I am about to describe, but there is no doubt that Ld. Lucan gave orders to the Light Cavalry, the 4th.–11th.–13th. & 17th. to charge the whole Army of the Russians!, & to try & take their guns. They obeyed their order only too gallantly, & with Ld. Cardigan at their head (by himself almost), riding as if down 'Rotten Row', they charged up to the muzzles of the guns, under the most tremendous fire. They sabred the men at the guns, & took 26 guns! Of course they could not hold them. The whole Russian Army closed on them, & they wheeled about to cut their way out. Out of nearly 800 only about 100 returned from that fatal Charge. Yesterday about as many more turned up. Our Light Cavalry in fact no longer exists.[11] I went down yesterday to enquire about many acquaintances & friends I have among them, & found in the whole Brigade only something under 200! There is one universal feeling of disgust throughout the whole Army at this murder, for it can be called nothing else. As a French Colonel [de Noé] said to me yesterday (who saw it all), 'They might as well have been ordered to Charge the walls

---

[9] Dallas is mistaken here, and he subsequently annotated the family's copy of his letters with the note 'an error – the Highlanders received them in line.' Sir Colin Campbell's men, the 93rd Sutherland Highlanders, rose in line two deep from behind the crest of a hillock to form the famous 'Thin Red Line', and, by three volleys (somewhat ineffectual by many accounts), turned back a probing advance by two Russian cavalry squadrons. At that moment, however, the 93rd, including the Grenadier company, some invalids and a number of scared and demoralised Turks were all that stood between the large Russian Army and Balaklava Harbour.

[10] The Charge of the Heavy Brigade was a brilliant success, in stark contrast to the more-famous charge of later in the day. General Scarlett, an officer with no previous experience in action, led the Scots Greys, the 4th & 5th Dragoon Guards, the 1st Royal Dragoons and the 6th Inniskilling Dragoons in a charge uphill against a much larger force of Russian cavalry, driving them off.

[11] The Charge of the Light Brigade is probably the most famous single action in the history of war. Dallas summarises the action reasonably accurately, and, like so many others, then and since, attempts to find someone on whom the blame could be placed.

of Sebastopol.' Who will answer for it, I don't know. Ld. Lucan *I am told* lays the blame on the A.D.C. who brought him the order, poor fellow! I knew him pretty well, a most promising Officer, Captain Nolan, 15th. Hussars. He was the first killed. He charged with them and fell the first. Ld. Cardigan, extraordinary to relate, escaped almost untouched. He charged quite by himself at the head of his Brigade right up to the enemy's guns. 'Maude' of the Horse Artillery (you know him) was badly wounded in the arm, but as I hear, doing well. The most extraordinary thing happened: a Shell hit his horse in the chest, went inside him & there burst, blowing the horse and rider up. Odd to say, he escaped with some flesh wounds in the arm!

My Division came down just in the middle of this,[12] and all we could see was the ground strewed with dead horses & men, & countless horses tearing about riderless. We were only 2,000 strong & consequently could not attack the enemy in the good position they were in, 20,000 in number. But we kept them in check all day, our men burning to avenge the poor Cavalry. My French friend, a Colonel of *Chasseurs d'Afrique*, with whom I have struck up rather a friendship & see a good deal of, tells me he never saw anything so splendid & gallant as the way these poor fellows charged up to almost certain death. We all pray that whoever is to blame for this may be made to answer for it. An 11th. man to whom I was talking (who survived it) told me that he really thinks the only circumstance to which the few who escaped owed their lives was the utter astonishment with which the enemy saw hardly 800 Light Cavalry charging 20,000 men, with Artillery playing on both their flanks & in their faces.

Yesterday the same Army coolly marched up to our right, but got a bitter lesson. Our Field Pieces got them within easy range & mowed down ranks of them. They soon retired & lost many

---

[12] Colonel Windham, on the Staff of the Division, recorded, 'The 4th Division got there just as this charge was being made.' They had been summoned to the battle earlier in the day, but their commander, Sir George Cathcart, had delayed in bringing them into action. Maxwell Earle, recorded, 'part of our Division (which had been sent for from the front in the morning) were [sic] marched up to retake our loss [i.e., the redoubts] and to replace the Turks. This was done easily as the enemy showed little inclination to remain so near us.' In fact, the 4th Division recaptured only the westernmost redoubts, leaving the main positions in the hands of the enemy.

prisoners.[13]

Altogether we are not in great force now. We shall have, we expect, to abandon Balaklava & our Authorities are blamed for having such extended lines in our rear, as we have not nearly men enough to keep them & carry on the Siege too. Balaklava, however, has now served our purpose, as we landed all our guns &c. there, & we have another Bay nearer where we can disembark anything more we want.

The news of the Cavalry Massacre will cause frightful excitement in England I fancy. I can only tell you the facts of the case. As to who is to blame, we only have rumours, & no place is so full of rumours, false & true (generally the former), as a Camp.

You ask about your friends & acquaintances. I will tell you all I know. All the Divisions are so worked in the Trenches that we have no time for writing to each other, & ever since we landed have had such work that we really know nothing of each other. We none of us have taken off our clothes to sleep since we landed. Blackwood I see occasionally, much altered in appearance from the 'ineffable' young gentleman I recollect in London – grown fat and coarse looking. I rather like him but see him seldom. Maxwell Earle I see often. Maude as I told you was wounded rather seriously in the arm, but I was told was doing well.

Always recollect that I say these sorts of things as I am told & cannot vouch for anything, as there seems a regular combination to disseminate falsehoods about here as elsewhere. For example, yesterday I met a 17th. man & asked him about a friend of mine, 'Webb' of the 17th., who had been wounded. He told me he had had his leg taken off, & was doing well. I met the Doctor who is attending him 5 minutes later. He said there was no need he hoped of his losing his leg! Blake of the 33rd. I see in the papers lost a hand at Alma. I have not seen him, but I firmly believe he was not touched. Will you send this letter to Sir William & tell him I will write soon, but have not time by this post. It is for him I gave so long an account of the Cavalry Engagement.

---

[13] Known as the battle of 'Little Inkermann', this reconnaissance in force by the Russians presaged their attack of 5 November, 1854.

P.S. I am not sure whether I named the Cavalry who were cut to pieces, the 4th. Light Dragoons/13th. do/8th. Hussars/11th. do/17th. Lancers.

Letter 11

Before Sebastopol, 6 November

We had yesterday a most tremendous engagement with a large Russian Army. We beat them well but with frightful loss. I was not touched thank God! tho' in the very worst of it![14] Our Division lost Sir George Cathcart & General Goldie killed, General Torrens very dangerously wounded, Colonel Swyny 63rd. Killed, Col. Seymour half killed, & I dread to learn how many others. We (46th.) had two officers wounded.[15] I am now in command. Our men lost very severely, but behaved splendidly. It was I hear (tho' one only knows what occurs in one's own neighbourhood), a much severer affair than 'Alma'. Maxwell Earle was not there having been slightly wounded a day or two ago in the foot with a Shell. I will write more particulars when I can. The Russian loss was frightful. We fought from 7 A.M. till 5 P.M. nearly. Adieu dearest. I am not in good spirits as you may imagine having lost many friends & acquaintances killed and wounded. Noble old Sir George died close to me 10 yards from the Enemy like a Hero. How grateful I ought to be that I am here & well to write.

P.S. I got one shot on my breast plate[16] which saved my life.

---

[14] Dallas was amongst those who took part in the disastrous charge led by Sir George Cathcart down the slopes of the Kitspur at Inkermann. He was probably never in greater danger in his life, and his efforts in leading a charge back uphill with five men against an entire regiment of Russian infantry led to his being awarded the French Légion d'Honneur and the Turkish Order of the Mejedie.

[15] Captain Hardy and Ensign Helyar.

[16] Infantry officers in the Crimea did not wear breastplates as we would understand the term. Dallas here refers to his shoulder-belt plate.

Letter 12

Before Sebastopol, 7 November

I am full of a tremendous engagement we had the day before yesterday. I do not think 'Guy Fawkes' day' was ever celebrated by more Gunpowder and fire. I can only tell you my part of the affair, as it was a very general engagement & lasted from 7. A.M. till nearly 5. P.M. We were all alarmed about 6 A.M., by a good deal of Musketry on our right, where there has been an Army hovering about for some time. The 'Assembly' sounded, and we all fell in, our two Companies forming with the two Companies of the 68th.[17]

We marched as fast as we could to where the fighting evidently was, our Brigade under Gen. Torrens (old Sir George was with us too). We found the Guards on the extreme right engaged with a large force of Russians on the brow of a hill (on which the extreme right of our Camp rests). We immediately formed line, & set to work – here poor Torrens fell badly wounded – the fire was very heavy. At last the enemy began to waver, & we took advantage of it & made a most splendid headlong Charge on them, pushing them down the steep side of the mountain, in utter confusion. The slaughter of them was here immense, for we charged right at them, & every man had shot away his 60 rounds (or nearly so) before we could get them to pull up. We then came leisurely back up the hill again, (of course scattered all over the side of it). When a few of us got nearly to the top from whence we had started, to our astonishment a most astounding fire opened upon us, from the very place we had come from. The men came up gaily, & we formed as we could, & with a mere handful returned the enemy's fire, as long as our ammunition lasted. We were placed, I should say 50 of us, with most of the Staff of the Division, on a small sort of natural platform, about 10 yds from the Russian Infantry Regiment which had outflanked us & had come round to the summit of this fatal hill, to receive us on our return from the Charge. How many of us escaped I can form no idea (few indeed did). We were so close to the Enemy that they threw stones, & clods of earth in our faces.

---

[17] The 46th fielded 6 officers, 15 non-commissioned officers, 3 drummers and 180 men on 5 November. The two companies of the 68th present comprised 6 officers, 15 non-commissioned officers, 14 buglers and 198 men.

Poor Sir George Cathcart fell there, shot, I believe, through the brain.[18] As I was coming up the hill he was just in front of me. As I passed him he recognised me & said, 'There is nothing for us but the bayonet, Dallas!' Noble hearted old Hero! I shall never forget him sitting quite calmly on his horse, certainly not 12 yards from the front rank of the Enemy. He was wounded in the head when he spoke to me. If ever a man lived who knew not what fear was, he was the one. By his side fell Colonel Seymour (on his Staff) who was much attached to him having been his Military Secretary at the Cape. Also Colonel Maitland badly wounded in the arm – Major Wynne 68th killed, Colonel Harry Smyth, 68th. badly shot thro' the body, another Officer of the 68th. killed [Barker], all of our little Party.

We held our position till we had no more ammunition, & until few of us were left, & then retired a few paces down the Hill, just as a Cloud of *Zouaves* came dashing out of the right flank of the Russians.[19] I was not touched myself except by a ball which hit my breastplate, & glanced off tearing my Coat & by the way was hit with a large stone of which the enemy for a second or two threw quantities. Our men behaved splendidly. We lost of course many. Nothing but their

---

[18] In a letter to his family, Maxwell Earle writes, 'Fred Dallas begged me to inform Flo [his sister, Emily Florence, the wife of Fred Dallas' eldest brother, Robert William] whether Sir George Cathcart was wounded in the head. He was only wounded in the body. A shot struck him in the heart and he was bayoneted also in the left breast. I myself saw him brought out of action and superintended his being laid out on his couch. The body of his Adj. General, poor Seymour, I had laid beside him.'

[19] Lieutenant Colonel Colin Campbell, 46th Regiment, arrived in the Crimea on the day that this letter was penned. He recorded the story of the Kitspur Charge in a letter which was later published,

About 12 or 1 o'clock in the day poor Sir George Cathcart turned round to Dallas (whom he knew intimately), and said, 'Dallas, I believe all is lost. We must try the bayonet!' They were then within about forty yards of the Russians. Dallas took the five men next to him and attempted as he described 'to boil up a little charge.' But when he got within about ten yards of the Russians, finding himself totally unsupported, he ran back again as fast as he came; extraordinary to say, he got back untouched, although he says that every man in the Russian line seemed to be firing point-blank. Three out of his five men were killed, and Sir George was shot at the same moment. (Colin Campbell, 1894.)

indomitable Pluck saved the whole of us being either killed or taken prisoner. I certainly do not think there were more than 60 men, holding their position against a whole Russian Regt, & having the lower ground.

All that I had to do afterwards was to retire with what we could collect of our Division, & form again, get fresh ammunition & then lay ourselves down, as a sort of reserve or rather support to our Artillery – under the hottest cannonade for about 5 or 6. hours. We lost a good many men here for we were in very bad cover. I can give you no general account of this battle which took place on a mountain, & in a valley called 'Inkermann'. Our loss was decidedly severe. My Division lost – killed – Sir George Cathcart, General Goldie, General Strangways (Artillery), Colonel Swyny 63rd., Colonel Seymour, Staff, Major Wynne 68th., Col. Harry Smyth badly wounded, Brigadier General Torrens shot badly thro' the body & many other Officers of whom we interred a portion yesterday. I hear today, but will not answer for my Authority, that we leave 2,000 & 90 Officers killed and wounded.[20] Of my little Band we had 38 killed & wounded & 2 Officers wounded (not badly), out of 150 men & 6 Officers. The Russians had I believe, & there can be no doubt 40, or 50,000 men, & we fought about 11,000 [i.e., our strength]. Their loss was something fearful. We had to fight fresh batches of them all day. They had a very large force of Artillery also, which they worked very well. After we had fairly beaten them off, I amongst others, was sent to get in the Prisoners, slightly wounded &c., & this was a part of the field where I had not previously been. I should say that the loss at Alma was trifling compared to this.

Our Siege in the meantime seems to be at a standstill, however the Authorities say it is all going on very well, so we must be satisfied. Another Victory like 'Alma' or Inkermann will, I fear, leave few of us to take the Town.

---

[20] The official casualty return for the British Army at Inkermann was:

	Officers	Sergeants	Drummers	Privates	Total
Killed	43	32	4	380	459
Wounded	101	121	17	1,694	1,933
Missing	1	6	0	191	198
	145	159	21	2,265	2,590

P.S. I am a 'Commanding Officer', now. Poor Hardy, my senior, was wounded – not badly tho'.

Letter 13

The Heights before Sebastopol, 16 November

It is not one of the least of the enjoyments attendant on good health to know what a relief it must be to one's poor anxious friends at home to hear of it, & I certainly have been blessed with almost uninterrupted health. I tell you about my own personal well being as I am afraid my letter is likely to be rather a melancholy one, and from such a scene as this, who could write otherwise!

I wrote an account of the battle [Inkermann] to Lady Napier for the General, & I do not propose writing you a long account of it further than my own personal adventures. The history of this battle was that, on the 5th. of November, we were attacked & altogether surprised, owing to the culpable carelessness & inefficiency of our Leaders, on the right of our present position, by an Army that partly came from the Town, & partly had been collecting under our very eyes for some time. They were about 50,000 in number & had their guns in position & were quite into our Camp before we knew anything about it. Nothing saved us but the extraordinary bravery & splendid behaviour of our troops. Leaders we had none.

We fought, 10,000 (or so) in number, from 7 A.M. till 3.1/2 P.M., & killed & wounded at the lowest computation 15,000 Russians, the French say 20,000! It was a scene of utter confusion. I was with part of the 4th. [Division] on the extreme Right & after a good deal of firing we charged, & drove down a Hill, a large party of the enemy, with frightful slaughter. On our return from that Charge, we were altogether surrounded by a part of the enemy, who had come up, somehow, in our rear, & a small party of us fought till very few were left (consisting of Guards, 68th., & ourselves, & a few 20th. men, in all about 100), with Sir George Cathcart & most of the Staff, within a few yards of a Russian Regiment. It makes me grieve to look back and think what noble blood was spilt in an almost hand to hand fight with these Slaves. What was the use of killing 15,000 of them when we lost such men as we did on that day! Within 10 yards around me, in half as

many minutes, I saw Sir George fall, Seymour his Adjutant General,
Wynne of the 68th., Torrens our gallant Brigadier, Maitland, Seymour's Assistant badly wounded, Colonel Smyth 68th. the same, &
many other noble fellows. Our Clergyman read one service for all the
next day, a very sad day for the poor 4th. Division. At the head of the
list were 3 Generals: Strangways, Sir George, & poor Goldie, Maxwell
Earle's Brigadier much beloved by all.

I escaped unhurt except by a shot on a buckle that fastens my belt.
A shot flattened against it & it saved myself. It was a great victory for
our men, & a great disgrace to our Leaders, that such a slaughter
should have been necessary. A few hours work would have rendered
our position unassailable, but they allowed us to be surprised, &
nothing but our noble men saved our Camp & our Generals' reputation.

The French, by the bye, came up just in time, & helped much to
pull us through. Our little Band, after Sir George fell, would certainly
have been utterly annihilated. We had not a single round of
ammunition left when the gallant *Zouaves* rushed up and attacked our
foe in Flank.

Such a loss as we sustained cast a great gloom over our Camp. I lost
many friends and acquaintances. Poor young [Cavendish] Greville, I
was much grieved to see in the list. His brother [Algernon] introduced
him to me a few days before, such a nice looking boy, just joined!

In the midst of all this my Regiment arrived. How glad I was to see
them! all my old friends, & looking so fresh & clean & English. How
sadly a few days has altered them too![21] Three days ago what our
Authorities had wantonly shut their eyes to, & had made no preparations for, took place: namely, Winter approached us, & with great
severity. I will not harrow your imagination with the dreadful sufferings of the troops, & recollect that what I say does not so much
apply to us Officers who can afford ourselves luxuries, or rather
necessaries (that are considered luxuries). Three days ago a hurricane

---

[21] Lieutenant Richard Lluellyn was one of the new arrivals. He wrote of Dallas and
the others of the regiment who had been present at Inkermann: 'The poor fellows
seemed half ashamed to claim our acquaintance and indeed it is difficult to recognise
in their haggard faces and ragged clothing the gay soldiers who left us the other
day.'

came & blew down the whole of our Camp. It was accompanied by a fall of Sleet & Snow. The tents remained down for 24 hours. The Commissariat declared that they could not supply food owing to the state of the roads, & since then the men have hardly had enough to support life, all this time having to go every alternate 24 hours to the Trenches, where they lay half clothed, half starved, & worked to death.

All this time we never see Lord Raglan, who is either unmoved by all this, or unable to find any relief for it. There is one general outcry against him. We are told that those about him don't like 'talking Shop' (to use the slang of the day). We all feel that something must be done, and that soon, or there will be no Army left. Our gallant Army of 25,000 that landed in the Crimea & has since received various reinforcements cannot now number 9,000 fighting men. If they go on as they do now, & in all probability the weather will get worse, there will not be 900 in a month. We are to stop here for the Winter, & I believe we are to build huts! We have no wood at present! You must remember, my dearest mother, that we Officers can always buy (of course at an extravagant price) food & drink, so that there is no danger of our being starved, but I do not mind telling you the Truth about the Army as I suppose you will hear it in the papers. Lord Raglan has a dreadful amount of death & misery to answer for when called upon to do so.

The Siege meantime goes on languidly. We are all night in the Trenches, for if we were not there the Russians would take them, but we fire few shots & all seems at a stand-still. There is no danger of our being attacked again, for independently of the dreadful lesson the Enemy got on the 5th., deserters tell us that their sufferings are threefold greater than ours! Today a rumour is about that the Enemy in our rear have all gone away & that the starving survivors are trying to get to Simferopol.

The cold is very great & the hurricane has done dreadful injury to our Shipping. The *Prince* (that the 46th. came out in), loaded with warm clothing for our poor wretches, went down with all hands, & many other ships the same.

I live in a tent with Arthur Wombwell. We have a tent apiece, but find it warmer & pleasanter being together.

A medical report has gone in to Lord Raglan to say that the men cannot do the work imposed on them, & that there will be none of them left if it goes on much more. It is signed by the Medical Officers of the Division & the Colonels of Regiments. I hope it will move him from his miserable apathy. We have not seen his face since 'Inkermann'. I believe he does not go out in bad weather.

I hope I shall be able to send you more marching news in my next. I have a commission for you to do for me which is to get me at 'Cordings Waterproof Shop' in the Strand a large-sized thick waterproof Coat with a hood, & a pair of fishing boots large ones and long, also 3 or 4 pairs of thick blankets, & send them by the first ship you can. Our 'Kits' that you recollect our getting were very good for what we expected, but not quite warm enough for a Russian Winter in huts, or rather tents for where the huts are to come from we don't know! A great many poor fellows lost much of their little possessions in the Hurricane. I lost none of my things except my horse. He was very thin I must say, & I honestly believe was blown away, for I have never seen him since. All the poor horses by the bye are starving as well as the men. What will the people of England say to all this?

You ask me about Sir Colin Campbell. I have never seen him, not having been near him & not having much reason to go about. He is very highly thought of & liked in the Army. Would to Heaven he were Commander in Chief.

P.S. I wish by the bye that when a mail is coming out you would send me a *Times* or two. You can't fancy how we devour a paper here & we have nothing to read.

We are having the most extraordinarily beautiful weather like an English Spring, cold in the evenings, lovely in the day. The troops are getting healthy though they have suffered dreadfully since we landed. As yet thank God, I have had nothing wrong with me, but nearly everyone is suffering from 'Diarrhea' ('Saving your presence' as an Irishman would say).

We get lots of food, such as it is, 1lb & 1/2 of meat a day & 3 rations of rum. With such work as we at present have, men require some stimulants. As it is we find it almost impossible to keep them awake when sitting down 'on Piquet' in the Trenches tho' we are in the face of an enemy.

The French are doing well shelling on their side of the Town, gradually pushing up their works close to the Town. We cannot advance our Works as the ground is all rock & the French side is expected to be the real attack. We only harass the Enemy & our guns endeavour to silence theirs that play on the French. The French are next the Sea, on the S.E. side of the Town.

Poor Lord Dunkellin an acquaintance of mine, very near sighted, walked into a Russian Piquet thinking it was one of ours & was quietly taken Prisoner. Fancy, What a bore![22]

Letter 14

Before Sebastopol, 26 November

By this time you have the sad news of the losses at Inkermann. Since then we have been having bad weather & its effects upon our poor men has been fatal beyond belief. They are said to die of Cholera – I don't believe in Cholera at this time of year here, & a clever Doctor to whom I have been talking on the subject says that he firmly believes that they die of want, overwork, & insufficient Clothing, combined with sleeping (not much of that by the way) on the wet soaking ground. An additional argument in favour of my, and his, theory is that the Officers' health is not worse than might be expected from the life we lead, if we were anywhere else. We are pretty well fed (by ourselves & pockets), not so hardly worked quite & have a dry wrap or two to get into when we come home from the trenches.

The greatest trial here is seeing the sufferings of our men, without being in any way able to alleviate them. They are positively worked to death. If they were well fed (instead of being half starved), & if the weather was fine and warm (instead of constant rain and wind), & if they had a change of clothes in their camp; if they had all these benefits I don't think any but the very strongest could stand it. As it is they die miserably, not singly but by tens! I know dearest it will make your heart bleed to hear this of the poor fellows who fought at 'Inkermann' & 'Alma' but I cannot write otherwise.

---

[22] Lord Dunkellin was taken prisoner on 21 October 1854. The heir of the Marquess of Clanricade, Menshikoff initially refused to exchange him, and sent him to Moscow. He was eventually exchanged around 9 December 1854.

For myself I never was better in my life. Hard work suits me I think; that I am the least happy I cannot say. Who could be here? The Siege goes slowly on. To our unlearned eyes we make no progress but still our accursed trenches have to be occupied. We have (our Division) constantly about 1000 men, I had better call them spectres, sitting 12 hours at a time knee deep in that horrid ditch. Today has been a Summer day but the rain and wind has been constant for a fortnight previous. If we could only get one or two like it it would be better than all the medicine in the Hospital, and the Commissariat would be able to bring up food for the men from 'Balaklava'.

Our officers are all pretty well, 'The Brigadier' (Garrett)[23] well enough in health but in wretched spirits. He takes the gloomiest view of affairs. Indeed he arrived at such a time, that one cannot wonder at it, particularly as he sees his poor men suffering so much. The history of the dreadful work that is expected from our men is that we have to do the duty of an Army three times our number. We are now in number (daily decreasing) about 10,000! & we still do the same work as if we had the Army we landed with, 25,000 about, & keep going on the same every day. This of course cannot last much longer. Some of our men tell me that they are sometimes 4 or 5 consecutive nights in the trenches! We, the Officers, have to go back 3 nights a week & that with a dry bed to come into & a sufficiency of food, we find quite enough to do.

Our party on board the *Harbinger* was sadly diminished by 'Inkermann': Sir George, Seymour, Torrens, Maitland; the 2 first dead, Torrens mortally wounded, Maitland dangerously & poor Greville gone home having lost a brother, & [a] dear friend & Patron in Sir George. Sir John Campbell now commands the 4th Division. I have never seen him, in fact I think nobody appears to see him. He is, I hear, an amiable and fearless man, but he lives in a small cave he has found somewhere near here & does not seem to bother himself much about us.

---

[23] Robert Garrett was acting Brigadier-General at this point. Another officer of the 46th, Lt. Frank Curtis, recorded in a letter dated 22 December 1854, 'We hear that it is all right – our Colonel is to have a brigade, and so become a double-jointed Brigadier instead of a Lance one as hitherto.'

We are all told to 'build huts for the Winter', the only objection to this being the having no wood, & the men having no time to do anything but cook their scanty rations, & snatch a little sleep in their soaking tents when not in the Trenches. Some of us have dug holes in the Earth & covered them with skins & dirt & old sails. Wombwell and I still live on in our tent, which happens to be a good one and we get on pretty well. We fortunately have got all our baggage. Our little iron bedsteads are capital things. I only got mine a few days ago, until then I had never taken off my Coat to sleep or ever laid on anything but the ground since I landed, & odd to say it had agreed with me wonderfully.

About the progress of the Siege I cannot tell you much. We shoot very little & I believe are making one or two new batteries (I hope they will be of more use than the old ones) & the general opinion seems to be that we are awaiting some large reinforcement of the French to regularly 'Invest' the place which means to completely surround it & starve it out. At present we only cover one side of it, & forces, provisions &c can come in & out of the town with impunity. The French have a very large force here already, about 50,000, & are constantly receiving additions.

Our Rifles (1st. Battalion) who are in our Division, did a very gallant thing the other night. There were some Russian Sharpshooters who had established themselves a few hundred yards from our Battery behind some rocks & stones that they had heaped up, & did us considerable injury, as well as the French on our left, picking off our Artillery men at their guns. 200 of the Rifles went down in the night & charged them, drove them out of their holes, & with some working men (soldiers) with spades &c made themselves a little cover to protect themselves, & held their advantage all night against 3 separate attacks the Russians made upon them (the beaten Sharpshooters having got reinforcements & come back to retake their posts). Canrobert was so delighted with them that he published the affair in his general orders to the French Army, & then, & not till then, Lord Raglan was shamed into saying something in our orders about it. It was a very gallant affair. Poor Tryon, the Subaltern who led them, was unfortunately shot. They lost about 10, or 11, the Russians many men.

Letter 15

Before Sebastopol, 6 December

You will have heard by this time all about 'Inkermann' & many other 'griefs' that we have been getting into, I mean in the way of rags, starvation &c. I wonder what the people in England think of it all. I trust they do us poor devils justice, for nothing can exceed the behaviour of our men. It is a great sight for a reflecting man on a pouring day, or rather night, at 4.1/2 A.M. with a wind that cuts you in two, to see 1000 men of our Division (& the others of course the same) parade to march down some distance to do duty in the Trenches for 12 hours, many very ill, all wan and haggard looking wretches, who had been told the day previous that 'there would be no meat for that day' & given a handful of biscuit & a glass of rum. It is a curious sight to see these men half clad march off without a murmur, many of them having been only 12 hours off duty, and this you may see here every day at 4.1/2 P.M. & 4.1/2 A.M., & this is the Army that started so gaily, so splendidly equipped, so thoroughly furnished in every department (as poor John Bull was told). As a French friend of mine said to me today 'Ce cher John Bull wants something to show for his money' & with, I imagine, almost unlimited means at the disposal of Government the present state of our Army is such that (if ever the truth is known at home) it will excite one universal feeling of indignation. It is melancholy work writing in this strain, but I feel that you would not like me to write & deceive you about affairs here.

For myself I never was better in my life. We are *now* commencing to get warm Clothing which we want, of course, sadly, & if the dreadful weather would only improve & even if we could only get 2 consecutive dry fine days I think there would be a very visible change in the health of the men, but we never have more than 12 hours at a time of dry weather (& that seldom) & then rain such as would wet through a hairy dog. Everything is one great marsh. By the way, I see in the paper that they are going to send us out 50,000 hairy caps which will be very comfortable *when they come* (rather more than 3 caps & a half apiece for we have hardly 15,000 men here).

The dreary old guns go on shooting occasionally. Some of them, I am glad to see, have worn out, and some have had their noses knocked off by the enemy, but the dismal old survivors still keep up the farce. I do not believe they are the slightest good, & nobody seems to say they are now.

All this time, I must tell you, that *there is not one of us that has a moment's doubt* about our taking the place, with 70,000 French (& 40,000 on the road) & ourselves. One General's opinion is, that we could take it whenever we liked to assault it; of course, at great loss of life, but the question is amongst us, whether it is not better that say at the outside 15,000 men should be lost & we take the place & save the lives of the remainder, than remain sitting opposite to it watching battery upon battery rising against us, & losing steadily 80 men a night by disease. The loss in a battle is a trifle compared to what is lost by disease.[24] Look at the present expedition. We have fought two most bloody battles & I think 5,000 killed & wounded would include all our loss. How have 10,000 gone? You must recollect also that the Winter has only begun.

I am writing this in bed. I recollect, dear Puss, you & I always held similar opinions about our beds. Mine is now a great fact & I get into it (whenever I am not in the Trenches) at about 7. & quit it reluctantly at about 8. or 9. next day. I bought an immense blanket the other day & with a quantity of Plaids and Turkish great coats (odd to say, called 'Grego') I pass many pleasant hours. Wombwell does the same on the other side of the Tent & we hold much intellectual conversation across the hole in the middle. Our tent is rather a good one, that is to say that when it rains hard outside, it only rains slightly within. We passed one very wretched day the day of a great storm I think I told you about. Every tent in the place came down but ours, & we kept constantly prowling around it with mallets, knocking in the pegs that hold it up, of course perfectly wet through. At last we got quite exhausted & crawled in, determined to live or die with it. We packed up everything, & sat drearily down opposite one another on our saddle bags. I found a pot of preserved Turtle soup, we then, somewhat sadly, cut up a little table we had made & lit it & made a little fire in the middle of the tent, which nearly smoked us out, cooked our pot of Soup, & certainly had quite the most delicious meal we ever fell upon.

---

[24] Dallas's observation was all too true, and was borne out by the official statistics of the Crimean War which show that out of 20,813 deaths between 1854 and 1856, 16,297 were due to disease.

Our tent never *quite* came down, & the storm abating next day, we repaired our damages & strengthened our 'position', & now listen calmly to the furious winds that often blow upon us.

We used to be constantly harassed by night alarms & whenever there was a little more shooting than usual in the trenches we used to have all to fall in, armed & dressed. Lately it has been found out, I suppose, that we must have a little rest to do the considerable amount of work we are called upon to do, & that we cannot be alarmed into the bargain, so that we hear the most furious cannonade without scarcely turning round in our beds. The Russians make the most furious attacks on the French, every night. They do not do much harm I believe, but they certainly make a most awful noise; one has just ended about half an hour ago; they last about 5 minutes. They fire every description of missiles for that space of time, into the French lines, which are very close to the town. The French do not appear to care much about it. I see them from our trenches (when there) & it is a most beautiful sight on a dark night, the noise of the guns the flash of the muskets, & the flight of many shells in the air all at once. These attacks never last long.

I see a good deal of a French Regt. that has, I am glad to say, come to live near us: the *1st. Chasseurs d'Afrique*, a magnificent Cavalry Regt. I am much *lié* with the Lieut. Colonel, a Baron de Noé, a most agreeable fellow & much attached to anything English, his mother having been English. I breakfasted with him today & always enjoy myself much there. The French seem the most cheery fellows after being with us solemn old British. He talks English about as good as my French. I find my French improves, & my spirits certainly do, by association with them. Their Colonel is a very fine soldierlike old fellow & de Noé tells me, inquires always 'Where "Ce cher Capitaine Anglais" is', when I don't go there for two or three days. De Noé was a Page of Charles X & has been 20 years in Africa, when not there on leave at Paris, what a singular life!

Letter 16

Before Sebastopol, 11 December
We have heard that Lord Raglan is a Field Marshal. We here are not so delighted with him, as you all seem to be at home. Nothing is

done for us here. You will scarcely believe that the mail has been in since Saturday morning, this being Monday night, & except Ld. R's own bag, not a single officer has yet received his letters! The mail has been wandering about & no one knows where or why. The postmaster tells us that every obstacle also has been put in the way of the mails going away from here & it is shrewdly suspected that Ld. Raglan is at the bottom of it, as he does not like our accounts getting to England, as soon as his. This however is merely suspicion. There has certainly been some very mysterious delay about our two or three last mails going out.

Sir de Lacy Evans is gone home I hear, thoroughly disgusted, they say, with affairs out here. Our men are still nearly starving, but patient. It is sad work altogether. We have a new Siege train in the course of being 'put in position', our old one having completely worn out & been knocked over by the Russians. The French have, I believe, 150 large guns ready to open when ours are ready. I trust the new Siege Train will be more successful than the last. I don't know when we shall be ready. We see spectral Artillery horses dragging up immense guns every day. You will laugh at what I am going to tell you, but it is perfectly true. The horses have all been so starving that they have eaten each other's tails! & it is a fact that not one horse in ten of the Artillery has any hair at all left on that ornamental part of their persons, which adds considerably to their ghastly appearance.

Letter 17

In my bed before Sebastopol, 22 December

Do not imagine from my heading that I am not well or bedridden for I was never better in my life, but the weather today is so utterly disgusting that I have not yet got up, & from the little peep I got at the *Lake* surrounding my canvass house, I hardly felt justified (being a bad swimmer) in going out at all. It is raining and blowing, & *has been* raining and blowing ever since 6 yesterday morning (now noon), without one moment's intermission with a force & determination peculiar to this favoured spot. By the way I read the other day in some paper an extract from some French news from here in which it stated 'that the troops had been somewhat inconvenienced (*gênés*) by rain'! I should rather say we had! It is the most extraordinary climate in the World. Every five (or six) days, we have a Summer's day, not a bright Winter's day but a *real* Summer's day for sitting on the grass, (if there was any). Then comes rain, then sleet, then a Hurricane & twice we have had snow. I don't think it is colder here, as yet, than in England, but living on high ground, in canvass tents, is not treating any climate fairly.

Yesterday when I was sitting somewhat gloomily in my tent, smoking a very short black pipe, (my 'constant pardner' Wombwell being in the Trenches), disagreeable and unworthy reflections coming over me as to the advantages of being a Crossing Sweeper at home, over being a 'Hero' in the Crimea, then your letters & papers came quite unexpectedly & I had pleasure & amusement for the remainder of the day, & the hero got altogether the better of the inglorious sweeper. Apart from joking, you cannot conceive the pleasure with which we get letters out here, I am so much obliged to any one who will write to me, & your & Mother's letters you can well believe are a weekly source of delight. Papers too, I must thank you for, much, they are priceless out here.

Campbell [46th], who has foolishly got up & came in here just now to see us, says it is quite bitter out today, I can quite believe it, for my hands and nose (the only parts of my person out of my blankets) are nearly frozen. You might guess from my more than usual bad writing, that something was wrong. It does not much signify tho' if you can decipher it, does it?

My servant went yesterday to Balaklava on a ghost of a Pony he had found, or stolen, to get me stores, & came back pretty successful. I must tell you by the way we eat nothing but ham, *ever*. Of course he brought one, & some potatoes, very valuable things here, costing about as much as oranges at home – but almost necessary to people constantly eating salt meat.

Thank much my dearest mother, for taking so much trouble about a coat for me. I cannot follow exactly your kind injunction as to writing to tell you what I want, as it takes at least 2 months to get the things, & you seem fully to have anticipated my wants in the approaching box. Our wants are literally, food, clothing, & lodgings and Government, somewhat late in the day, is sending them out. We are still miserably fed. I can only answer for my own Division: they do not get enough to sustain life considering the work and exposures they undergo, and consequently life is not sustained, as will be seen by the sad return of sickness & death, in mine & other Regiments. There is no Epidemic amongst them, Cholera (real) very rare, but my Regiment now numbers about 300 men fit for duty! We had about 100 before the Regiment came out! & they brought 700. We, the Officers, are very well on the whole. We have only 2 sick, & they have gone to Balaklava & are going on well. I was talking to a Sergeant [Hampson] of mine, whom I left on the shore at Alma (apparently dying). He gives a much better account of affairs at Scutari. When he first went there, he was left, he tells me, with several others in the Hospital there, in a room, & for 7 days they never saw a Doctor! He survived it, & says that now all is much better arranged. Miss Nightingale & her attendant Angels, he speaks most enthusiastically of. They were everywhere amongst the sick, doing more good than any doctors, & as he somewhat naively observed 'there was no sort of delicacy about them, Sir.' Heaven help them & sustain them, in the dreadful path of duty they have chosen!

As regards your kind offer of sending things out for my men, I think that now all descriptions of things seem on their way out for them, & they have already, & are daily bringing up, with much toil & pain, (10 miles to Balaklava & back & deep mud all the way) various sorts of warm clothing, & by the time anything you could (as you so kindly offer to do) send out I fancy that they will be pretty well clothed. One of their greatest hardships now is having to fetch everything, rations &c from Balaklava themselves, in addition to the constant Trenches, for the Commissariat has altogether broken down. All the mules and horses are dead. I hear 300 new ones have arrived, for the whole Army! We have not seen them.

Letter 18

                                    Before Sebastopol, 30 December
[The following is a copy of a letter to Capt. Dallas which was enclosed with Letter 17.]

My dear Fred,

Lord Raglan *'disch' 'I likewise beg to solicit Yr.. Grace's attention to the Services of Col. Horn 20th. Regt., Capt. Inglis 57th. Regt., & Capt. Dallas 46th., on the occasion of that Skirmish at Inkermann'.*

Yrs. Most truly,

A.M.E.

I was of course much gratified in reading my name in Lord Raglan's dispatch; a pleasure much enhanced by knowing how pleased you would be. I do not understand exactly how it got there, for Hardy commanded us going *into* action, – I only coming out. That fact prevents my getting any promotion by it as everybody else I see in a Gazette of the 13th., who were mentioned, have got Brevet Rank. It is no disappointment to me as I knew that if there was any promotion given to us, Hardy, as Senior, would get it, & it is quite honor enough for me seeing my name at all when so few but Staff people ever are mentioned.[25]

I have not of course yet got any of the things you have so kindly sent me. There is such an utter want of system out here that there is a considerable amount of luck in getting anything when it has arrived. Everything is shied onto the shore, or else remains in the Ship, & very likely takes another trip back to England. An acquaintance of mine gave me a striking example of the state of things at Balaklava. He had been expecting a box for some time, & went down often to look for it. No one could tell him anything about it, but one day he accidentally saw the lid, or something resembling the lid, of a box, the box itself buried in the mud, & he dug away at it. His labors were rewarded by finding that it was his long-looked-for friend. A small ship was fastened to it, viz: the cable tied round it (it was on the shore). He released the ship with his knife & got his box carried home for him! A more striking type of the whole of our arrangements here I could scarcely pick out.

The Siege is at a standstill, tho' I am sorry to say our labors are the same as ever. A great many things for the men (clothing &c) have

---

[25] Dallas' indifference to his lack of promotion does not last. As the war goes on and other officers with lesser claims leapfrog over his head in seniority he becomes more and more embittered. Eventually he receives his Brevet Majority nearly two years after the action in which he had distinguished himself.

arrived. Some of them the men managed to fetch up. The greater part are lying in the mud at Balaklava. A great friend of mine, by the way, has been given the Command there, Col. Haines, a most disagreeable command. He is a first rate man, & if it is possible will get things into some sort of form.

General Pennefather, who has now got our Regiment,[26] is very ill at Balaklava. We are all much pleased at the appointment. He is a most popular man, a capital Officer, & we are most of us acquainted with him, having known him in Dublin. Our Colonel (R.G) [Garrett] had a very gratifying interview with him yesterday.

January 1st. 1855. Many happy returns of the year to you all at home. As I rather expected another order came back last night, that letters were to go at 9. A.M. (this A.M.) the proper time being 12 P.M. tomorrow. I have found out why all this bother and inconvenience takes place now about our letters. Our Postmaster, a capital man (from Constantinople) has gone away in disgust from Balaklava & the Post Office is removed to Lord Raglan's. The Head Quarters Staff having anything to do with it quite accounts for the ridiculous way in which it is now managed.

By the way, my Papers wandered in sometime yesterday. I read Lord Dudley's speech[27]. I liked it much, very eloquent, but I don't think he knows enough about affairs out here. If he knew more he could have made a more severe attack upon Government. For instance, he cites the loss of the *Prince* as one of our greatest calamities here. Now we here further than the actual loss of valuable things, do not and did not think so much of it, as its loss could and would have been easily replaced if we had transport for troops from Balaklava. Here, her loss was to a great extent an accident. What kills us out here is the utter want of system & arrangement in every department. Balaklava is strewed with wooden houses. The sailors make rafts of them; when nobody is looking they make firewood of them, but not a single Soldier has ever slept yet in anything but a tent. Hay, oats,

---

[26] Pennefather was appointed to the Colonelcy of the 46th Regiment with effect from 19 November 1854.

[27] There was no Lord Dudley at this time; however, the Earl of Derby made a speech in this vein on 12 December 1854. It seems probable that it is Lord Derby that is intended.

Biscuits, vegetables are rotting in the mud; yet the men, until 3 or 4 days ago when they sent the Cavalry up with our rations, have been starving. It would be endless writing of all the mistakes & absurdities committed.

Part Two
1855

'We are certainly the worst clad, worst fed, worst housed Army that ever was read of.'

Letter 19

Before Sebastopol, 5 January

You are all at home, (I mean all England are) so kind about us here but our Authorities seem to care so little for us. Except a few flannel waistcoats, the men have nothing more to face the dreadful winter with than the old rags they landed in & we are still in our tents & the snow a foot deep on the ground!

I always write in bed & I have waited till the last moment so as to get your letters before I wrote. Our mail goes out in one hour. The one we have just received ought to have been here 3 days ago. All but Ld. Raglan's bag were left at Constantinople, nobody knows why! This is not the way to treat men who have to do, & do pretty well I may say, such duties as ours here. I have just been melting the ink in bed with me! It has been a beautiful but bitterly cold day, I think colder than England, a dreadful wind blowing, but what is very wretched is having no fire to warm oneself at. I suffer from cold feet a good deal. The truth is one wants regular boots & stockings for the purpose. I don't know what the poor men can possibly do if the weather continues! They have great difficulty in getting fire-wood, only roots they dig up with a Pick-axe, & bushes, & now that they have the snow to get through God help them! poor creatures, for no one else can now I fear. It is no use telling them houses are coming. Why, the winter has come! They may read or hear of furs, of coats, of food, of railways to be made in a month or so! Why, our whole Brigade, 4 Regts., now musters 800! How many of those can one hope to see living in a wooden house or clothed in fur?

Last night a funny incident took place on our advanced post. We have sentries placed out at night about 100 yds or less from the Russian sentries. They are instructed to hide themselves, of course, in holes in the rocks, or behind bushes, or in fact conceal themselves anywhere that they can – but last night they were so cold that they could not remain in their holes & both English and Russian sentries, as if by some mutual agreement, walked up and down to warm themselves, not at all shooting at each other. A soldier told me that he found one of them an exceedingly pleasant fellow!

Letter 20

Before Sebastopol, 6 January

I am very glad to see that you seem thoroughly to understand all my letters. I thought & still think it an unworthy thing to write cheerful letters & say nothing of facts that you must know sooner or later by the papers. You seem altogether to comprehend that when I talk of misery & suffering here, I do not in any way, (or in the least degree) refer to myself. The utmost suffering I have is extreme discomfort & seeing the men hungry, starving & dying around me, & knowing that I can do nothing, & that those who could have prevented it all, (in great measure) stand idly by. Nothing that England can now do can possibly save the Army here. It is the very outside of what the *whole of the remnant of the Cavalry* can do, to bring up food for the men. It is useless to talk of wooden huts at Balaklava, there is no means of getting them up here. There are no means of transport, the Commissariat up here has failed, the Ambulance, or the force that was called the Ambulance, no longer exists & when the food is brought up, there is no wood for them to cook with. With great toil & pain they dig up a few roots & they must fail in a day or two completely, & I have heard no word of any supply of wood coming! Lord Raglan rode up on a sleek horse a day or two ago, & all he is reported to have remarked was that the 'Artillery horses appeared insufficiently clad'. God forgive him! *Two months* ago he could have got as many ships as he wished and loaded them with wood, with mules from Constantinople, with forage, with in fact every preparation for fighting against Winter, but no, nothing was done. Wrecks that might have made huts, were allowed to float out of the port to sea. We have lived from hand to mouth & the only prospect that I see to save the remnant of this gallant Army (if the other Divisions of whom I know nothing, are in the same state as ours, and I believe they are) the only hope for us is to cower away to Balaklava, or elsewhere, & try to live until Spring. I am by no means 'a croaker' & I have thought, & think, more of our position than perhaps many others, & I see no other prospect for us. The Regiment next to us turned out 7 men (seven men! I put it in writing as you might think I had left out a 0) for duty this morning. Can Lord Raglan know this? or if he does not, ought he not? Government may be at home, & I believe have been, totally unprepared for so great a Campaign, & now are sending out, & will continue to send out, probably, reinforcements, but, as regards us who are here, they can do nothing. What *could* have been done, could have been done by the Authorities here.

We don't the least care how many Russians there are. When anyone says 'There are 30,000 Russians come into Sebastopol today', we only say 'Are there?' & don't think any more about it. But, if anyone had said to us, a month or two ago, 'We are going to Winter here, & huts will be got for the men immediately, winter clothing, stores of forage, & food will be made, fresh mules shall be immediately brought' (& there was not the slightest obstacle to all this being done), we should have seen that we were cared for, & we could have done and lived through what we now do and die doing. We have daily & nightly to furnish 1200 men for our Trenches (I mean our Division have to). Our Brigade now number barely 700! (4 Regiments). This was the same number we furnished when we were 3000 strong & the weather was fine, provisions, wood and forage plentiful! We have now 700 men for duty, over 2,000 sick! & as I hope to be saved! I firmly believe that decent foresight & care would have kept up our numbers to the original amount, for we have received constant drafts, & of actual diseases, excepting those arising from overwork and destitution, we have had but little.

We read with pleasure that I cannot describe all that our country so generously says of us, & perhaps feel that it is not undeserved, but I don't think you know half enough in England, about us and our state here.

The medals will be received with delight. Of course I am delighted at seeing my name in Lord Raglan's despatch. It was there through the kindness of the officer who was left in command of our Division who mentioned my name favourably [Windham]. In general we don't look with quick interest on a Despatch out here – The usual form, & it was not departed from in the last one, is 'The whole of the Staff & part of the Commanding Officers, behaved with great gallantry &c. &c.', and we look with no great jealousy on the promotion being given to the Staff (not half of whom were present) at what is called emphatically 'the Soldiers Battle'. It is what we always know is, & will be, the custom.

7th Evening. I think I told you that poor Campbell [46th] was very ill. I am happy to say he was rather better this morning & we got him off to Balaklava, having begged a French Ambulance mule to carry him there.

I am glad to say a box of Wombwell's turned up from England & two boxes of Provisions that he and I had wisely ordered about six weeks ago from Malta, so that now when my boxes come we shall be pretty well prepared for the next month or so. I am rather in grief about my Company. My two best Sergeants are for the present *hors de combat*, one of them having lost his leg & getting on but slowly [Brummell], & the other, a most valuable old Soldier, is in the midst of a low fever, poor old Chap! I have just come back from seeing him. He sent for me about a quarter of an hour ago, & I went away to see him in a great fright, but happily found him only dreadfully alarmed at having broken out into a profuse perspiration. The Doctor, who I had also dug out of his tent, & I explained to him that it was the very best thing that could have happened & would probably leave him free of his fever. It was an affecting sight to see 3 or 4 hairy old soldiers of my Company sobbing about him like women. They seemed so fond of him, & were so delighted when the doctor explained his Case to him. I expostulated with them, & was trying to persuade them that it was not exactly the way to cheer a sick man, but he told me, poor dear old chap, 'not to mind them for that he was not the least uneasy about himself, it was only those good old Donkeys'. I always go once or twice a day to see my other sick man who today is better than I have seen him yet. He was shot in the leg & had it taken off. Thanks to Chloroform he had no idea it was off till a day or two after the operation! & odd to say complains of pains in the foot which is off. Does not that seem extraordinary? I believe however that is not unusual! He is very fond of me & looks forward with great delight, he tells me, to my visits. I send him anything I can to eat or drink, but of course he is not allowed much & whenever I ask him what he would like he always wants the most dreadfully unwholesome things! The last thing he asked for was Pickles, & of course the Doctor told me that 'two pickled Walnuts would probably kill him'. However, I had sent him 3 or 4, & he is better than he ever has been yet!

Our part of the Siege goes on very tranquilly. We just go down and sit in the Trenches & we don't shoot at the Russians (having no guns) & I am happy to say that they don't shoot at us, not, however, for the want of guns for they seem to have guns all over the Town. The French on their side have the most furious rows every night with the Enemy – I never know what the result is. They have just finished one about 5 minutes ago. I fancy they don't do much harm, for if all the guns they fire were to take effect there would be no Russians or French left. They generally last about half an hour & take place about twice every night. We are now quite used to it, & the only excitement it causes in our small house consists in either Wombwell or myself turning in our Cribs & saying 'I say old fellow?' 'Yes?' 'Are you awake? (a silly question by the way) 'Just listen to those blessed French again', upon which we do listen to the blessed French for a second or two & go to sleep again. When we were less fagged & there were more of us, half the noise would have sufficed to have us all 'under arms'. We find that we can't afford to do our present work & be alarmed as well.

Letter 21

Before Sebastopol, 12 January

We got a wretched sort of mail last night consisting of old newspapers but no letters. I got by the way ... an *Illustrated* with pictures of us here only dressed as we *ought* to be not as we *are*. I can assure you that to this date, the 12th. Janry, we have neither the huts, fur caps, boots, or anything in the 'picture'. About 20 men yesterday who, odd to relate, were not in the Trenches went down to Balaklava & brought up the 5th. part of one hut for the Hospital! By about summer I have no doubt we shall be housed.

Excuse this little letter, but it is better than none. I am going down to the trenches tonight or would write you a longer one in bed. I can't write with my hands like ice, & have no fire to thaw them.

Letter 22

Before Sebastopol, 14 January

I must beg my best of mothers to excuse a very miserable note I sent her by the last Post but I only had a few minutes to write it in, &

then to cut down to the Trenches, & a very cold night it was, I can tell you. The Russians made a furious cannonade on all our Trenches that night. I myself was posted in advance, on a road (the Woronzoff Road as it is called) leading into the town, with 150 men, & the Russians came out in force, made a feigned attack on my place & a rather brisk one on a trench on my left where I am sorry to say they took 13 men & a Sergeant of the 68th. prisoners, but were driven back. It was a very beautiful sight from where I was posted, their Batteries being rather over my head, a very black night. We suddenly heard a most tremendous yell, & immediately afterwards, about 60 or 70 guns opened upon our trenches, all their shot passing well over my head. It lasted about a quarter of an hour. They came up my road, & fired a volley of musketry at us, but as we were behind an earth breastwork dug across the road, they did no harm & did not come near enough for us to fire with any certainty. It was I believe a great Fête day of theirs, and they were probably more drunk than usual. They always yell, by the way, whatever they do or are about to do – odd to say they did not kill a single man with all the fire they kept up. Shells at night, one can see coming all the way, & if not coming straight at one they are the prettiest things on a dark night you can imagine.

It is certainly dreadfully cold. We have had great falls of snow the last 2 days & it is about a foot and a half deep on the plain, but quite dry, & when it does not blow, I manage to stand it well. My feet are the only part of my person in grief, & they feel frozen from the time I get up till my return to my dearly beloved bed. The men suffer, of course, a good deal from frost bites, but on the whole I think their health is a good deal better than it was. We have got up this last day or two more warm coats for them, & tomorrow send for some more. The poor 63rd. have at last almost disappeared, & have, I believe, no one fit for Duty. Lord Raglan, who I think must have read *The Times*, came up here today, & is going to send the 63rd. to Balaklava, & we get the 18th., a strong Regiment, in their place, which will relieve our men considerably. None of our Regiment, except of course us 'old Campaigners' (the two Companies) had ever seen him before, except in the distance!

Our present great want (after fuel) is wooden houses; those I see no prospect of getting up. It takes, they tell me, 100 men to bring one hut up from Balaklava & we never have but few men 'off duty'. Conceive a tent with 2 foot of snow on the ground & of course in drifts many feet of it. This morning we literally had to dig our way out of ours. The Cavalry, to their great disgust, are turned to the only possible use that can be found for them, viz: to bring up our food, so that now we are pretty well off for food, tho' the cooking of it is a sad affair. There is hardly any wood left. There has been a little charcoal lately at Balaklava for anyone who could fetch it, but we are rather frightened about using it in tents for 3 wretched officers, who had little pans of it in their tents were found dead 'asphyxied' [sic]. One was a Major of Artillery 'Swinton'. I don't know the others' names or Regiments.[28] They also use the Cavalry for Ambulance purposes & a very ghastly procession of poor sick & dying creatures perched on gaunt horses goes away from up here terribly often. It is a great thing tho' getting them away at all for they never seem to recover in our Hospitals here. Heaven knows what they do when they get away. The Survivors of a six mile jolt on a rough road may benefit perhaps from change of air & at any rate more attention can be paid to those left behind. The weather has been so dreadful that I haven't been near my French friends for some time, so that I don't know how they get on. I should say that they must suffer a good deal, but their work is so much lighter, their Commissariat, Transport, Hospitals & in fact all their arrangements so infinitely superior to ours – that one may conclude that they suffer much less than us.

I must give you an instance while I think of it, of the clever way in which everything connected with the Army is done, at home as well as here. We got up at last about 20 pair of boots per company, a great want as the men were all in a wretched state. Would you believe that they are all too small! & except for a very few men useless! How curiously the vein of Incapacity seems to wind about thro' everything, not omitting even the humble boot. With endless wealth, great popular enthusiasm, numberless ships, the best material for Soldiers in the World, we are certainly the worst clad, worst fed, worst housed Army that ever was read of. Our wealth may be seen rotting in dif-

---

[28] Major Swinton died on 2 January 1855. Lt. Ramsbottom was another of the casualties of charcoal. The identity of the third officer, if there was one, has not been discovered.

ferent forms at Balaklava; our ships bring out the wrong things to the wrong people & generally leave them at the wrong place. Our soldiers die of inanition & our fine horses die of the Heavy Dragoons they have to carry & want of forage which rots about the Port! Let us hope to learn wisdom: it is an astonishing thing, how long John Bull (who is in most things a business man) has sat quiet and got so little for his money!

Letter 23

Camp before Sebastopol, 19 January

Last night I came home from a very bitter 12 hours in the Trenches, and enjoyed a good read in bed, after a good dinner, provided for me by my faithful mate. A thaw is now going on, fortunately not a very rapid one, or else we should soon be drowned, for we are surrounded by heaps of snow.

We are still in the same melancholy state, with perhaps a few more articles of warm clothing, but not half a single hut yet. We fade away daily, but quite patiently, and if one did not see such constant funerals, & enquire about affairs, no one would know what was going on. About 100 die daily in our Army. I do not include of course those who fall sick, & those who are carried away by the remnant of Cavalry. Lord Raglan has been seen (somewhat) about lately, & is supposed to have read the *Times*. I am almost inclined to think, that the 'faithful band' round him, have not allowed him to know the truth, not that I consider that any apology for him, as he ought to have found out, & looked about for himself.

Duncan Davidson suddenly came up the other day, having manfully walked up from his ship, about 8 or 9 miles, thro' the deep snow. He dined with Arthur [Wombwell] & me, & slept in a bed we made for him, intending to go to Balaklava next day, & get round to where his ship lays in some boat, but it was such a dreadful morning, we did not let him go, and as it cleared up a little, I took him round our Camps. I think he was much shocked with what he saw, and his astonishment & horror struck me very forcibly, for he & his ship have been now 2 or 3 weeks close by. Fancy how little can possibly be known in England of the real truth, tho' we know that everything is being done, that can be done, by the people.[29]

Letter 24

Before Sebastopol, 26 January

I did not write to you last mail, as it went off rather unexpectedly, furthermore I had nothing to tell you. *Now* I have rather more important news. Although Sebastopol has not yet fallen, my boxes (two of them in the *Oscar*) have arrived! & I got them up last night. They were full of the most charming and useful things, tho' almost too abundant. I intend to distribute amongst some of my cold friends the things that I can spare. Will you thank the Blakes for the nicest and most comfortable cap I have yet seen of the many varieties that have come, & the Col. [unknown] for a box of delicious cigars, a great treat! I have not had time to carefully look over the endless comforts of the boxes yet, but *one* I slept last night in, and enjoyed myself immensely in, & that was your delightful fur wrap, the softest and jolliest affair I ever saw. It is wrapped round me at this moment, also a rug I found in one box. They were the things I wanted much.

The nights are dreadfully cold, & I have occasional touches of Rheumatism. We are having now beautiful weather: a hot sun for a few hours of the day, & such a frost in the shade, & at night the ground like iron, unless for about 5 hours of the day when it becomes impassable for sticky mud. My hands, by the way, are frozen at this moment, for I cannot write, unfortunately, in some most delightful fur gloves, or rather pillowcases for the hands, that you have sent me, much the best I have seen out here yet. We have got up a good deal of warm underclothing (a great boon) for the men lately. Indeed there are so few now that it does not take much to bring up their things. 'Huts' we do not believe in. There are one or two put up as Hospitals, but the men and we are still in tents. How little does anyone seem to

---

[29] After writing this letter, Dallas went out to dinner, as noted in Maxwell Earle's letter of 19 January 1855: 'Fred Dallas and I dined with Col. Windham this evening to celebrate the arrival of his box.'

know about this climate! One person says winter is over, another that February and March are the dreadful months. I hope we shall have nothing worse.

Things are a little improved. The Guards have begun to relieve us in the Trenches, & now the men get a little more rest again. The woollen things we have some of, but we all feel bitterly how our Regiments might now be numbered by hundreds, instead of tens, if these things had been done in time! I think I told you that one Regiment had gone away, the 63rd., I mean they marched away 25 in number! Poor fellows. It was not a very nice Regiment, but they fought like fun at Inkermann. The Rifles, just in front of us, have now under 100 men for duty, if I recollect right they had 1000 not long ago!

We have great rumours of Peace here, tho' how the Emperor [Nicholas] can possibly swallow the terms I can't conceive. We shall all be perfectly delighted at it, at Peace I mean, if it does come off. Conceive a soldier saying that! Such has been the treatment we all have received, Men and Officers, that there is not much enthusiasm left.

I passed through the Turks' Camp yesterday, and positively they were considerably more comfortable than our men, each tent having a stove smoking away like fun. Odd to say, Ld. Raglan has been riding about a good deal lately. As regards the *Times* Correspondent, altho' he writes forcibly and truly, I don't wonder at his being in disgrace, for one must remember that everything we read, the Emperor also reads at St. Petersburg, and independently of his stating the exact position of our forces, our batteries, numbers & reinforcements. It must be most inspiriting to the Russians to know that we die by the hundreds, that our Generals are incompetent, & that our transport is worthless, like all the rest of our arrangements.

Altogether I don't think we bear our misfortunes with much dignity. The French manage these things, as they do everything connected with military matters, much better. They regularly send 6000 sick away monthly, & tell no one. They are getting, I should say, rather sick of us, were it not for their innate politeness, & their immense admiration of us at 'Alma' and 'Inkermann'. Naturally they must be tired of carrying away our sick, guarding our Batteries, carrying up our shot and shell, & in addition to all, having to fight about three small battles every night with the Russians, waiting for our new batteries to be put up. On their side of the Attack they have the most hideous fights. Last night they appeared to have regular engagement all night long, but I fancy from the darkness they don't do each other much harm.

The Russians, I am happy to say, leave us comparatively quiet in our Trenches. The only times they have come (except once or twice) they have found all our men fast asleep, & I don't think they suspect us of doing much harm. It is almost impossible to keep the men awake, they are so utterly fagged out. I regret to say that the man I sent to inquire about Bolland's poor protégés has come back from the Orderly Room to tell me they are all three dead! We have only about 80 left for duty, so that I hardly expected to find them here, but I hoped that they might be at Scutari, perhaps. I will give the things to some other poor fellows, as you directed me, but I must tell you that now we have heaps of warm clothing for the men (those that remain) & therefore tell you not to send any more things. The only difficulty is getting them from Balaklava, where they all remain for want of transport. Wombwell and I are still miracles of health.

I am happy to say that I have found out that one 'Elijah Johnson' of Bolland's 3 friends is not yet dead: he is sick at Scutari, and I will try at once and get him his parcel somehow when I can. W. Brooks died 25th. November (a Corporal), Jacob Johnson, 1st. January (a Corporal also).[30]

Letter 25

Before Sebastopol, 28 January

All the things you sent me were most useful and acceptable – the coat is charming, the fur apparatus the most comfortable thing I could have wished for, & the handkerchiefs and socks peculiarly fortunate, for I was rather short of both articles. I can hardly enumerate all the things that I have raked out of the welcome boxes so must thank you for them 'in masses'. In fact I am set up for this & the ensuing winter, if I may have the misfortune to spend another

---

[30] Pte Johnson died of diarrhoea at Scutari on 28 March 1855. Corporal Brooks died of cholera and Corporal Johnson of dysentery, on the dates shown.

one here. I am going to ask you not to think of sending me any more clothing, for I really should not know what to do with it, after the arrival of the *Zumarra* to which I look forward with great expectation.

I receive all your letters and papers & I don't understand exactly why other people don't get theirs. We get everything a day or two later after its arrival here than necessary, but that is a private discomfort arranged for us by the authorities out here. The weather is now pleasant enough, frost at night but lovely days, the only great bore being the mortar (I cannot call it mud) that is made by the sun in the day, about a foot in depth, which renders walking a great labour. The men are much the same in health, perhaps a trifle better. We got a draft of about 50 a day or two ago. I am always sorry to see these miserable drafts arrive, they never live, and look so nice and clean! We are getting new guns at last into our Batteries, what they will do I can't tell. My own suspicion is that the Russians will knock them down as they did the last lot, as they have now about 3 guns in position for 1 that they had before.

I went all over our new works, on the extreme right of our position by 'Inkermann' at the head of the Harbour, & had a most charming view of the whole Port. It was a beautiful sunny day, and nothing could be more lovely than the whole scene. The harbour is itself most picturesquely situated, & the water was like a mirror. I saw three of their line of battleships, 3 deckers, at anchor in the centre of it. The only break to the perfect quiet was an occasional puff of smoke from one of their batteries, & the whistle of the shot as it flew over our heads, for they were firing occasional shots at a working party in a battery behind where we were. The Russians hardly ever molest us in our Trenches, not so with the French, for they keep up a most constant fire of shells on their works & I should fancy must in the long run do some damage. The French have been ready with their guns, about 170 in number, for some time. They are all masked, as it is called, which means that the embrasures, or holes they shoot through, are filled up with earth which can be knocked away when necessary in a few minutes.

What do you think of Peace at home? I cannot conceive that the Emperor [Nicholas] is at all likely to accept such terms as we are likely to impose on him. Here, we don't believe in it at all, but the rumour of it had apparently done some good for there has been more done in the way of arming our Batteries this last week than during the previous six.

We have now some new mules from Spain who will be useful, but I should say not a twentieth part of the number required. The Cavalry still continue their cheery employment of carrying up biscuit and conveying back the sick. The only people who seem at all comfortable are the Highland Brigade who are, and have been, much too long doing nothing at Balaklava. They have escaped the whole of the horrid Trenches & the bad weather, much the most trying part of the Campaign. All the regiments, or nearly all, have two or three Captains going home owing to the late promotions. I believe our two junior ones will.[31] I made a good fight that the ones who have out from the beginning should have first claim, not with any reference to myself, for I should not have offered to go, but for a Captain [Shervinton], a most good natured hardworking Officer, with a wretched wife & two hungry infants at home, but I was defeated as the Colonel [Garrett] was somewhat obstinate about it. Poor old chap, he does nothing but sit over a brazier of charcoal until he becomes quite stupid. I was very sorry that I had not better success in my endeavour. I pity excessively any miserable man out here with a wife at home. They have no business here to begin with & if a chance of getting home turns up for anyone, why not let the only person whom it suits get it? None of us wish to go home. For myself I have perfect health and nothing but sickness would induce me to go till the affair is over one way or the other. Vesey is going to command the Depot, & he is another unfortunate with a wife at home who I suppose cries about him, as a decent woman ought, her greatest delight being perhaps reading his stupid little Irish letters. Shervinton, who is a blundering good natured chap (an Irishman) has struck up a cheery little friendship with me (from our having been out here so long together I suppose). He came and told me the other day in great glee! that his wretched wife had produced a baby, and always since comes and tells me how she is getting on whenever he hears from her. She is nursing it herself he told me! Where she gets the milk from I really can't conceive for I know he has only got his pay to keep himself and her & another (child

---

[31] The two junior Captains of the regiment, Fane and Waldy, left the Crimea for the Depot on 6 February 1855.

who eats with a knife and fork) but he is quite cheerful: ought not I to be, who has a warm coat, 12 handkerchiefs, socks & gloves, and no children?

I have just come back from Balaklava. No more boxes yet, the mud the same as usual. I am perfectly convinced that directly hot weather comes, some pestilence will rage in that dreadful place. I saw some nurses from Scutari (Heaven knows they're wanted) as I was leaving the place. The sick had just come from the camp on Cavalry horses, & they were putting them on board like bales of goods, nobody caring for them. 2 had died on the road & 1 died in being shoved up the ship's side!

Letter 26

Before Sebastopol, 30 January

I am sorry to hear poor Whyte-Melville is coming out; he would be much better writing songs at home. Today is such a cold day I have got on everything I possess; on the top of all Susan Blake's cap, (thank her much for it) Katie's and her sister's mitts, the mother's coat, and I don't know whose, (God bless them for them) fluffy bags for my hands, (not while writing tho').

I am sorry to hear that Mrs. Duberly is a friend of Susan's as she is a female of whom I have the greatest horror. We have not seen her for some time now, but she used, to the disgust of all of us, to be constantly looking on, with the great apparent glee, at the Siege, when it really was a Siege, and every half an hour or so poor mangled wretches were being carried up from the trenches, not to speak of the thousand horrors that a woman could not help seeing in a camp of this sort. Almost the last time I saw her, she was quietly looking through a Lorgnette, at the whole of her Regiment being blown to pieces at the dreadful Balaklava affair by the Russian Guns, (and if scandal speak truly) a lover of hers being one of the first killed.[32] *We* were there, sad spectators of it on duty, what she was there for, Heaven knows! What a mistake women make thinking to excite men's admiration by not being womanly.

---

[32] Captain Nolan was rumoured to be her lover.

I took a pleasant ride on a moke I borrowed today, went over to a *Zouave* camp close to the Guards, and listened to their capital band. The French Officers, who are always by the bye most smartly dressed, & always look like soldiers, get on capitally with us, and have got quite accustomed to our extraordinary appearance. We have a great pull over them in one way, we all can understand, & most talk, more or less badly, their tongue, whilst not one in (certainly) 50 of them can speak a word of English. The *Zouaves*, and *Chasseurs d'Afrique* are our principal friends, they formed the African (Algerian) Army, and are the most finished soldiers I ever saw. The *Zouave* band that I went to today, is a very good one and a favourite lounge with us when it is fine. The *Zouave* men (such splendid picturesque fellows, with immense beards) certainly do look with astonishment at us all. I was much amused a few days ago there. I was talking, myself in a sailor's shirt, to Prince Edward, whom I had happened to meet at Alma, & on the march once or twice, a most capital fellow by the way, he looking rather like a respectable Under-keeper on this occasion, when Canrobert & his brilliant Staff all came up. The blank look of astonishment on the *Zouaves'* faces, when they saw Canrobert come up, cap in hand, & making the most ceremonious speeches, to so homely looking an individual, were very rich. It must seem very odd to them, I always think, seeing our officers, for whom at the same time I think they have a great respect, walking about in clothes that no respectable servant could be induced to appear in.

General Bosquet & his Division, who came up so opportunely at Inkermann seem to me to have orders to look after us. They do now most of the outlying picquets & Vedettes duties on our right (Inkermann), duties by the same token that we do very indifferently. Bosquet is constantly about. He seems to be aware that if he did not look after us, we should be fighting some ridiculous battle, or doing some absurdity or other. We are well off for supplies now, as the shops have nearly everything that one wants, at a little (very little) less ridiculous price than formerly. The 'Crimean Fund', and the 'Plum Pudding Fund', &c &c exist as yet for us only in the columns of the *Times*. When we do get everything that our grateful country sends, or tries to send us, we shall die of repletion. I have got heaps of clothes, warm things &c. Now I want to explain to you [that] I should not know what to do with any more, so don't think of making me up any more boxes, when I have got the ones on the road, & the men have also now lots of warm things. But the baccy you are sending will be a treat to them.

Things on the whole are looking up within this last day or two. The work is lighter, & the weather certainly less severe, and I dare say that we shall not lose many more men. I look forward with dread to rains, that we are told of in February, & March. The huts are so dreadfully cumbrous, and the transport so inefficient, that one hut for a Hospital is all we expect to get up, and we must face it all in our tents. I really do believe, that we have seen as cold weather as is likely to be this winter, and here I, for one, am as well as ever I was in my life. Wombwell is another of the fortunate few, that have as yet held out. Poor Campbell [46th] is sick, on board a ship, looking such a spectre. He was never ill for an hour in his life before, and has an iron constitution. He starts tomorrow for a trip, a fortnight to Constantinople, and I think will get all right again.

The *St Jean d'Acre* has arrived, & I conclude Ld. Rokeby & Barnard in her, tho' I have not seen them. One meets men out here in the oddest way. I was riding the other day, & overtook a most dreary old Plunger, with whom I entered into sweet converse. Somebody happened to holloa out my name, and he afterwards asked me if I was any relation to a Mrs. Dallas at whose house he had once been to a capital ball, in Harley Street. His name, I think, was Forrest. He seemed an amiable but dismal old creature, and seemed to retain most vividly the memory of his wild dissipation in dear old Harley Street. (I wish I was there now, & not sitting on my bed writing on my knees, with my back dislocated).

2nd. No news. Heavy rain for a change this evening.

You ask me whether I am covered with short hair, I can relieve your mind, by telling you that I have continued the cleanly habit of shaving, with the exception of a pair of moustaches which are getting long, & which I eat a good deal with my food: not so my 'constant pardner', who looks like an amiable terrier, and is, (with some reason) annoyed at having a reddish sort of nail brush, growing all over his face, his hair on his head being very black.

Letter 27

Before Sebastopol, 5 February

Three of our men go home 'on Promotion' tomorrow: Vesey, Waldy & Fane. Everybody says 'lucky dogs' out here; I do not envy them much for as I have perfect health, & have seen everything as yet, I hope to see the end of this affair soon. Heaven knows whether I or many of us will! It is extraordinary how completely a long course of neglect & indifference in our welfare, & comfort, have utterly anni-hilated any enthusiasm in this poor Army. I honestly think that there are not ten Officers in any Division that would not be delighted at any chance of getting away. I was standing close to our camp the other day, talking to a Clergyman who has recently arrived here, & Lord Raglan rode by at some little distance. He asked me who it was. At the commencement of this Expedition the shouts and acclamations of every soldier & Officer in the camps would have told him. Now he rides (rarely) through the middle of a camp, the soldiers don't know (!) who he is & the Officers run away to avoid having to salute him!

I have just heard I have a box come for me at Balaklava & shall send tomorrow. I think it must be 'Cordings'. I hope so, for his things, & the blankets, are really my only wants now. I cannot write any more, partly for lack of news, mostly from the paper flapping about on my knees, and driving me nearly distracted.

Letter 28

Before Sebastopol, 9 February

The French keep continually receiving strong Reinforcements, & must have now a very large army, constantly increasing. I fancy we have nearly 100,000 men between us of which we have only about 10,000, & the French 90,000. About what our movements are likely to be, we have none of us any notion. Our Batteries are getting ready, & I really don't think that the French will allow us to dawdle any more, as they have been ready on their side for some time, & as they are very close to the town, must lose a good many men in the constant 'Sorties' the Russ make on them.

The 'Navvies' are here & have begun to make a railroad & as they have turned all the shopkeepers out of Balaklava & most of the Turks seem to be dead, the place looked to me rather better than usual a day or two ago when I was down there. I only pray to Heaven that we shall not be here to travel on the railroad when it is finished, for it can hardly be done for two months or more, & to the Summer here I look forward with great dread. I trust before Summer to be in the Town, or driven from the Country! The horrid pestilence that unavoidably must come amongst us in the hot weather will be something fearful. The amount of dead animals, & every description of horror that the whole of the plain is literally strewed with, & from which during the cold weather there is hardly any effluvia will, when the hot weather sets in, become a dreadful source of disease. As yet, one must recollect, we have had no disease (epidemic) amongst us in this Country, nothing but death & illness arising from causes that would have been equally fatal on Wimbledon Common or elsewhere, such as overwork, want of clothing, sleeping on damp ground & insufficient food. Cases of cholera have been isolated & on the whole I think that it is a healthy climate. We all earnestly hope for something being done speedily. We are all still in tents; we still have no fuel.

By the way, a 'Crimean Fund' Ship has come in,[33] & has been here for some days, full of things, but it was arranged that the Field Marshal [Raglan] should make some plan for the sale of the things & consequently the dreadful spell that seems to fall on, and paralyse everything that comes within the shadow of 'Head Quarters' has had its usual effect on the well-intentioned Fund & its efforts, for one cannot get anything on board the Ship & the Captain told me 'he didn't know when we should be able to get anything'. They were waiting (Heaven help them!) till Ld. Raglan had decided about it.

Letter 29

Before Sebastopol, 16 February

The French I believe, under Bosquet (our old friend) are going out in force, to thrash the Russian Army on our rear & right, a very judicious thing to do. They are getting much too plucky & want being

---

[33] The Crimean Fund schooner *Erminia* docked at Balaklava Harbour on 13 February 1855.

put in order. I fancy a small portion of our people will accompany him, but I don't know. In fact the whole thing is as yet only a rumour, but I think that is probably true.

We hear that the Turks have beaten the Russians at Eupatoria: this I doubt. Perhaps a few Turks may have discomfited fewer Russians, but they must be very different Turks or different Russians from the specimens of the two races that we have come across, for such to be the result of any great fight, with anything like even numbers. However, I sincerely hope it is true. I fancy that we have perhaps here only the scum of the Ottoman Army, & that there *are* good 'fighting Turks'. I believe we have here the Egyptian Levies, not the pur-sang Turks.

We have as yet no news about politics, further than Lord John's [Russell] resignation, and even with a totally new administration, I myself don't see what is to be done. If Ld. Raglan is recalled, I do not know what General we possess of talent enough to take us out of the mire we are plunged into. Sir Colin Campbell has, I fancy, too many seniors in the Army to get the supreme command. Lord Rokeby is, as I told you, arrived & is going, we hear, to have the 1st. Division. I saw him the other day, but not being personally known to him, of course did not speak to him. Sir Colin, by the way, I have never seen! isn't it odd? Barnard is to have the 3rd Division, I trust they will both turn out great Generals, (I mean Barnard and Lord Rokeby). We have lost a good man in Pennefather (our new Colonel),[34] & to say the truth, we are all rather sick of Generals. We suffer from two varieties, principally the one I may call the Gentlemanly helpless variety, the other variety are given up to leathern 'stocks', and foul language, and tho' I personally prefer the former, I really think the latter do more work & good.

I saw old Yea today. He was looking, and told me he had been, seedy, for some time, & looked not unlike a sick bear. I fancy being constantly in a rage, cannot be healthy, & I believe he has been so for some months, with everybody and everything. I observed tho' that he had got up various huts for his Regiment, & upon inquiry, found that he manages to do more than almost any Commanding Officer owing to the dreadful fright in which everybody was in of him, Doctors,

---

[34] He was temporarily invalided out of the Crimean Army on medical grounds.

Commissaries, Officers, Servants, & Horses, which goes in favour of my argument that the second variety of my 'Generals' are more useful than the first, in their generation.

I am sorry to say that my poor old Sergeant [Hampson] of whom I told you once, went away to Scutari, very ill, and died there.[35] How few ever seem to recover, either wounded or ill, in any way here! My other patient tho', who lost his leg [Brummell] is doing well, & will I hope soon be able to get home. He is one of the few who ever have recovered from an amputation here. The weather has been so fatal for wounds; in tents it is found impossible to keep the frost away from the injured limbs. He was hovering between life & death for a day or two, but a strong constitution pulled him through. I had written, when he could not himself, to his wife, a nurse in some family in Liverpool, & I got such a pretty letter from the 'lady of the house' the other day, thanking me for a little Xmas present I had sent her, (not the lady but the nurse). It appeared that the Sergeant's wife was not a very good scribe. He himself told me that she was 'a first rate woman', but that her spelling was indifferent, & then showed me a letter from her, & insisted on my reading it from one end to the other, smoking a little pipe on his stretcher & making the quaintest comments on it. 'Have you come to the part, where she says, Captain, she doesn't care if I come home with no limbs'? She spelt it, poor dear woman, 'lims', & seemed to have a sort of idea that her husband would return a 'torso'. I shall be quite sorry to part with him, when he goes, & he asked me if he might write to me when he goes away. I have now only about one Sergeant [Clapham] & seven men doing duty in my Company. Sad work, isn't it?

Letter 30

Before Sebastopol, 16 or 17 February
We are still leading the same uninteresting life that we have been doing for so long. There is hardly any firing going on on either side. The French, by the way, occasionally having a row with their opponents, the results of which we seldom hear. We go to the

---

[35] His death was misreported – see Letter 48.

Trenches 'seldomer' than we used to do, & on the whole I think our prospects have somewhat brightened. We trust, or at any rate we hope, we have 'broken the neck of' the Winter. We have been having high winds, which I personally dislike, but they are healthy and dry the ground, in our present position, an immense thing. We know little (probably less than you at home) of what our future offensive movements are likely to be. There was a rumour of an intended attack upon the Army outside the Town, but I have not heard anything definite about it. The French still keep on landing troops in hundreds, we in tens, & I almost begin to fancy that we shall wait until some measures can be taken to completely invest the town, and stop their supplies. This must of course be done by some other force landing on the north side of the place, and engaging the Russian force there.

We have two new Engineers here, a famous new French one, & an English one, 'Jones' (I don't know the Gaul's name) [Niel]. Of course they say (or it is said for them) that we have been doing everything wrong. Whether they will do anything right I don't know & it remains to be seen.

The railway is getting on, & people seem to say that it will succeed, Navvies at any rate work like fun at it. I only trust that we shall not be here to travel on it.

We rather expect a Mail tonight, & of course are anxiously waiting to hear whether we have a Government, not but what I think we should get on just as well without. I am not one tho' that lays everything on the unfortunate Ministers. I think they have been placed in a very false position. One can hardly say that the want of organisation in our Army can be laid to their charge, as they found the Army just as it had been for years, & I think any other Government would have equally found its organisation to be one suited for Peace, & not for War. Until there arose a War, I don't really see how anyone could say how it would work. They sent out a man, in Lord Raglan, whom all England wished to see in Command, & gave him every power. They have sent out everything that they were asked to send, & I really think that if they brought & delivered everything at the 'basis' of our operation, Balaklava, they could hardly be expected to carry it any further, & might very well expect the Authorities here to get it up the remaining six miles. Soldiers they sent out as fast as they could, &

one can hardly blame them for our having a small Army instead of a large one.

By the way, the 10th Hussars are not coming on until the Spring. People in England make a mistake in laughing at the idea of Arab horses living in this climate. It has been found that Arabs are the only horses that get on here, & the *Chasseurs d'Afrique*, who are all mounted on Arabs, are the only Cavalry that have weathered the Winter, & have lost hardly any horses. It seems extraordinary the horses accustomed all their lives to an African Climate, and coming straight from thence, should endure cold so well, but such is the fact.

Occasional Deserters come in from the Russ, & of course give the usual account, viz: that which will be most pleasing for their new friends to hear, & always say that the Town is in a great strait, no food, & constant mutinies &c &c. I never believe them. There was a capital joke the other day. A soldier of the 1st. Royals appeared after a long absence, & said that he had escaped from the Town, having been taken prisoner, & was taken according to custom, to 'Hd. Quarters' there. He gave a most graphic account of how badly he had been treated, & how everybody in the place was starving, all to the great delight of 'the wiseacres'. To our great amusement, it has been found out since that he never was taken prisoner, & that he had been living in some remote French Camp until tired of it, & then came home with his acceptable news.

Last night some of our men in the advanced works, took five Prisoners, all as usual drunk. As all their English consisted in saying 'Bons Ingliz', & our people in saying 'Bons Russ', there was not much information got out of them. I suppose they have been setting the Interpreter at them since, but I have not heard if any news was obtained.

Today we hear almost for certain, that the Turks have had an Engagement with, and discomfited the Russ at Eupatoria, I trust it is true, I told you of the rumour in my last.

The *Canadian* has come in, & I have got my box off her, but not up here, my 'moke' being rather unwell. I shall have to wait a day or two for it, unless some philanthropic brother officer brings it up for me. How it rained the other day, to my intense delight, for I went out in my waterproof Boots, Coat &c, & defied the elements most successfully.

I am glad by the bye, to see that the Cavalry are going to get a clasp for Balaklava, not because I and the rest of the 4th. Division will get it, but because they certainly do deserve some mark of approbation for such a 'ride'. What our Army wants is some 'order of merit' (I saw some talk of it). It would be peculiarly applicable to that occasion, for a medal has usually been considered a symbol (as it were) of victory, & in that sense I think it unsuitable for an affair where we met with such a loss, & left the field with our dead & wounded in the Enemy's hands. Again, a medal is given to all who are engaged, or 'under fire'. Now we who were merely spectators, & happened to have a few shots amongst us, & one or two men killed or wounded, will get (they say) the same as the Light Cavalry.[36]

I saw someone the other day who confirmed the story in the papers, I suppose you saw it?, about the signal sent up by mistake on Old Dundas's departure. The Middy who had charge of the signals, sent up 'May Hanging await you', instead of 'May Happiness await you'. It was hauled down, but not before the whole fleet had read it. Good, wasn't it?

We got yesterday our Winter Coats, and very jolly little coats they are too, tho' a trifle late; they are grey tweed short shooting coats, lined with the skins of domestic animals, some with cat, some with dog, others with rabbit. Mine (I think) is cat! & very comfortable.

A day or two ago, Wombwell & I rode over to a 'Monastery' called St. George's about 4 miles from here. I don't think I ever saw anything so lovely as the scenery, in a rocky, blustery way. It is perched on the edge of a tremendous cliff, and there are winding paths down to the sea. There are 16 most filthy old Friars, & a few even filthier Greek families, & one old naturalised English-Russ. There were a few French Officers with whom we as usual 'fraternised'. They were having a warm dispute when we first saw them, about St. George. One was saying that it was St. Michael that killed the Dragon, another St. George. I told them I thought it was St. G. as he was our 'Patron', but even that would not convince St. Michael's admirer, so I suggested that there might have been two brother Dragons, and by allowing

---

[36] 'They' were correct. The entirety of the 1st and 4th Infantry Divisions received the clasp for Balaklava, as well as the Cavalry Division and the men of the Thin Red Line.

that St. Michael killed the eldest, everybody was appeased. We walked up the cliff afterwards behind Mrs. Duberly & party, & very nice black Trousers she had.[37]

Letter 31

Before Sebastopol, 23 February

The weather, I am sorry to say, has gone back to real Winter again, such cold, & frost, & snow, & sleet, & wind. I have got boxes, by *Oscar* 2, by *Canadian* 1, by *Clyde* 1, & by the *Loire* 1; so that I am quite independent of the weather now, & have clothes enough to smother me if necessary, an operation by the way, I shall be sadly tempted to perform, unless the weather improves. I made a good many men happy with the tobacco &c, & we really don't want now any more winter clothing. There are so few left that we are at last pretty well supplied. I got a box from the *Loire* yesterday, I don't know exactly who sent it, but amongst other things there was a Plum Pudding, alas! so wretchedly packed that it was all green with salt water, or mould, fancy that! If ever (tho' I am sure I don't deserve any more) you *did* send out, or had the opportunity of sending out, a box, I am going to ask you not to think of sending any more clothes of any sort, but I will greedily ask you to send out some food. I think a large pie of Mrs. Vailey's, to steady the box at the bottom, would be a most wonderful good thing, & whilst I am so quietly telling you what to do, or not to do, I must tell you that we have not any difficulty in getting 'condiments' such as mustard, pepper, pickles & those sort of things: people thinking kindly that one wants sadly those sort of things send out whole boxes full, & one cannot very well live on them alone.

We all went down (the Regiment) & got new arms yesterday, from Balaklava, & very beautiful Arms they are.[38] I only wish that we

---

[37] Mrs. Duberly's habit of wearing trousers was a shocking departure from the accepted standards of the time. Dallas was not the only officer to comment upon the practice.

[38] An officer of the 68th reported, with some pique, 'Started at 8 o'clock for Balaklava to get the new Enfield rifles. Halted at the 18th Regt. to give them our Miniés, which delayed us some time as the 46th were also there. Old Garrett ordered us to halt & let the 46th go first. They consequently got their rifles at Balaklava first.'

required 1100 of them instead of about 300. I am just going to the Trenches, now merely a very cold uncomfortable way of spending the night, seldom any firing, & the men, from not having such hard work, are livelier, & give one less anxiety & trouble on night-duties.

There was a most absurd expedition, a 'Reconnaissance', made by the Highland Brigade the other day, in which the French were to have assisted. By some mistake they did not go, & when Sir Colin [Campbell] had found the Enemy, he had to come back again, being not strong enough to attack. It was a dreadful morning, or rather night, & the absurd manner in which 'the Staff' hunted each other, & Sir Colin, to fetch him back, & tumbled about in the dark, would have been only most amusing, if it were not disgraceful.

Letter 32

Before Sebastopol, 25 February

We are still in much the same position as before. Sir Colin [Campbell] went out on a little expedition in the middle of the night with the Scotch Brigade, after an army that had been poking about near Balaklava, for some time, (a few days ago this came off) & having found the Russians had to come back again the way he came, his force not being strong enough to attack. The truth was there was some 'hash' about the whole affair. Bosquet, our French Friend, was to have gone out in another direction & to have caught the Russ, but he did not go, & Sir Colin did, I fancy, rather prematurely, for the Staff from Lord Raglan's were hunting for him all night, to get him back, & could not find him in the dark, & as it was without exception the most beastly day we have had all this Winter, the Scotch must have come home rather wretched. He started about 2 A.M. & came home perfectly frantic about 10 A.M. One Staff man hunted another, for nearly 4 miles, the hunted one fancying his pursuer to be a body of Cossacks (as it was very dark, & even in daylight the 'poudre' snow blowing so fearfully that one could not see 10 yards). I think the man was 'Sterling',[39] who was hunted by Wetherall, & tho' 'put up' about 4

---

[39] Sterling provides a full account of this débacle in his *The Highland Brigade in the Crimea*.

miles from Balaklava, he was only secured by him in the town. Altogether a more absurd affair in every way could not have taken place, & as the Highlanders have skipped all the harassing work of the Siege, & Inkermann, we up here are unfeeling enough to be amused.

The night before last there was a most furious fight on the right of where I was in the Trenches. The French have taken off our hands some Outposts & Redoubts on the right towards Inkermann, & to their disgust the Russians came one day & quietly built a battery facing them, about 500 yards from their works. Of course this could not be allowed, & this night was selected for the storming of it. I had some idea that they were going to do it, & consequently passed a somewhat anxious time, as it was not improbable that the Russians on being attacked would come out at all points. It was so beautiful a night that I could nearly read your last letter that was put into my hand just as I marched down: and I went round my sentries pretty often, being in the advanced Trench of all. Looking down a steep ravine, on which our furthest sentry is placed, I could see the Russian Sentry at the bottom quite plainly, walking about & stamping his feet to warm himself. It was a most curious scene altogether, not without excitement, standing looking into the town, so close that one could hear people talking, & men digging, & see their pipes. Sentries at night do not shoot at each other (I mean of course the Sentries of opposing forces) & I cannot fancy a more singular way of passing an hour, than standing or walking about on such a night, within easy shot of a Russ, who by the way, is not such a ceremonious personage, & thinks little of crawling up and murdering a Sentry who is not looking out. We found two poor creatures on the very spot I am speaking about 3 or 4 weeks ago, who had met with this fate. On going to relieve them (all sentries on these posts are 'double') they found them both dead with bayonet wounds.

After going round all the posts, about 1 o'clock, I began to look out anxiously towards the right. A rocket or two about this time was fired from the French on the left, & very beautiful they would have been, had not one nearly hit one of my sentries, & another pitched close to our Trench, where we had to lie down on our faces until such time as it chose to go off (the great peculiarity of a rocket being that no one has any idea of where it is going. Sometimes it turns round & comes back). I do not know if the rockets in question were signals, but soon afterwards we heard the most tremendous firing about the new Russian Battery. It lasted about half an hour, & then ceased, not a shot being fired all the time at us & I hoped that the French had gained their object. Of course we could have no idea of what had happened, but except at 'Inkermann', I never heard such volleys, incessant ones, of musquetry. It is to me one of the many horrors of war, & especially this sort of warfare, perhaps one of the greatest, the reflection, after looking on (perhaps, as on this night, a mere spectator) at a 'row' as we call it, knowing there may be hundreds or thousands of poor creatures killed & maimed, on a hill or in a valley a very short walk off. On this night we could tell from the obstinacy of the firing that there must have been hundreds killed. Then all was quiet, & until next day, when I cantered over to the *Zouaves*, I did not know who had won the day, or rather the night. Then I learnt that one or two Regts. of *Zouaves* & 1 *Infanterie de la Marine*, in all about 2000, went to the assault of this Battery. The Russians never fired until they were quite close, & then a fearful volley. The Marines ran, but the *Zouaves* (the finest soldiers, I think in the world) rushed up with the bayonet, & gained the Battery. But hordes of the Enemy came out, and after the desperate fight I had heard, drove them out. They were overpowered by numbers, & lost I am told 3 or 400 men, & many Officers: one General badly wounded, 'Monet' by name. I asked a *Zouave* who was there about his 'Marines'. He told me that they fairly ran away, & when I asked him why the *Zouaves* didn't fire at them, he said that they were too busy, but that some of the others, who had been left to guard the French trenches gave them a volley as they came running in! He had been at 'Inkermann' (my friend) & said 'Oh if you English had been with us, instead of the Marines!' I don't know if he knew that I was going to give him my last cigar (which I did do) but I hope he didn't. I dare say you will think this rather a tedious account of a 'night attack', & except for the encouragement it must have given to the Russians, an unimportant one, but I have little to write about, & perhaps it may amuse you. I am sick of telling you how we die, & how our last November clothing is soon expected, & all the ills and wrongs that the 'Special Correspondent' [Russell] tells you so much better.

Today, a party of us, Wombwell & two or three very good fellows, our allies from a neighbouring Regiment, the 68th, made a pic-nic to the 'Monastery' & passed a most pleasant day. We rode over there, with a servant with 'grub', & ate it on a most romantic little spot on the side of the cliff. As somebody observed, 'it was really not very cold'. The intense enjoyment there is, in getting away altogether from the horrors & noise of such a camp as ours, to a lovely spot like the one we went to, you may well conceive. There was a French General & his Staff there, Pellisier (I am not sure of the spelling), the man who smoked the African people in the cave in Algeria, a common looking man. He commands the Army *de la Siege*. I wish he would smoke the Russians. He was a visitor like us, & looked as if he would like some *Pâté de foie gras*, but as we had not enough for his numerous 'tail' we didn't invite him. We scrambled down, when full, to the beach: a most beautiful one it was too, with jolly sand like home, & I really think we should not have been much astonished if an old bathing-woman, or a Coast-Guard, had come round the corner of a rock upon us. Scrambling up the cliff was not so amusing as sliddering down we found, & we found a glass of cherry brandy very refreshing, with the most delicious cold water I have tasted since landing in this country.

We had a most interesting conversation with 'the Superior' of the Monastery, he talking Russian with great rapidity, & we, at intervals, taking off our hats & saying 'Bono Johnny'. The Monks were very nasty looking beasts, with long hair like women, & faces & foreheads like apes. They seemed happy enough, laughing together, & did not seem to feel much their position, & the desecration of their beautiful home by a Company of *Zouaves* who are quartered there. Odd to say, the storm of the 14th. did more harm than the French to their old nest. It completely blew off the roof of one of the houses, & inflicted great damage all about the place. It must have been so lovely in Summer, & even with us all here, it will again be. We cannot destroy the beauty of its position, & the wonderful broken points of rock, torn, to all appearances from the main cliff. I am in love with the place, & intend going often, weather and duty permitting, to hide myself from this loathsome 'before Sebastopol'.

Letter 33

Before Sebastopol, 2 March

People at home seem certainly greedy of any information from here, and in many instances having been lent letters to read, have most unwarrantably published them. To my astonishment, I saw in a Liverpool paper, a note of mine to a poor Sergeant's wife, whom I think I told you I had written to, about her husband. As it merely stated that her husband had been wounded and was unable to write, in a very few lines, I cannot conceive what interest anybody could have taken in publishing it. It is hardly safe to write an order to one's Tailor now.

The weather is now real Winter again, frost and bitter winds and a little snow. Nothing doing, in a military way. There is a story, I don't vouch for its truth, of a General Forey, a Frenchman, being found in communication with the Russians, and 'they say', he was shot on board ship a day or two ago.[40]

There was an hour's truce to bury the dead, asked by, and given to, the Russians, the day before yesterday. It was after the night attack on the Russian Battery that I told you of in my last letter. I did not hear what the evening's loss was, but I should think that it was considerable.

The railway is getting on rapidly, and is already in use, as it clears things well out of the filthy port of Balaklava. I don't know when it is likely to get up here.

I am writing this in a little hut, which belongs to a friend of mine in a neighbouring Regiment, the 68th.[41] My tent is flapping about in such a disgusting manner, it is not much fun writing in it. The hut I am at present writing in, is one dug out about four feet deep in the earth, then a wall of mud and stones about three feet more, and a roof of bits of plank with an old sail over it, and is perhaps one of the pleasantest in the country. This is the popular style of architecture here. Wombwell and I have not been able to manage a hut for various reasons: one, the miserable 'fewness' of our men, preventing one's getting workmen; secondly, our being some distance from any stones. However, we hope to be able to get through the Winter in our tent. With lots of clothes, I think it is a healthy place enough to sleep in, and we are out all day, except during particularly furious storms of snow or rain.

---

[40] This rumour about General Forey was widely accepted, and is repeated by Temple Godman in much the same vein. It was completely untrue.

[41] Probably that of Captain Savage. Savage's diary records Dallas and Wombwell visiting him again the following day.

Letter 34

Before Sebastopol, 4 March

The railway is creeping steadily on, and this weather is perhaps a trifle better. It is at any rate 'fine healthy weather', but I personally hate wind so much that I do not enjoy it as much as I ought.

We are looking forward, as you may suppose, anxiously for all sorts of news from home, political and other. Peace, no one seems to think of out here. I confess I have ideas of my own on the subject & privately think in opposition to everybody around me, that the Czar [Nicholas] is much more likely to make peace & come to terms, Sebastopol *not* being taken; but as I am no judge of political affairs, and everybody says both at home and out here 'Sebastopol must be taken before any hopes of peace can be entertained', I hold *my peace*.

I rode down today to the Cavalry Camps to lunch with some friends, and we had a really good afternoon's fun, pony races &c on the prettiest little 'plateau' of land among the hills this side of Balaklava., & afterwards we had a most capital race after a wild sort of dog, who led us a chase of about 1/2 an hour, as fast as a fox. There are a great many of these dogs among the mountains. In the midst of the races we suddenly saw the Cavalry 'Vedette' who is on a hill in the valley of the Tchernaya, and whom we could see well through a break in the hills that we were surrounded by. We saw him gallop in from his post, and at the same time saw a few Cossacks on the opposite hills wandering about. We suspected some advance of the enemy perhaps on Balaklava, & you cannot fancy a more curious scene that we must have formed for any spectator, about 200 of us suddenly tearing across the little plain to the edge of a ravine to look over towards the Russians. However, all remained quiet, and the races went on as before. I believe our Cavalry Piquet took two or three Cossacks, who came too near & that was all. A few French whom we rather disturbed in a very pretty little village in the hills, seemed much astonished at us and with some show of reason I allow. We tore through the village about 200 in number after a great savage looking white dog, all dressed in the usual eccentric clothes of the British Officer, some in fur coats, some in shell jackets, some in jackboots, some in gaiters, some on hairy ponies, others on hairless chargers, but all certainly cheerful. A French Sentry we passed was perfectly delighted. I don't think I ever saw a man so excited in my life. He put down his gun, and jumped on a low wall that was behind him, & danced with delight.

Letter 35

Before Sebastopol, 8 March

We are full of news that came here the day before yesterday of the death of the Czar [Nicholas]. If it is true, of course you will have heard of it for ages before you get this. The news came from Ld. John Russell to Ld. Raglan & it said, 'This may be relied upon' so that we mostly believe it, tho' how, or why, he should die in such an exceedingly apropos manner, I can't conceive. Nobody seems to know (granting the death to be true) exactly how it will affect the war, & us. I should fancy it will stop it eventually, the sooner the better say I, for I look forward with infinitely more dread to the Summer than the Winter here.[42]

We are now having the most charming weather, quite like an English Spring, & if there was a single blade of grass, or a tree, in our corner of the Crimea it would be charming. As it is I personally am happier than I have been for months. It is always a pleasure to me to look at a fine day, & when I have done the little duty that we have to do, I ride away from all the noise, & stench, & carrion, & roam about the hills towards Balaklava. There are, about there, I think the most beautiful cliffs I ever saw. They go down so abruptly about 7 or 800 feet into the deepest blue sea, & all the little platforms, or any spot where a pinch of earth can stay, are covered with jolly little green shrubs. Our health is, I am afraid, not much improved. The awful changes in the weather are very fatal to the sick, for you must remember my ink was frozen four days ago, now I am going about without a waistcoat!

I told you of my poor Sergeants I think, one dead [Hampson], the other almost recovered & now hopping about on crutches [Brummell], & very happy at the notion of going home soon. I saw a most absurd interview that he had yesterday with two *Zouaves*. He was sitting on a bank in the sun reading a paper, with his unfortunate

---

[42] Tsar Nicholas I died at St Petersburg on 2 March 1855.

stump sticking out in front of him, & the two *Zouaves* came wandering by, when one of them caught sight of his leg, & then they pointed to it, & one of them said 'Russe?' He nodded yes, upon which they both explained to him, with the most perfect pantomime, what they would do to the Russe if they ever came across him, & one eventually went through the outward forms of cutting off the obnoxious Russe's head & handing it to my old friend, who perfectly understood the whole thing & solemnly shook hands with them. I have, I am sorry to say, my only remaining Sergeant, a very good man, now ill, & very ill [Clapham]. He was merely complaining of a headache a day or two ago, & yesterday he went into the Hospital, & on my going to see him in the evening, I found him struck down by the worst form of Typhus fever. Of course nothing but a miracle can save any man in a Camp Hospital with such a disorder. Such occurrences every day as these would make the most zealous soldier shudder at his horrid employment.

I don't think much of your new Ministry, it is uncommonly like the old one.[43]

Letter 36

Before Sebastopol, 11 March

'They say' that we are to commence bombarding the town again on Wednesday, but so many days have been so often given for the same purpose, by rumours, that I don't much believe it. I don't exactly know why they are going to do it now, except perhaps the feeling that it would be a pity to waste such a lot of nice shot & powder which we have been at the trouble of dragging up, for they don't seem to talk now of any assault, perhaps they fancy that if the town was destroyed that Menshikoff might give in. I am certain that we cannot destroy their works, as they [are] stronger & much more numerous than our own. Anyway our Batteries are ready to begin whenever they give the word.

Lord Raglan politely sent in with a 'flag of Truce' to tell them that

---

[43] The Aberdeen administration had been replaced by one headed by Lord Palmerston.

the Emperor [Nicholas] was dead, as they could not hear it as soon as we could. Lord Burghersh took the message & they as politely told him that they did not believe it. The story goes (I don't vouch for it) that Burghersh quietly took out his Betting Book & offered to lay them £50 all round that he was dead. I don't think they took him up. I believe they know it in the town now.

Lord Rokeby kindly called up here to see me yesterday, but I had just gone out. I was going to see him today, but it is such a very wet day that I must defer my visit. How savage they are in the papers about him. How very tiresome it must be for him to see the various letters in the papers, one man saying he is as deaf as a post, another that he is not quite, another says if you holloa very loud, he *can* hear, & one very plucky man that he was very sharp of hearing!

The papers seem rather annoyed with us Regimental officers for not having died as quickly as the men. The answer is a very simple one. We fed and clothed ourselves, & Government did neither for the men. Unless we had all had some little means of our own, I think we should all have died in numbers enough to please *The Times*.

You a little misunderstood the question of my not having got a 'majority'. I fancied I had explained it to you. Hardy was senior to me, & tho' his name was not mentioned, it would have been impossible to promote me over his head, & very unfair as he was wounded, & did command at the commencement of the action. My name was mentioned by Col Windham, our Q.M.General who was left in command of the Division at Inkermann, a most capital and hard working soldier, & one who has been very kind to me always out here. He was by accident with me during most of the action, & was good enough to be very complimentary both to me, & of me to others, after the Battle, & now that Hardy is out of the way, I dare say I have a chance of getting the Brevet. I know Windham has done all he can. He has the great merit of being in bad odour at Head Quarters, as he is much too independent a man and too fond of the truth ever to get on.[44] Consequently, altho' the only

---

[44] Despite Dallas' dismal predictions, Windham rose to become a Lieutenant General and was Chief of the Staff in the Crimea.

man I (or any one else) saw giving any orders or doing anything at Inkermann, he alone of all the Staff was passed over, & not promoted. Many who were not even 'under fire' were. I have not set my heart on the majority: if I get it, *tant mieux*; if I don't, I am no worse off than I was before.

This fine weather has done us all good. When I say that, I mean that the men who are well, are more cheery, & even clean their arms, & have their clothes dry. Their work is much lighter than it was, & if we were beginning with healthy men, I think we could get on capitally. As it is the numbers in hospital don't decrease, and the poor fellows have not stamina to get well. Yesterday I read the service over my last Sergeant [Clapham]. I think I told you in my last that I had another Sergeant very ill. He died the day after, & yesterday I buried him.[45] We have no clergymen to the Division, 3 have gone within two months, & we have always to read the service ourselves. He was a very good man and one I valued much. My friend with the 'one leg' [Brummell] is getting on capitally, thanks to an extraordinary constitution, but of course he will never soldier again. He is going home as soon as we can get a conveyance for him, & he insists upon my giving him my mother's address as he wants to go and see her, he says, & tell her how well I am getting on, when he gets to England. So that you must not be astonished at having a visit from a great bearded man with one leg some day. However, he is not there yet. I wish he was, but few of them, poor fellows, seem to reach their homes. One of the most painful phases of this sort of life is the horrid sort of familiarity one has with death, every day hearing of poor creatures whom one has seen knocking about the camp being suddenly taken off. We [46th] have actually buried, since we came into the country, 432! Conceive that about as many more in Hospital, here and at Scutari, most of whom will probably never get home. I am always afraid to ask after any soldier, whom I perhaps have not seen for a day or two. I so well know what in 9 cases out of 10 will be the answer. The sun has quite come out so I will not write any more dreary news. I will finish this before the post goes out tomorrow night.

---

[45] Sergeant Thomas Clapham died of dysentery on 10 March 1855.

16th. The Court Martial[46] is just over (4 P.M.), & the weather has changed from fine and warm to cold and wretched since this morning. I, who am like the lady in the weather house, have gone in completely.

We have been enjoying the most charming weather & I have been spending the last two or three days, to my great disgust, in a fusty old Hut on a Court Martial, & am taking advantage of some informality in the proceeding, that has adjourned the Court for an hour, to finish this.

The Siege on our part goes on the same as usual. We have now nearly all our Guns ready, & we sit in our trenches, & the Russians in theirs, without any firing or trouble. The French who took some time ago all our 'Duties' on the right, viz outlying Picquets &c, have been making rather a mess of it. The Russians have built up work after work opposite to them, and the French have made one or two unsuccessful attempts to turn them out.

I am commencing a little to lose faith in our lovely allies. The Russian don't seem to care the least for them, & have repulsed them on two or three occasions lately. They had a great fight the night before last. The French attacked some Russian 'Rifle ambuscades' & at first turned them out, but the Russians came back, & regained them, & the French in a subsequent attempt, failed to recover them: this of course is rather disgusting & must give immense encouragement to our enemy. Personally I am rather amused at it, as it will make our allies a little more modest in their tone, which at present would lead the public to suppose (from their letters &c) that 'we were very charming people, but rather a log about their necks, & that without us

---

[46] General Order No. 5 of 11 March 1855 convened a General Court Martial under the Presidency of Col. T. Scott Reignolds, C.B., 18th Regiment. The Court sat for the first time on 14 March 1855, and continued by adjournment to 16 March 1855. The Prisoner, Lieutenant Arthur Maurice Richards, 77th Regiment, was found guilty of 'Conduct unbecoming the character of an Officer and a Gentleman, in having, in Camp before Sebastopol, on or about the 19th February, 1855, deliberately and wilfully stated to a Regimental Court of Enquiry that a certain paper writing, then produced to the Court of Enquiry, was not in his hand-writing; he well knowing the said Statement to be false.' He was sentenced to be dismissed Her Majesty's Service. Raglan, in approving and confirming sentence, recommended that he be allowed to receive the value of his Commission. It is unsurprising that Dallas fails to mention any details of the proceedings.

delaying them, they would have done the whole affair long ago', totally forgetting that we have done all the fighting, & in my opinion, fighting they could not have done.

The way in which poor Tryon (who was killed) with some of the Rifles & others, took a similar ambuscade, (to the one that they failed in taking) & held it against two or three attacks to regain it, forms a (to them) mortifying contrast, to their proceedings the other night.

A sad thing happened the other day, a poor engineer, Capt. Craigie, was returning from the trenches, where he had been for the last time, just going away to be married to a girl at Corfu, when a stray shell burst some way in the air, & one piece came down & struck him on the head. He never moved again.[47]

Letter 37

Before Sebastopol, 19 March

Our batteries are nearly finished. The French have been making rather a mess of that portion of our lines that we gave up to them. The Russians build Redoubts & 'Ambuscades' for their Riflemen opposite our Allies, & they make in return most noisy attacks upon the 'Russe', without any apparent result, except a wretched troop of wounded passes us on their ambulance mules almost daily. They had such a furious fight the night before last, that we turned out & marched down towards the row to support them. However, after waiting some little time, we marched back again. 'Sir Brown' (as the French call him), who wears a tight leather stock, & is by way of being very vigilant, turns his Division out about 3 or 4 times a night, with his usual accompaniment of curses & noise, whenever he hears any firing anywhere. Thank Heaven, I am not under him! He is second in command, & anything happening to Lord Raglan, I conclude he would be A.1. As I much prefer a gentlemanly 'King Log', who is at any rate loved by all that know him, & hated by none, to a 'King Stork', who is quite the reverse, I hope nothing may happen to our present chief.[48]

[47] Captain Craigie was killed on 13 March 1855.
[48] King Log and King Stork are characters in Aesop's fable of the *Frogs Looking for a King*. King Log (being a piece of wood) did nothing; King Stork devoured his subjects.

There are various reports about the camp: one that the Russe are getting short of shot, a report probably arising from the fact that the French having shelled the town most terribly last night, on the Sea side (the left) without any reply. I hope it is a true one; it is at any rate *ben trovate*. Another, is that Menshikoff is dead; that, I can't tell the origin of, but he is known to have been wounded some little time ago, & there is evidently some 'swell' dead in the city, from the flags being half-mast high, and the tolling of bells heard from our advanced trenches.

The men are getting, I think, healthier. Those that are not *ill*, are at any rate much more cheery. They are able to keep their things, blankets, coats &c, dry, the great desideratum. I do not think I exaggerate, in saying that they, none of them, until a month ago, could possibly have had anything dry thoroughly for 3 months! Lord Rokeby called up here the other day, & I was out, but I went down the next day, & he was out. I am going tomorrow again if I can manage it. He lives on the top of one of the sharpest & highest hills round Balaklava, some way from here.

The Railway is creeping up towards us. Today (I think, for the first time) it brings some guns up part of the way, an immense help.

The *Jason* went yesterday to Alexandria, to fetch the 10th Hussars. They cannot be here for 3 or 4 weeks I suppose, but we want Cavalry much, & a fine strong regiment mounted on hardy Eastern horses, will be invaluable.

We have been having some Races this last week here, & great fun they were. I don't think I have seen or heard so many laughs from Men and Officers for many a month. We had some 4th Division races & a capital 'attendance' as we have a very good course, lots of Frenchmen, who were much delighted. Tomorrow, or the next day, we have some races for the men, foot races &c. Sir John Campbell, who is a very good natured man I believe, came out of his Hole for the occasion. The last race was one of 'Mokes', or rather 'Mules', and was great fun. The men have all sorts of races tomorrow, 'foot', & 'blindfold', & in sacks. An impious Sub. wanted to have a race of General Officers in sacks! These sort of things to the men, are an immensity of good. There is nothing, I am convinced, keeps them from moping and catching fevers &c, like amusing them in some way.

By the bye, as regards my poor Sergeants whom you were

interested in, I am sorry to say I have come to the end of them. My nice old one died somewhere on board ship [Hampson], my next I buried a week or so ago [Clapham], & my third [Brummell], I am happy to say, has escaped home, tho' with only one leg, & now I have the Sergeant of the Band to assist me, his own occupation being gone – two boys left of all our band!

Letter 38

Before Sebastopol, 23 March

We are having showery windy spring weather with occasional fine days. Things are going on pretty well in general now. We have huts for the sick, & food and transport for all. General Simpson is out, but I hear has no orders, so that one does not see exactly what to do, and he is only at present one more nice old man added to our original lot.[49] The Siege, or rather the preparations for it, are getting on pretty vigorously, both on our side & the enemy's.

Last night the French on our left bombarded the town most tremendously, & must have done much mischief. I was smoking a cigar at Maxwell Earle's, & went out to see it, & a very pretty sight it was. They were sending myriads of shells, & rockets, right into the best parts of the town, & got up a rather promising fire in the town, which burnt brightly for some time, but seems out today. After we had gone away to bed, about 1 A.M., the Russians (I suppose finding the town an unpleasant séjour) came out, & made a general attack on all our trenches, &, although they seem rather to have taken all our people by surprise, were gallantly repulsed, & left a good number or dead & prisoners, I am very sorry to say tho', not without loss on our side. I hear we lost 5 or 6 officers, killed, wounded or missing, but cannot tell you the particulars. One man only I knew, poor Cavendish Browne of the 7th. killed. My Brigade was not on duty. The French on their side did well, as the wretched Russe strewed, they say, outside their trenches, testify.

[49] Simpson was effectively a spy for the Government at home, which had been led to believe that Raglan was an incompetent, and was covering for equally-incompetent members of his Staff. Simpson's considered judgement was 'I consider him the worst used man I ever heard of!'

The Russe are the most extraordinary engineers: would that we had any half as energetic & clever! They build up work upon work, in miraculously short periods of time, & that with an army that all Deserters & spies say is in a dreadfully demoralised state.

A Pole who came in a few days back says that there is a very bad feeling in the town, and that they have constantly to change Regiments from one place to another. They have made a certain work on a 'Mamelon',[50] opposite the French, that Engineers say must be taken before anything can be done, but our Allies don't seem to find it an easy job. Night after night they fight about it, & it still belongs to the Russe. They will not let us take it, (which I am certain we could do whenever we were told) but insist on doing it themselves. We only keep on a fire of Shells into it, fired most beautifully, each one pitching right into the middle of the 'work'. The Pole told us that they lost 100 men a day, in that one redoubt. They are certainly the most splendid fellows, or their officers must be, to do what they do, with so much to contend against. On the whole, I think, we can & shall take this side of the town soon. There is evidently something wrong in the place. The Russians who generally fire 2 or 3 shots to our one, didn't reply at all to the tremendous French fire last night. I almost think that when we commence the real bombardment, the enemy will bolt to the other side. Whether they can blow us out, when we get in from the north side, no one can say, & that I fancy is the great problem to be solved. This side contains all the town, & arsenal, &c, & of course gives us the command of their ships. Menshikoff, we are told on good authority, is dead, & an admiral was killed in the fatal 'Mamelon', that I told you about.

We got papers yesterday to the 9th., & Wombwell a Punch, with a picture in Punch's worst taste of 'General Fevrier'.[51] Odd to say, I was talking yesterday morning about Punch, whose advent we look forward to with some excitement out here, & conjecturing as to what would be the subject of the 'big pictures'. I said I was sure there would

---

[50] 'Mamelon' – a mound.

[51] The Punch cartoon in question showed a skeleton in the uniform of a Russian General beside the Tsar's death-bed. The caption read: 'General Fevrier turns traitor', referring to Nicholas' boast that 'Russia has two Generals in whom she can confide – Generals Janvier and Fevrier.'

be some loathsome or insulting picture of the dead Czar [Nicholas], wasn't I right? I hope you agree with me as to the 'taste' of such a picture in such a paper? All their pictures of the Czar have been I think worthy of being at the head of some penny-a-line Ballad.

Letter 39

Before Sebastopol, 27 March

We had a truce for a couple of hours, two or three days ago, to bury the unfortunate victims of a rather important sortie that the enemy made a night or two before, & which I think I mentioned in my last.[52] At a given hour a white flag is run up at the different batteries on both sides, and immediately crowds rush out from the 'Embrasures' of either Party. On this occasion, the principal loss of life had been opposite to the French lines on our right, at a point where the advanced French lines & the Russes are not above 70 yards separate, so that when both sides came out to bury their dead, they were mingled together, talking, laughing & helping each other in their dreary employment. They must have fought very hard at that spot, for I had seen a large heap of dead all the previous day, and people who went down there tell me there must have been at least 200 Russes killed on that one spot. The Russe was [sic] very friendly on the occasion of the truce, though any conversation beyond mere civilities, was forbidden with them. The French lost terribly, I suspect, on that occasion. They always conceal their losses, but I hear they lost 20 Officers. We had 6 killed and wounded. The enemy were led on both sides (I mean against our 'Right Attack', & our 'Left Attack'), by two most gallant Albanians, beautifully dressed in their national dress. They both fell. On the whole I think it was a rude repulse for the enemy at all points, and I am glad of it, for the French have been so unfortunate on our right in their attempts to take some wretched little 'Rifle-pits', that we were getting rather disgusted with them, and the Russe we may suppose proportionately elated.

The dear General [Napier] need not be at all afraid of our having lost caste by this war, & our having lost the prestige of our Arms, for I am quite sure that nothing will ever cement our alliance with France

---

[52] This truce took place on 24 March 1855.

more securely than their having seen us fight. I can now understand their admiration of our *Solidité*, which I always attributed to their politeness in great measure. The Russians don't care the least for them, (and quite between you and me) I think would turn them out of the country, if we, with our poor little 15,000 were not here. I do not write this at all unadvisedly, for I was a great admirer of them, & of their Organisation, & all their military arrangements, & of their fighting, having only seen them fight at Inkermann, where we had to bear the brunt of it all. But now I am coming back to our fine old English creed, of one Englishman being a match for two Frenchmen, & I think they know it more than ever they did. The *Zouaves* are the *crème* of them, & fine soldiers, & I am happy to say that nothing can be more cordial than the feeling between the French and ourselves, for our men – with a good taste that I did not suspect them of – are particularly friendly with them now, & I saw an English Regiment turn out & cheer some *Zouaves*, who passed them yesterday, a thing which I had not seen since our first arrival when we cheered everything and everybody. They say the Russians have a great respect for us, & during the truce saluted our officers, paying no attention to the French whom they detest, altho' the French were much more friendly (as is their custom) with them, than our people, who walked about among them with great 'solidarity', & solemnly assisted in their dreary employment.

Letter 40

Camp before Sebastopol, 30 March

I saw Lord G. Paget yesterday. I think he has been roughly used by the people at home. I don't see why he should not go home as well as the Duke [Cambridge], & Lord Cardigan. I think he is a hardish case. Before the war broke out he wanted to sell out, his whole possession being his £14,000 for his commission, & then he can't go because his Regiment is ordered out. He comes, behaves on the only occasion he had of so doing, exceedingly well, & then goes home (his regiment 30 or 40 in number being employed in carrying up our biscuit) & then the 'Donkeys' of the 'Senior United Service' discuss whether they should turn him out & elect a man whom they had previously black balled, Lord Cardigan (both having done the same thing); the opinions, by the bye, of those 'in the fight' being by no means unanimous as to the Earl's splendid behaviour. There are no two opinions about Lord George's.[53]

I have no more news, & will write you a longer letter next mail, you must 'take it out' in violets. Wombwell I have just seen write [only] half a page to his sister & the rest violets![54]

Letter 41

Before Sebastopol, 6 April

Our 'Monastery' is shut up now, at least the French will not allow anyone to go nearer than the edge of the cliff, as they say that *we* have destroyed the trees & walls &c about there. That is indeed a joke, for a more cursed Flight of Locusts in an enemy's country, than our lively Friends, you cannot conceive, burning, & destroying, & abusing all before them.

The weather has been so favourable for transport, & we have on all sides been so busy with the Siege Works, that I think we shall open fire on the town in a few days, probably in about a week. We have the most tremendous Siege Train that ever was dreamt of. You may form some conception of the magnitude of it, when I tell you that the French on our Left have in position, ready to open, nearly 200 of the largest sort of guns, in the place of about 40, (and those not the largest) which they had on the previous occasion. One must also recollect, that their Batteries, (the French) failed from an accidental explosion, & their own weakness, about two hours after the last fire opened. Ours has been proportionately increased, & of ammunition we have a most ample supply.

---

[53] The reference to Cardigan's behaviour in the Charge relates to a rumour which started to circulate some weeks after the event, that Cardigan had turned back before reaching the guns. There is evidence to suggest that another officer of Cardigan's regiment, who had been wounded and who had to turn back, had been identified as Cardigan in error.

[54] Dallas is not being entirely candid here. A letter from Maxwell Earle of the same date notes, 'I am to dine with Fred Dallas this evening, when he promises me all the luxuries of the season.' One cannot but suspect that Dallas cut his letter short to allow himself time to prepare for his guest.

Nobody of course knows the 'programme' except the swells, but our general impression, & my hope, is that they will fire into the town, which they did not do last time, & I am inclined to think that if they do, no living creature will be able to remain there. If the fire has that effect the Russe will of course evacuate, & go over to the other side, a contingency that I think they look forward to, from their immense busyness on the other side. Whether our object will be considered to have been obtained by the destruction of the town, Arsenal &c, & the Capture of the South side, I do not know. It is also a great question whether they will not be able to drive us out by a fire from their Batteries on the North, across the Harbour.

There is a good deal of fighting on the right of our position (the works you may recollect that we gave over to the French) I do not know with what result. The Russians to all appearances are stronger there than ever, and sometimes open a tremendous cannonade on all points, to which we answer but slightly, keeping our ammunition for the event. Last night they made an apparently vigorous Sortie on our right trenches, & I hear were well met by the Light Division, tho' I have not heard the particulars. There was a good deal of musketry, some heavy guns, & then all was quiet for the rest of the night.

Arthur Wombwell & I went to a rather jolly pic-nic at the Monastery last Sunday, a very pleasant party, & lots of champagne. Sir John Campbell was the chief of it, & a very nice fellow he seemed. I never met him before, & he was very civil to me. He considers Peace as likely to put an end to our troubles soon, & told me he thought I was certain to get a majority which, as he commands our Division, and (I believe) kindly sent in a claim for a majority for me, gives me hopes that I may get it.[55]

I was down at Balaklava yesterday. I went there with Earle to say good bye to Street, a man in Maxwell's Regiment, who is going home sick, a very good fellow, & an ally of mine, as he was of poor Henry's [Dallas], having come from the 98th to the 57th. I found him

---

[55] That is, a Brevet-Majority. Curiously, Maxwell Earle wrote in a letter of 4 March 1855 (over a month earlier): 'Fred is, I am happy to say, recommended for a Brevet-Majority, with a fair chance of success, which he richly deserves, as he has not missed a day's duty since landing in the Crimea.' Whether Earle knew something that Dallas did not is unclear. Dallas' promotion was still many months away.

stopping at Sir Colin's, to whom he introduced me, & who was very kind: such a guy, dear old chap, as he looked! He was standing at the door of his hovel with a Welsh wig on, the wrong side foremost, with the fluffy curls of it in his eyes.

There is a great rumour here that all beards are to be shaved off. It will not affect me, but those who have found the comfort and protection of them, independent of the trouble of shaving in a tent, will feel it much. This order emanates from 'Sir Brown', whose principal military talent appears to me to be the happy knack he has of making everybody about him uncomfortable. He has already got an order for us all to wear our swords when going about the camp.

Letter 42

Camp before Sebastopol, 9 April

I have not much to write about to fill a long letter but that little is important, for today we opened fire, & commenced the '2nd. Siege'. It has been a fearfully rainy & windy day, & we have not been able to see any distance, so that the effect of the tremendous cannonade that has been kept up since 5 A.M. this morning, is a matter of surmise only. The weather has been considered by the 'cognoscenti', as in our favor, for the cutting wind and rain has been mostly in the faces of the enemy, & the breaking up of the roads, & overflowing of the 'Tchernaya', will prevent, or seriously impede, any attempts on our flank or rear. The principal feature of the affair as yet, has been the exceeding feebleness of the Russian fire in answer to ours. On the former bombardment they answered always as many, generally 2 to our 1 gun. Today they have answered one to our 10. The dense rain and mist have prevented us from looking on at the affair, but the most tremendous fire has been, & is, carried on, & is certainly scarcely replied to at all, altho' the Russe have battery upon battery raised against us. There is evidently 'a screw loose' somewhere, either they fail in ammunition or in men to work their guns, or they may be saving up for some grand effort. I trust that tomorrow may be clear, & that we shall be able to see the effect of today's fire, as well as the shooting tomorrow. Tho' we could not even see our guns firing today we have once or twice counted the No. of shots in the minute, & the average of shots we found to be about 40 in the minute. Such a number from the largest guns ever made, fired for so many hours into the town, must have done fearful mischief. My own fancy is, that the whole of them will bolt to the other side, finding the side which contains all the town, arsenal, Barracks &c, untenable. I trust such may be the case. The Russe's fire has been so weak that in the whole of our half of the works, we have lost only 3 or 4 men.

I am much obliged to you for getting Cording's bill, which I thought dear on the sunny day that I read your letter, but I have found such comfort from his raiment today, that I really think I will some day pay him!

I will try to make enquiries about Bolland's friends, but it takes some time to find out any authentic account of any soldier who is not actually here. They say, & I believe it is true, that there are 4000 of the army who cannot be accounted for any way, & they don't know what has become of them.

Letter 43

Camp before Sebastopol, 13 April

I have to acknowledge two jolly long letters dated the 26th. & 30th. March, & before I go any further will answer one or two of the questions. The Sergeant's name is Brummell, not, I imagine, any relation to the Beau's tho' a very good looking fellow. I mean the one who lost his leg. He went away some time ago now & will stop I fear some time at Scutari. I say I fear, for I am certain he was quite able to go straight home & no one gets better at that horrid place.

The two men whom you asked about are Havelock who is here & quite well, & Johnson, of whom I cannot find out anything certain but will tell you if I do.[56] It is extremely difficult to find out about men who go away from here. For instance, two of my men of whose deaths I had had official accounts from Scutari came quietly back here with a party of convalescents, & putting aside the pleasure I had of seeing

---

[56] This is presumably the same man as Elijah Johnson mentioned in Letter 24; there is no record of anyone by the name of Havelock serving in the Crimea with the 46th Regiment.

them alive, put me to considerable inconvenience as I had (according to custom) sold all their possessions except the things they went away in, & the proceeds had been forwarded to their friends. One of them, by the way, asked me particularly not to mention his being alive to his wife, whom he told me was not at all a nice person & with whom he appeared to think I corresponded regularly.

I think I told you in my last that the second Bombardment had commenced. It began on Monday & that was a particularly dark day with wind & rain so that one could not see more than fifty yards. Next day was fine & clear & I am sorry to say that upon carefully looking over the town & its Batteries & works, that I never saw them look better in my life & to this day I see no alteration in the place, nor is there any material injury done to their works though we have thrown in an almost fabulous number of shots & shells. Of course they must have lost many men & perhaps the town opposite the French (who are much nearer to it than we are) is destroyed to a great extent, but we can only see from our side but a small strip of the town.

The Russians have fired well and steadily (very few shells) but have knocked about our batteries considerably. Our casualties have been few; a large proportion of those sailors, who are particularly reckless & have always suffered most in the trenches. I was in the trenches the night before last & was lucky in having a most lovely night, and the Russe did not fire a single shot. The French, tho', kept up the most constant & tremendous fire into the town all night. It was a beautiful sight, four or five shells constantly in the air & the tremendous noise of them, with the crash as they fell into the town & burst, together with the excitement & anxiety of being in charge of our most advanced 'parallel' made the night pass quickly.

We are but seldom on duty in the trenches now as Captains & at any rate this Bombardment will be over before my turn again. What we are going to do I cannot conceive. I have no doubt but that this attempt will be as fruitless as the last & I can hardly believe that we shall begin again. 25,000 Turks are here under Omar Pacha, and altogether we have a most splendid force, those who are left of our men all soldiers such as few Generals have ever had the fortune to command. The day after the firing commenced I was sitting on the grass about half way down to the trenches examining the city through a glass when Lord Rokeby came up & I introduced myself to him & he was most kind and good natured & told me to send his love & all sorts of kind messages to you both.

I have got a rather curious little souvenir of Sebastopol for dearest Puss which I will send her by the first opportunity. It is a little china lamp taken by a Frenchman, one of a most desperate body of volunteers called the *Enfants Perdus* who go nightly into the Faubourg of the town & have the most extraordinary adventures and escapes. This lamp he took out of a house that he & his brother *Enfants* got into some nights ago. These *Enfants Perdus* are the *élites* of the most desperate character in the *Zouaves* and their extraordinary adventures would form a most curious book. They go only armed with bayonets, no firearms as the noise of them would betray them, & I have no doubt commit frightful atrocities.

Letter 44

Camp before Sebastopol, 15 April

I told you in my last that we had commenced the Second Bombardment. It began last Monday, exactly a week today & to all outward signs, the town is just as near being ours as it was 6 months ago. The French & ourselves have kept up a most constant and tremendous fire on the place all the time & further than the horrid destruction of life which must have taken place in the town we have done nothing towards gaining our object. I who take considerable interest in the affair and go down as near as possible every day with a good glass to watch for an hour or two, cannot see that we have shut up any of their batteries yet. Our loss has been comparatively trifling, I don't know exactly the amount. The sailors here lost most. The Russians made two desperate sorties on the French on our left, on what is called the *Bastion du Mat* (Flagstaff Battery), (if you have a map you will see it), & were repulsed on both occasions with great loss, I am sorry to say, on both sides. The first time was two nights ago and the French (they say) lost 4 or 500 men, and last night, a very black night, there was the most furious fight I ever saw for about 1/2 an hour on the same spot. We can see it from our camp and I never saw anything so beautiful as it was. The Russians lost fearfully as it was, and the French followed them back into the battery (Flag Staff) from whence they sallied and destroyed it, which is considered a good thing.

I have just come up from looking on at the Siege. The firing was very heavy & I was in time to see a magazine of ours blown up. It is the first one we have lost, but they say it was not a very large one. It was a horrid sight though, for one does not know how many of the black specks up in the air are poor Artillery men, or sailors, or whoever may be near it when it bursts.

We have now 25,000 Turks under Omar Pacha here, much better looking 'Johnnies' as the soldiers call them, than our old lot. The 10th Hussars arrived here yesterday and disembark tomorrow. I am anxious to see them & their Arab horses. They came from Alexandria in the *Himalaya* and the *Etna*.

We have a few amateurs[57] out here. I have met one or two London acquaintances, to my astonishment. I dare say it is an interesting sight to men who are sick of London and don't know what to do with themselves & perhaps suffer from what my friend used to call 'le Spleen'. We, as you may well conceive, are a little weary of it and the new Siege is singularly tiresome as there is no sign of any success about it. We used to silence some of their Batteries during the last fire for an hour or two sometimes, and occasionally blew up their magazines, but now we merely keep grinding away at each other with no visible result. What we are to do when our powder and shot is finished, which it must be in a day or two, I have no conception. We shall be just where we were after the last fire tho' without the dreadful winter to look forward to. I hope we shall go out & thrash the Russians who are outside, for we certainly can't get at them in the town.

A man who has just come from the batteries tells me that the magazine that blew up was not a very important one but killed and wounded 31 men, most of them wounded.

Letter 45

Camp before Sebastopol, 20 April

Our second siege must now be numbered among the things that have been. It is over & has been a more ridiculous & disgusting

---

[57] Tourists.

farce than the first. The Russian Batteries & works are as good & strong as ever & further than the mischief that such a tremendous fire must have caused in the town, we are no nearer our end than we were months ago. There is one universal feeling of disgust and humiliation amongst us at this second ridiculous exhibition. We were led to believe that after a few day's firing some final assault would take place & then an end, at whatever cost of life, would be put to the miserable spectacle that we present to all the world. In fact we expected the assault the night of the last letter I wrote, but no, the firing died away as it began, and we were exactly where we were. What our next move may be no-one knows but there is every symptom of the same farce being repeated when we have replenished our store of shot & shell. Rumour says that the French threw us over & at the eleventh hour refused the assault. I don't believe it but something must have happened to alter the evident intention there was to storm the town.

We are now, as we have been for months, ourselves the besieged in our corner of the Crimea. We have a most splendid army thrown away on our chiefs, either by their dissensions or their incompetency. The Tenth Hussars are encamped at Balaklava and are to my idea the *beau-idéal* of Cavalry, both men and horses looking splendid. Ships have gone for the 12th. {Lancers} from Cairo.

An absurd 'Reconnaissance' took place the day before yesterday in which Turks and our Cavalry took a part. They solemnly went out & killed one Cossack & took another and our loss consisted in the capture by the enemy of two Navvies who went out to see the fun! Our only other attempt at offensive operation consisted in an attack on some ambuscades that annoy our Batteries on the right. It was conducted as all our operations seem to be. A body of the 77th. went out last night, drove the Russians out of their holes & were left totally unsupported to hold their places against whole columns of the Russes. They were of course cut to pieces but fought splendidly & held their ground in one of the ambuscades. They lost their Colonel, Egerton, a very fine fellow, and a Captain, a little boy named Lemprière, who had just got his company, about 20!, killed, & two officers wounded. All this is very sad & has caused a great feeling of disgust amongst us; men's lives, if one may use the term, being frittered away, in wretched little mismanaged attacks of this sort that do nobody any good & that are only redeemed from being ridiculous by the gallantry our poor soldiers always show.

Lord Stratford [de Redcliffe] is either here or expected immediately, why, no one knows but there is a pretty general feeling that our only probable release from our present disgraceful position, will be as disgraceful a peace. As to dictating terms, Heaven knows we are not in a position to do that, the Russians must be laughing at us. When we have just recovered from our personal discomfort & the remnant that is left in the best spirits, our numbers amounting probably to 150,000 in all, our winter over, & the weather lovely, it is heart-breaking to think that we have to wait for a broiling sun & probable disease to commence again the horrid farce of bombarding Sebastopol.

Letter 46

Camp before Sebastopol, 23 April

The 25,000 Turkeys who came with their Omar Pacha have gone back again, and except to give us the pleasure of seeing them and of hearing their pretty bands, no one exactly seems to *know* why they came at all. They seemed an improvement on the old lot we have had here & if practising at it could make them drill well, they ought soon to be perfect for they appeared to be out at it morning, noon and night. There were among them some exceedingly funny ones, 'Tunisians'. Anything so frightful in the face & hideous in dress you cannot conceive. We used to go & see them sometimes. They all wore long grey dressing gowns and grey extinguishers on their heads, & their band was too killing and the solemnity with which they all played I won't say different tunes, for nobody played anything like a tune, made me laugh more than I have done for some time. As the sun went down every evening they all gave a frightful howl & ran like rabbits into their tents. Omar Pacha is an exceedingly pleasant man, very unlike his pictures, with a cheerful roundish face and a square cut beard, almost white, very plainly dressed & riding a priceless horse![58]

Tomorrow there is another 'Reconnaissance' & one or two of us are

---

[58] Omar Pacha was 'white' – he was born Michael Lattas, the son of a Croatian army officer, converting to Islam later in life.

going as Amateurs. I dare say it will be interesting, I should like to see the country about here. It is rather an early affair: 5 A.M. we start. The Sergeants you mention are neither of them my one-legged friend, but one, 'Hampson', is an old ally of mine & came out with me in the '*Harbinger*'. I have a very pleasant recollection of him once, just after we had landed, bringing me a leg of mutton when I was very hard up for food. Some of my little party had stolen it somewhere & had deputed him to present it to me. He left us apparently at the point of death at the Alma & when I parted with him I never expected to see him alive again. I am very glad to hear that he has got home.

The Siege has subsided again into its usual state. We have left off firing again '*faute* de powder & shot', & I suppose when we have scraped together enough we shall shoot again, and unless you can manage to make a Peace for us, at home, we seem likely to pursue the same lively course for many years to come. However, the weather is now very fine & we are all very well. So are the Russians.

Letter 47

Camp before Sebastopol, 26 April

Lord Stratford [de Redcliffe] is here: why or wherefore we none of us know. The weather's lovely & the health of the troops pretty good. We have nothing to do in the way of duty, at least compared with what we have had & we find considerable difficulty in passing the day. We have occasional races which are rather fun & our principal occupation is speculating on our future operation (if ever we get as far as an 'operation'), & a few sanguine ones talk of the possibility of peace. Omar Pacha went away as suddenly as he came, taking with him 10,000 of the 25,000 Turkeys that he brought. He is supposed to have gone in a hurry to Eupatoria.

I have just been interrupted by two of the Officers of the old *Harbinger* which has come out again here after having gone home to England with Invalids. They were talking about & asking after the Officers that came out with dear old Sir George, but of about 14 or 15 that came out, there are just four of us left here!: Colonel Windham, Major Smith, one Commissary [Coppinger] & myself, the rest dead or gone home wounded or sick. A sad list, isn't it? I fancy that that is about a fair average of those left of the whole expedition that landed at Kalamita, I do not think that above one third would be left here now.

The French had a grand review here yesterday of what is called 'the Army of Observation' under Bosquet (to distinguish it from the 'Army of Siege'). They looked uncommonly well. The *crème* of them, the *Zouaves*, were splendid. Their dress is the most picturesque & Eastern looking costume you can conceive, and in addition to that is the most comfortable & serviceable. At the Review they wore *Grande tenue*, their Green Turbans looked very pretty; in undress they wear Fezzes. There is a reckless sort of *degagé* air about them, heightened by their loose dress, that is to me charming, after the prim stiff helpless absurdity that is our ideal of a soldier.

We have a good many 'amateurs' out here now, one or two acquaintances of mine amongst them. They seem to think it great fun, which of course it is to anyone who comes now in the fine weather, with the immense advantage over the 'professionals' of being able to go away whenever they like. We are all delighted to see them & show them everything. Part of the programme is to go down into the trenches at night & if a shot will only come at the right time they are quite delighted & we always tell them that it went quite close to them, which completely satisfies them & they wisely go home again. Altogether I cannot fancy a pleasanter trip for a man with many acquaintances in the army than a week or two here: everybody only too delighted to see & entertain them & just 'roughing it' enough to be amusing. They do not find champagne at dinner & a bed in a tent in this weather at all disagreeable.

I hear that General Bentinck is coming to command our Division. I shall be sorry to lose Sir John Campbell who is a pleasant gentlemanly man & lets us alone, a great blessing now, tho' one might call it 'neglecting' us when we wanted a champion during our winter troubles.

Letter 48

Camp before Sebastopol, 4 May

We are all in affliction at the present time, Death having snatched from us one whom we all loved for qualities that one values more, the more one sees of the world. A more kind hearted, utterly unselfish, being never lived than poor Frank Curtis, who was taken from us the night before last.[59] He was on duty in the trenches, when a shot (almost the only one fired all the night) came & killed him (instantaneously) & a poor young Engineer, who only lingered for a few minutes.[60] We bury him today, poor boy, on what is called Cathcart's Hill, where he will rest in noble company. It has been a great blow to us all for we were very fond of him. He was just going to get his Company. Probably we shall see his name in the next Gazette! I don't think you know his family, poor people!

An expedition starts today, for where, we do not exactly know: Kertch is named and Eupatoria. It consists of the Highland Brigade and French, altogether about 12,000 men. I think Eupatoria the most probable destination for them, for I don't exactly see what 12,000 men can do anywhere up the country. I should like to go with them. Everybody would, of course, but I fear that our numerical weakness will stand in the way of our ever going anywhere & look forward somewhat gloomily to many more months of the dismal uninteresting duty that we have now spent 8 months at.

I told you my one-legged Sergeant's name, 'Brummell', I think in some former letter. I have no idea in what ship, or when, he will go home. The last news I heard of him was from Scutari where he was detained – why I can't conceive, for he was quite able to go home, and they could hardly expect another leg to grow on him, so that except to catch some of the horrid fevers which abound there, I cannot imagine why his voyage for England should be delayed, as he of course must be discharged immediately he arrives home.

I was glad to hear a good account of the 2 Sergeants Doucherty & Hampson & can only say that a little kindness seems to go a long way with our poor fellows, for I really feel rather ashamed of the way in which they seem to speak of the little I have been able to do for them. You were right in your surmise that Hampson was the one that I supposed was dead. We had the most authentic (apparently) accounts of his death & that combined with the state in which I left him at the Alma satisfied me of the truth of the report, tho' we heard since of his

---

[59] A friend and fellow-member of the 46th Regiment.
[60] The 'young engineer' was Lieutenant Carter.

being all right at Scutari. It is very difficult to get correct information about men that leave the seat of war: men that have been officially reported dead occasionally turn up.

Letter 49

Camp before Sebastopol, 11 May

I think I told you of an expedition that started for 'somewhere' we did not then know where for: Kertch was its destination, & they got within an hour or so of their destination, when all the Captains of the various ships got sudden orders to return to Balaklava, and to the immense disgust of everyone engaged in the affair, they found themselves next morning instead of in Kertch, off Balaklava. It appears that an express steamer was sent after them to stop them. No one knows why, but it is imagined that it was done by the French, owing to some telegraphic orders from Paris.[61] This miserable indecision is enough to destroy the 'morale' of any army, & has utterly disgusted all parties. The troops were landed again & if ever they again set out on the same errand they will find Kertch as strong as Sebastopol. In a few hours it must have been ours as they were entirely unexpected by the enemy! Now they will of course have time to fortify it.

We are all of course disappointed at the fruitless result of the negotiations, as we feel that we can only make ourselves more ridiculous. If we try to continue this ill-fated war, with such an army as we have in the field now rotting on this barren plain, and with leaders, how different would be our tone! However it is no use growling. Here we are & until you can manage to patch up some sort of peace, here we are likely to remain for many a day.

I hardly think it is likely that we shall attempt to take the field until Sebastopol has fallen, which is an event to be looked forward to as something remote.

Lord Raglan very kindly sent to ask the Chief [Garrett], if he thought any letter from him would be a comfort to poor dear Curtis' friends & I conclude the Chief said he thought it would. It was very

---

[61] It was.

kind and thoughtful of him wasn't it? to think of it, harassed as he must be with such great cares and troubles. It is a proof to me, if I wanted such, what an ample cloak kindness of heart & amiable manners & address make, for a multitude of sins. For, with all his many shortcomings (his neglect of us in our distress in the winter, his want of energy & purpose & the utter failure of the whole affair under his command), notwithstanding all these, I don't think anyone dislikes him.

I just read an advertisement that delighted me in a paper I never heard of before, *The London Journal*, that someone sent to either me or Wombwell. It was under the head of 'Marriage' & (amongst many others) the young lady's name was Violet & she wants to meet with a well-formed Protestant under the age of 30, of moderate Income. Isn't it jolly? She described herself as quite lonely. When the Siege is over, if I am still under 30, which I begin to have my doubts about, I shall look out for her. Perhaps she may be less *exigeante* by that time.

Letter 50

Camp before Sebastopol, 13 May

The Russians took advantage of a desperate dark rainy night (2 nights ago) to try & surprise our Guards in the trenches. They made a very furious sortie, and were most gallantly repulsed by the 68th. & a party of ours, tho' not without loss on our side. The 68th. lost a very good fellow, a Captain Edwardes, killed & 29 men killed & wounded, ourselves 4 men wounded, two I fear mortally. Edwardes we regret much. He had just purchased his company. Almost the last time I saw him he was talking to poor Curtis & myself, joking about his being a Captain before Curtis as they both expected to be in the same Gazette. We bury him side by side with Curtis today. It is very sad losing those we value & like in these sort of affairs, no honor or glory or victory about it except dying in their wretched posts, nobly doing their duty.[62]

---

[62] Captain Edwards was killed on 11 May 1855. Captain Savage of the 68th Regiment noted in his diary, 'Buried poor Edwards at 2 o'clock in Cathcart's mound – all the 46th attended, also Brigadier Garrett.'

Our men behaved very well on this occasion. It was so dark that one could not see 10 yards, and the Russians all were killed almost in our trenches, many actually inside them. Their Officers behaved as they always do, splendidly. Two of them were killed in the trenches leading on their men.

One cannot exactly see the object of these sorties for they are always repulsed & never do our works the slightest injury and their loss is always infinitely larger than ours, tho' they invariably drag away their dead & wounded so that we hardly know the amount of their losses.

We are reinforced up here by the 71st. & the 3rd., two strong Regiments that came up a few days ago & lighten the work a little. Part of the 12th [Lancers] have landed & some 'Sardines'.[63] I went down to the 'Sardines' yesterday & was pleased by their appearance. They are well dressed & look like soldiers. They wear little hats somewhat like 'wide-awakes' with a cock's feather in them and are picturesque.

Sir Colin Campbell has resigned the command of the army at Balaklava, I suppose to be in a position to take the field in case we make a move.

Letter 51

Camp before Sebastopol, 21 May

Another expedition starts tomorrow, we suppose again for Kertch, I hope with some less absurd result; the same lot go. A great many French have been landed here these last 10 days & we have altogether an immense force.[64]

Canrobert as of course you know has been replaced by Pelissier. I

---

[63] The 'Sardines' were the Sardinian army. Sardinia had no quarrel with Russia, but joined the war on the side of the Allies in the hope of gaining international recognition and status. Their one battle (see Letter 72) in the Crimea saw them emerge the victors.

[64] The 'immense force' by now totalled around 200,000 men, of which the British contingent amounted to some 30,000. To minimise the discrepancy in the relative sizes of the British and French armies, the Sardinian forces were counted as British; however, the French army far outnumbered the combined forces of the British, Turkish and Sardinian troops in the Crimea.

know nothing of him. I fancy he was the man who baked the Arabs in the cave in Algeria & I hope may find out some equally successful plan of cooking the Russe.

The weather is lovely, much too hot for being in tents tho', but if we had trees & a stream or two it would be charming.

Letter 52

Camp before Sebastopol, 27 May

We have just come from Church Parade, where, after a brief service, Sir John Campbell announced to us the successful issue of the expedition to Kertch. They took the place with no loss, got 550 guns and prisoners &c. What they intend doing further in that direction we don't know, perhaps come back, after destroying it.

We have taken some more territory on our right. When I say '*we*', I mean the French. They went out in force, about 60,000 or 50,000, and after a very trifling skirmish with the advanced Guards, the Russe, who were in no great force, retired, and now our camp extends into the valley of the Tchernaya, as far as the river. I rode over the day they went there & enjoyed a most pleasant wander amongst long grass, trees, and a river, pleasant objects on a roasting day which I has not seen for many a day. The Sardinians are encamped in advance towards the village of Tchorgoun and their outposts all amongst the most romantic looking hills remind one much of a scene of an opera, the riflemen's dresses being correct copies of 'a chorus' with drooping feathers in their hats. All our Batteries are again ready to open when wanted.

The French & Russe had a most desperate affair on our extreme left (towards the Sea). They fought from about 11. P.M. till 2. A.M. without a moment's intermission, about 4 nights ago, & the loss was very great on both sides. I do not know the numbers, but the French lost nearly 2,000 they say, & the Russe in the usual proportions. The French were mostly Imperial Guards & tho' they behaved very well they say that they did not know the ground well & made various blunders. The French advanced considerably the next night with no loss.

28th. They say that a good many despatches & private correspondence were got at Kertch which describes the state of the inhabitants of Sebastopol as very very dreadful & their expectation of another immediate Bombardment. This can well be believed for, tho' we don't appear to advance much yet, our dreadful fire into the town must make it a most horrid place to live in. I wonder what they think there of the fall of Kertch. They have hardly fired a shot for the last 48 hours. We talk of opening fire on Wednesday or Thursday again. Another rumour is that General Jones (the Engineer) says he won't do anything until our allies take a certain work called the 'Mamelon' which they ought to have taken ages ago.

Letter 53

Camp before Sebastopol, 1 June

We have various accounts from our expedition at Kertch. They took 100 Guns (between you and me, I fancy very seedy ones) and what is more to the point, over 100 ships laden with all sorts of grain &c: a heavy blow, I hope, to the Russe. We don't know exactly what they are doing now but we suppose them to have gone to Arabat, or Anapa. The value of the Grain taken was over 1/4 of a million! The Russians have blown up 6 or 7 of their own steamers in the Sea of Azoff. And we had commenced the Bombardment of Arabat & a lucky shell had blown up a magazine & with it half the town. This is news straight from Head Quarters, but of course I cannot vouch for its truth. I only hope it is true.

Our present plan of operations (here), I believe, is to bombard for a certain time & then to assault two important outworks of the Russe. The French assault a work called the 'Mamelon' which seems to be thought the Key almost of the south side, & we take a Quarry in which the enemy have built a battery in front of our Right. When I say we I mean the Regiments who guard & man the 'right attack'. Ours is the 'left attack', & if you will promise not to tell anyone I will confess to you that I am much pleased to say that owing to the nature of the ground, we can go no further! You will know from this (understanding probably as little of fortification as I do) that the present plan is to take the place in detail, one Fort after another & I think there can be no doubt of the success, if carried on with vigour.

The French, I hear, assault the 'Mamelon' with 15,000 men, I should say too many. We go at our place with 1,000. I expect both places will be ours in a day or two.

The move of the French into the Valley has been a most charming thing for us, has opened the most lovely country you can imagine for us to ride and wander about. Wombwell & I generally go out late & enjoy our ride through such a smiling luxuriant country all the more for not having seen a tree or blade of grass for so long. The scenery is quite equal to Killarney & very much the same style. There is an outpost of Sardines on a hill overlooking the entrance to the valley of Baidar that I think the most delightful spot I ever saw. I have never seen anything to equal the beauty & quantity of wild flowers. Everywhere the whole ground is covered, amongst a hundred other varieties, with jolly little roses. The camps scattered about, & the picturesque 'Sardines' add wonderfully to the scene. Their 'Bersaglieri' (sharpshooters) are very smart looking troops, perhaps a little theatrical in appearance any-where but amongst such appropriate scenery. I was much amused with one the other day. I was making a most beautiful little Italian speech asking him to hold my *cavallo* when he quietly said 'I'm afeared, Sir, I shall have to go away directly, but *this* cove will, I dare say', pointing to another 'Brigand'. I asked him where he had learnt such beautiful English but found him mysterious: he 'had travelled', he said. I think he must have been an Englishman.

The French are in great numbers here now. I should be curious to know, but I don't suppose it will ever be known, the amount of their losses here. The number must be something frightful what with disease, frost bite &c in the winter & the constant deadly fights in the trenches.

My friend De Noé, who I told you had left the Crimea, has been given the command of a regiment of *Spahis* in Africa, a good thing I suppose. They are the most extraordinary looking troops, all Arabs 'pur sang' & dressed & mounted in the Arab fashion on fiery little Arab horses. There were a few here as poor St. Arnaud's body guard, splendid wild looking fellows who looked as if just caught in the desert & half tamed.

Hesketh of ours went home yesterday. A medical Board sent him home very ill. I am glad he got away for he could not have lived long here.

I cannot hear anything of my poor friend Brummell, but I hope
that he is on his way home. He promised to write to me but I am
afraid that he is not very skilful with his pen.

Letter 54

Camp before Sebastopol, 2 June

The Kertch expedition (as you perhaps knew before we did here)
has done well & has secured large quantities of stores and booty, 240
ships, 100 odd guns &c taken. We are still waiting here, why I don't
know. All the Batteries are, & have been, ready for some days & every
day we are told that we open again tomorrow & the tomorrow seems
never to arrive.

The French by the way made an expedition in some force to
Baidar (*vide* your map) & found a few Cossacks & quantities of wine
& tobacco & came back in consequence very drunk & much pleased
with the entertainment. I am beginning to think that the Russe is
not in such force in the Crimea as we supposed. It has been rather
the fashion with the press & indeed with all the world, to suppose
that there are always 100,000 Russes wherever you go. Now my
notion is that they have the Garrison here & the Army which we
see the other side of the Tchernaya 'et voilà tout'. If they had so
many thousands to spare they would not have given up Kertch &c
so easily, nor would they have had only a few Cossacks at Baidar.
They say, I don't know with what truth, that the French, & following their example, the Turks, have behaved everywhere in the expedition to Kertch with unheard of atrocity, plundering &c. Heaven
help this wretched town when we get into it! & I really think that
event not far off now. I don't think that there will be a soul spared.
The Russes have brought it on themselves & our men have heavy
debts to pay them. A more barbarous and mean enemy no one ever
had to contend with. They have murdered our wounded, crept up
& stabbed our Sentries on their posts & constantly fire large guns
at 2 or 3 wretched men whenever they see them, all these enor-
mities being unheard of among civilised nations.

We have got a new General of Division in General Bentinck. I
know nothing of him. Wombwell and I have just come back from

dining with some Guards at Balaklava & they did not seem to like him (an old Guardsman). Greville, one of dear old Sir George's A.D.C.s has come out with him.

Letter 55

Camp before Sebastopol, 8 June

I received your letter of the 25th. at a moment of perhaps the greatest anxiety & excitement that I ever endured, whilst watching from our hill, for the signal of the simultaneous assault upon the whole of the Russian outworks on the right, to begin at the commencement of this, I trust, our final attack. We commenced opening a most tremendous fire from all our batteries the day before yesterday at about 3 P.M. & a most magnificent sight it was, the weather most lovely. The plan laid out & executed (as I shall tell you) was to fire all we could for 24 hours, & then for the French to rush into the Russian out-works on their side (our right) and some of us, 2nd & Light Divisions, to assault a Quarry in front of us, where the Russe had commenced making a battery.

At about 5 P.M. yesterday we (who were not to be engaged) began to collect on our Heights, the weather perfect, a delicious cool breeze blowing. Every gun we had was firing all it could to endeavour to silence the points to be attacked, & our eyes alternately strained through glasses, first on a flagstaff where the signal was to be raised, then on the Mamelon, the most important work to be taken. At about 6 p.m. up went the Union Jack on the flagstaff & like magic the whole of the side of the Mamelon (on the top of which is the Russian battery) was covered with French (looking like ants) tearing up to the Assault. The leading men get in & are followed by hundreds hopping on to the parapets & down the other side. The Russe are entirely taken by surprise, & apparently the French are in possession with but slight resistance opposed to them, but they rush on through the Mamelon out on the other side, & I fancy without any orders, charge up to the Malakoff Tower (a most tremendous work, in fact the Citadel of Sebastopol). Thousands of Russe come out and drive them back, tho' fighting splendidly. The Russe still advance & drive the French through the Mamelon & back into their own trenches. At that moment I, who saw it all through a good glass, thought that all was over, knowing what a stake depended upon the affair. But the French come out in thousands again & dash up, a glorious mob, to the embrasures of the battery & after a most tremendous fight almost hand to hand again clear the parapet & jump over amongst their enemies. This time they hold what they take and the Mamelon is ours, but again they make the same fatal error and the *Zouaves*, who can never be restrained, go on again to the very mouths of Malakoff Tower guns & then is their great loss. Shower upon shower of grape is sent into them & still they fight on. Eventually they are driven back to the Mamelon which they held and now hold. This part of the row I saw. There were also assaulted & taken by the French two or three redoubts of the enemy's, very strong works, & about 500 Prisoners taken with but small loss. Their loss at the whole business (of course a mere rough guess) is supposed to be about 1000, most of them cut to pieces through their fatal impetuosity in going on further than was intended, the object being to take the Mamelon alone. On our side we had a most terrible fight. Three times were our fellows repulsed in the attack on the Quarry. They found it full of the Russe, & were first beaten back.

I must explain to you that half the party in an attack of this description carry tools, 'picks & spades', to make protection for themselves when the storming party have done their work. On this occasion, when the storming party were repulsed, they came on again with part of the 'working party' who had thrown away their tools & insisted upon fighting. Again they are too weak & have to fall back. Then the remainder throw away their tools & after a most tremendous fight, force their way in & the Quarry is ours. All night long the Russians come to dislodge them, & as often are they repulsed with frightful loss. Altogether it has been a most splendid feat; our loss, I fear, very great in proportion to the number engaged. The loss I have heard no estimate of, but from Rumour I should say that we must have lost about 2 or 300 men & the usual proportion of Officers.

I had just written the above when I got a hurried note from 'an official' telling me that there was to be an armistice at 3. P.M. & as it was 2.30 P.M., I packed up my writing, and saddled my horse, rode off to the Brigadier [Garrett] to tell him & we started to go down to the French side, but found it was not the case, as I indeed expected, for it was very improbable that there would be anything of the sort at so critical a time. However, we heard various scraps of news: 1st that the French had lost about 2,000 yesterday; that Lord Raglan had had telegraphic news of still continued success of the expedition at Kertch, that they are making most important captures in & about the Sea of Azoff with no loss to us, & what seems a most unintelligible thing, that a large body of Russians were leaving the Army before Eupatoria & marching up the country out of the Crimea, their number about 10,000! why, one cannot conceive.

I have no doubt now but that this dreary siege is drawing to a close & that the curtain will soon rise on the last act. I hear & believe that tomorrow at daybreak, a further assault will be made on their two strong places, a fort called the 'Redan' and the Malakoff Tower, the former falling to the lot of the English to take, the latter to the French. If successful, (and if attempted I have no doubts about it) this will give us the entire command of the whole of the South side of Sebastopol, and it must fall to us in a short time. If done before the post goes out tomorrow & it may be, I will tell you of it, as the post goes at 8.1/2 A.M.

Pelissier is just passing by cheered by our men, a peculiar looking ruffian as ever I saw, gorgeously arrayed, and a white short *'Bournous'* over all, a pretty dress on a less common looking man.

Letter 56

Camp before Sebastopol, 11 June

I grieve to say that our loss was very much greater than we had fancied. I fear somewhere about 40 Officers killed & wounded, but I have seen no returns of the numbers. We had a flag of Truce for 3 or 4 hours the day before yesterday to inter the dead. I went down there to see the scene of the two assaults, and of course it was as horrid a sight as can be conceived, but exceedingly curious and interesting. The Russians looked to my eyes most wan and haggard. They had lost most tremendously at the Quarry. Our men had fought splendidly, but, as you may guess from the disproportionate number of Officers who fell, they, poor fellows, had all they could do to get them on under the very heavy fire. The French had taken the 'Mamelon' as I told you in my last, and had lost frightfully. It is a most tremendously strong work. How they ever took it excites all our admiration. 'They say' that there was a Council of War held after the affair, concerning the propriety of a general assault immediately, & that Ld. Raglan entirely refused to have one, as we had lost so terribly at the 'Quarry'. I have no idea whether the story is true, but I think it very probable, as he has shown himself such a advocate for half measures. Perhaps he was right. I have not the slightest doubt about the South side of the town being ours soon, and I imagine we are only waiting until the French make a battery on the Mamelon that they took. When it is made, it will command most of the place.

Letter 57

Camp before Sebastopol, 13 June

We have been having the most charming weather for some days that you can possibly conceive, not nearly so hot as it was before, and what with our successes at Kertch & our advantages here, we are in great force. We all think that the town must fall soon. Altho' I am afraid people will be horrified at the loss in the taking of the quarries, yet the moral effect of the success – independent of the local advantage it has given us – is immense. The French took much the most valuable work from the enemy. Ours is daily a source of great loss of life. I am sorry to say it is dreadfully exposed to the enemy's fire, but we all look forward to a speedy termination to 'trench life'.

We had yesterday the most pleasant day we have passed for many a month. As our men were in the trenches and we could not possibly be wanted, Wombwell and myself and one or two others rode out to the extreme advance post of the French towards Baidar along a road called the Woronzoff road about 12 miles. It is a beautiful road and winds about thro' a narrow gorge before entering the valley that, I think, almost the prettiest thing I ever saw. The advanced Picquet of the French was quartered in a '*Maison de Chasse*', supposed to be Prince Woronzoff's, in the midst of a beautiful wood, cut in every direction with shady paths, and I must say we envied them, and turned to go home with many a regret to our dusty parched up Camp. However, it was dark when we got home, so that we could not make offensive comparisons between our Bivouac and theirs, and we had a 'heavy

Left: Fred's father, Captain Robert William Dallas. Dallas served with the 9th Regiment of Foot during the devastating Walcheren Expedition of 1809, and in the Peninsular campaigns of 1810–1814. Injury compelled him to cease active service in Spring 1818. *(Editor's collection)*

Below: George Frederick 'Fred' Dallas, aged 17, immediately prior to his joining the army. *(Editor's collection)*

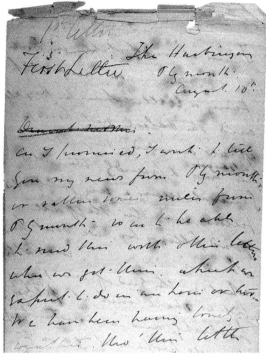

The start of Fred Dallas' Crimean correspondence in August 1854. The first line reads: 'As promised, I write to tell you my news'.
(Editor's collection)

Officers of the 46th Regiment of Foot in the uniform in which they went to war in the Crimea in 1854.
(Cannon, Historical Record of the Forty-Sixth Regiment)

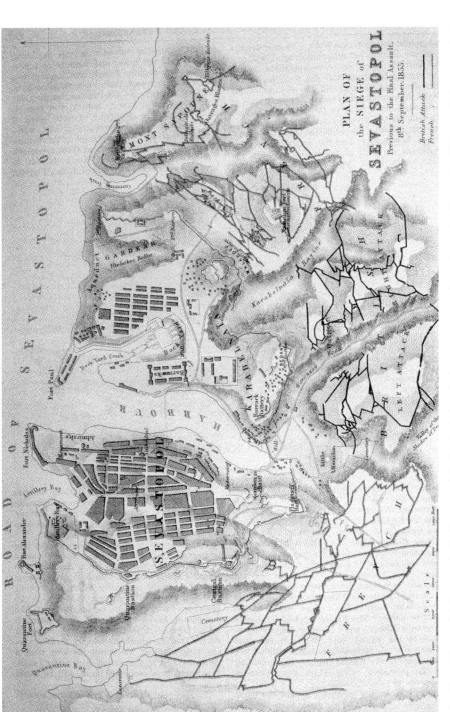

PLAN OF
the SIEGE of
SEVASTOPOL
Previous to the Final Assault,
8th September 1855.

British Attack
French

The Siege Lines of Sebastopol. Dallas served in the Left Attack (bottom centre) throughout the Siege. (*Dodd, Pictorial History of the Russian War*)

'We landed quite unopposed ... on a sandy strip of land ... between the sea and a salt lake, a most desolate place.' – Letter 6. *(Photograph by Michael Hargreave Mawson)*

'At night we were ordered to send out a Patrol, 400 yds further on the road, bringing it to about 500 yds of the City gates.' – Letter 8. The Worontzoff Road as it now is. *(Photograph by Michael Hargreave Mawson)*

Above: 'Sir Colin Campbell has had the command of our rear position which consists of Balaklava our port and the adjacent heights.' – Letter 10. The port of Balaklava and the adjacent heights as they are today. The church in the foreground dates from before the invasion. *(Photograph by Michael Hargreave Mawson)*

Left: 'I got one shot on my breast plate, which saved my life.' – Letter 11. *(Editor's collection)*

Right: 'When a few of us got nearly to the top from whence we had started, to our astonishment a most astounding fire opened upon us, from the very place we had come from.' – Letter 12. The view from the top of the Kitspur. *(Photograph by Michael Hargreave Mawson)*

Above: 'We ... made a most splendid headlong Charge ... pushing them down the steep side of the mountain, in utter confusion. The slaughter of them was here immense.' – Letter 12. The Eastern slope of the Kitspur. *(Photograph by Michael Hargreave Mawson)*

'Dressed as we *ought* to be, not as we *are*.' – Letter 21. *(Illustrated London News)*

'The men suffer ... a good deal from frost bites.' – Letter 22. *(Punch)*

"Well, Jack! Here's good news from Home. We're to have a Medal."
"That's very kind. Maybe one of these days we'll have a Coat to stick it on?"

'It was very dark, & even in daylight the 'poudre' snow blowing so fearfully that one could not see 10 yards' – Letter 32. *(Dodd, Pictorial History of the Russian War)*

'When I have done the ... duty that we have to do, I ride away from all the noise, & stench, & carrion, and roam about the hills towards Balaklava.' – Letter 35. *(Watercolour by Captain Hall, 4th Regiment, dated 1856 and entitled 'Entrance to Balaklava Harbour'; editor's collection)*

'I was sure there would be some loathsome or insulting picture of the dead Czar [in *Punch*], wasn't I right?' – Letter 38. *(Punch)*

'I had ... to lie in a crowded sort of trench from 2 A.M. until 10 A.M. and straight in the road of all the poor wounded who were carried past us in troops, and a very sad sight it was.' – Letter 58. *(Dodd, Pictorial History of the Russian War)*

'The Russians had the temerity, poor creatures, to come on against our lines in the Valley of the Tchernaya.' – Letter 72. The Valley of the Tchernaya as it now is. The causeway carrying the water-pipe was not present in 1855. *(Photograph by Michael Hargreave Mawson)*

An idealised view of the accommodation for officers in the Crimea. Dallas never enjoyed such luxury. *(Dodd, Pictorial History of the Russian War)*

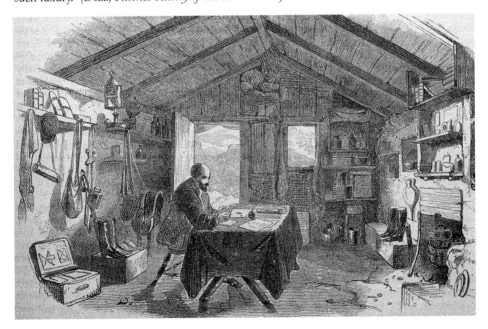

The Staff of the 4th Division, 1855–6. Major-General Garrett is seated in the foreground, passing a document to Brigadier-General Staunton. Dallas is the bareheaded officer in the centre of the picture. *(The Royal Archives © 2000 Her Majesty Queen Elizabeth II)*

'The loss of the Malakoff must lead sooner or later to the capture of the whole place.' – Letter 77. *(Dodd, Pictorial History of the Russian War)*

'On the night of that day we heard a succession of explosions & then fires broke out at all points in the Town, and we then saw that the Russes were evacuating & destroying their works.' – Letter 77. *(Dodd, Pictorial History of the Russian War)*

'I ... usually detest amateur Theatricals ... but out here it is good fun.' – Letter 104. *(Dodd, Pictorial History of the Russian War)*

The return of the Port of Balaklava to Russian hands, July 1856. Dallas is in the group in the centre. The unmistakable figure of Alexis Soyer is in the crowd of onlookers, bottom left. *(Illustrated London News)*

The medals of George Frederick Dallas: (left–right) Crimea with clasps for Alma, Balaklava, Inkermann, Sebastopol; Second China War medal; French Légion d'Honneur (Chevalier); Turkish Order of the Medjedie (5th Class); Turkish Crimea Medal. *(Editor's collection)*

Fred Dallas' wife and children; Maria Louisa, Fredericka, Lucy Clara and Alice Muriel Dallas. Collectively the daughters were known as 'the beautiful Misses Dallases' to Edward Elgar, who was their music teacher. *(Editor's collection)*

tea', 'the weight' of which consisted in an immense plate of Bacon and fine old camp eggs, and so to bed. You can fancy how we enjoy a holiday amongst the trees and grass of our 'new property' after the life we lead, and the scenes we live amongst. It is quite a luxury not even hearing the dreary old guns altho' they only go off at intervals at present.

Campbell [46th] was with us yesterday and was all the happier from having a great deal of duty to do now. He volunteered to Act as 'Assistant Engineer' and when he became a Major, which would oblige him to rejoin the Regiment, he obtained leave to continue his present employment for some little time more. I am very sorry that he was allowed, for it is a most dangerous employment, of course now more so than ever, as we are so near the enemy. Perhaps that is his reason for staying, for he is the most perfectly fearless fellow in the world. I hope he will get back to us safe. In an assault the engineers who accompany the party rarely escape: both of those who went with the party to the quarry fell. I only hope it won't come to his turn to do likewise.

The Party from Kertch are coming back, part already arrived. They have certainly had a most charming little campaign, and now they are sadly wanted here. The Highlanders, who have done nothing all the winter, will I trust be sent up to assist us here. When I say us I ought to say the regiments that man the trenches on the Right, viz: the Light, & 2nd Division who of course were dreadfully cut up in the quarry affair, and now lose about 50 men a day in the quarry guarding it.

I have not seen anybody yet that has come back from Kertch &c but I hear it was most delightful. They found in one house somewhere tubs of cream sunk in the earth, surrounded by ice! How sick I should have made myself. Pray tell this to the dear General [Napier], who I am sure would also have made himself sick, as he is as great an admirer of cream as I am. And conceive coming on it iced!, when in a tight red coat and the thermometer 90 in the shade!

I have been very busy these last few days. First of all, the night before last, a pony that I was very fond of broke loose, and lost himself and I hunted about for him all day, a pursuit somewhat similar to that of a 'needle in a bottle of hay'. I published his description in a *Hue & Cry* that we have here, and perhaps may recover him, tho' I have but small hopes. He is a great loss to me, for independently of my affection for him he was a very handsome and valuable one. Next, I was in the trenches for the night, always a harassing and somewhat anxious way of passing the night. Then this morning I have been making a sketch of poor old dear Sir George's tomb for Col. Windham, who wants to send it home to Lady Georgiana Cathcart, and the sun is so hot! Altogether I have become wonderfully active haven't I? The pony is a sad loss, tho' personally I have escaped as yet all dangers &c, in every other way. I have been so unlucky that I begin to think that I must have sailed for the expedition on some ill-omened day. I have lost 8 Sergeants from my Company, my last one being insane in hospital at present. A groom I got the other day, a very nice lad from my company, is dying of fever. And I have lost now two good horses since I have been here, tho' I took every precaution. The dreary subject of promotion I will not speak of again. Altogether, that is a goodly list of misfortunes isn't it? However, the weather is lovely, and I hope soon to see the end of the 'Camp before Sebastopol', both great aids in making one cheerful under difficulties.

Letter 58

Camp before Sebastopol, 18 June

Yesterday we got orders that today we were to assault the two principal works of Sebastopol the 'Redan' and the 'Malakoff Tower', the former our share, the latter that of the French. The 'Storming Parties' were of the Lt., 2nd., and part of the 4th. Division, the 46th. and other Regiments, Guards, Highlanders &c being the 'Supports'. We all paraded and marched down, at 1 A.M., full of hopes and almost certain of success. Instead of the result we so fondly anticipated there ensued nothing but mismanagement and frightful carnage. As we were, in the performance of our duty as supports, merely lying in one of the trenches and enveloped in smoke I can tell but little of what occurred. We remained there with a tremendous cannonade going on, until about 3 A.M. Where the proposed assault took place the result was that the French failed at the Malakoff, and by some misunderstanding, our Stormers (whose attack on the Redan was supposed to depend on the success of the French at the Malakoff) went on to the Redan under the most terrific fire of every description of missile. It was utterly impossible for them to get on as they were literally mowed down. It was almost a good thing that comparatively few faced it, or the slaughter would have been only more horrid. The Russians must have had information of the whole affair for they were prepared at all points.

Our loss is not yet known, but the proportion of Officers (who, in some cases, were not followed by their men) was immense. Sir John Campbell, who led the Stormers instead of commanding and directing the Supports as was his duty, paid with his life for his reckless gallantry, and fell one of the first. Poor Colonel Yea of the 7th. was killed. Colonel Shadforth was killed, & his Regiment, the 57th., suffered awfully, and hosts of others whose names I don't know, & many whom I did and liked, poor fellows. We know no particulars as to numbers but I fancy the loss of men was not much greater than the list at the taking of the quarries, but the list of officers is I fear double. The fire that came on them was so tremendous that nobody could face it, and they were forced to return back to the trenches. The whole affair was hideously mismanaged, and if it had all come off as intended, would, I think, have failed from the Russians being so perfectly prepared.

Some of the Regiments, I fear, did not behave very splendidly, and could not be brought to follow their officers into the fire. The whole affair is a very sad thing. It is the first time that our troops have been beaten. However, the feeling of the Army is I think good, and they are burning to avenge their comrades' slaughter.

I had, as I told you, nothing to do as it turned out, but to lie in a crowded sort of trench from 2 A.M. until 10 A.M. and straight in the road of all the poor wounded who were carried past us in troops, and a very sad sight it was, knowing as we soon did, after the commencement of it, that it was almost hopeless. Sir John Campbell, who had temporarily commanded the 4th. Division until Bentinck's arrival, we all regret much. He was the kindest-hearted gallantest man in the world, but lacked head. He commanded the 1st. Brigade, 4th. Division. The 57th. behaved very well and were much cut up, I think 7 officers killed and wounded.

Of the French part of the business I know nothing except that it failed and that they lost heavily. There was another part of the story —

about the 3rd. Division: I don't know what their orders are or were, but they rushed in under General Eyre somewhere about the outworks on the left and are there now, as they can't get out till it is dark. Nobody knows what their loss is, we hope that they have some sort of cover, Eyre is reported to be wounded.

We came home about 11 A.M. very tired and roasted by such a sun, having to lie quite still in it for some hours. Pelissier is, we hear, furious and is reported to say that he will take the Malakoff '*à tout prix*' and he ought, for it is the key of the town undoubtedly, & our sad affair at the Redan, in my belief, was intended originally only as a diversion to draw the fire a little off the French, and [only] in case of the French succeeding at the Malakoff, to be turned into a real attack.

Letter 59

Camp before Sebastopol, 22 June

We are all here as you may imagine in great disgust and grief at our fruitless and bloody assault of the 18th.: a more horrid piece of mismanagement never took place. Our loss was much greater than we at first imagined, owing to the frightful mess that General Eyre got the 3rd. Division into. Our loss on the right was not much more than I fancied, about 6 or 7 hundred, but altogether our loss amounts to nearly 1500 men and 80 officers. The French loss they say is nearly 6000. It is supposed that the Russians (from the evident complete state of preparation that they were in at all points) had got information of our intended attack. Their loss however is supposed to have been very heavy. I am sorry to say I lost a good many friends and acquaintances. It always seems that every bullet that does hit anyone picks out one's friends and the lives of those that everybody values. The only two killed in the 44th. Regiment[65] were both friends of mine, and the only ones I knew in the Regiment, poor Agar, a very good fellow and an old Harrow School fellow of mine, and Caulfield. I think by the way that he was a relation of the Plowdens.

---

[65] A third officer of the 44th Regiment was also killed on this occasion: Captain Bowes Fenwick.

We had a flag of truce next day, and brought in Sir John Campbell's body, Yea's, and others. We buried Sir John the same evening.

I don't at all know what our present intentions are. I do not know who will have Sir John's Brigade, as it usually happens after any sort of action half our dear old Generals find themselves very ill. Pennefather is going home I hear; Codrington is ill on board ship. The former is I think no loss to us, for he is a most excitable man under fire, or when anything is doing, tho' he is popular enough and has many friends. The latter is one of the best Generals we have, and if he goes, will be much regretted. We are sick and weary of our Generals, one seems as perfectly incompetent as another. Sir George Brown I firmly believe to be the head and origin of our disaster the other day, having given the signal for the attack, which he ought never to have done. Our attack at all was to depend entirely on the success of the French at the Malakoff Tower, and their success there was to be the signal for our advances. The French failed, & whether Sir George thought that they had succeeded or whether he fancied that we could assist them by a simultaneous attack I don't know, but certainly he gave the signal for our poor wretches to advance in most inadequate numbers to certain destruction. None of them got much more than half way to the 'Redan', our point of attack, owing to the dreadful fire that they were under. You may form some idea of the affair when I tell you that I really believe not more than 8 or 900 ever went to the attack and they lost 600! A wretched party of sailors, who had to advance with scaling ladders, got about half way, and only 10 out of 60 or 70 came back at all.

On the other side, Eyre advanced his party (with what object Heaven knows!) right into the suburbs of the town, and then having got a knock on the head with a stone left them, I believe, with orders to advance as best they could. A few got into some houses and saved themselves from being murdered, and the rest lay in the cemetery all day, being assassinated one by one, by an enemy whom they could neither see nor injure. They laid there all day and only got home at night having lost frightfully. The 18th. Regiment alone lost about 300 men. Eyre is supposed to be one of our best Generals here. Heaven help us!

Letter 60

Camp before Sebastopol, 25 June

We have a poor account to give of our Generals: poor Estcourt, whose name you must be familiar with from seeing his signature at the end of all officials, died of Cholera the day before yesterday, (his wife and I think his sister were here with him); then, as I told before, Pennefather, is just going or gone home; Codrington Do.; Sir Geo. Brown is ill on board ship, and altogether we have but few Generals left. If I might say it respectfully, I shouldn't wonder if we got on better without them.

I don't really wonder at the accounts of the weather here forming a large part of the Dispatches, for a more extraordinary climate no-one ever saw. A day or two ago without the slightest warning, after a most bright day, there suddenly came on the most tremendous shower of rain that was ever seen, tearing up the roads and nearly drowning lots of people, and falling in the most partial manner. A Regiment about 300 yards from us was nearly washed away, we again had not a drop of rain. Then there came on a thunder and lightening storm, more beautiful and grand than anything you can conceive. For about an hour the whole heavens were illuminated by constant flashes of fire. There was a violet tinge about the flashes that I never saw before. All this lasted about an hour, and began, luckily for me, just after I had come back from a 24 hour visit to the trenches, at about 9.30 P.M. Today there is a hot hurricane blowing, the most horrid visitation that we suffer from here, the dust penetrating all one's possessions here from one's hair to the clean shirt (supposed to be safe) at the bottom of a bag.

I fear that the success of the Russe in repelling our assault the other day will give them a renewed confidence. Fortunately they are too busy at work in the Town to think of 'Sorties', and they leave us pretty quiet. I believe we are going on with the old story of dragging up more guns and making more Batteries. There was a wise Russian Sergeant at a truce we had the other day [who] said, in pretty good English, to a Sergeant of ours who was there, 'Your men and Officers are Lions, but we know that your Generals are Jackasses' rather good wasn't it? They were very friendly at this last truce altogether, and had behaved very well to our wounded, giving them water &c. Poor creatures, they had been lying out ever since the fight, no-one able to go near them for nearly two days! Happily we found but very few alive, and they said that the Russes had come over in the night and given them water and sugar and bread, so that they seem [to be] getting more civilised? They were evidently a new lot of men that we saw at the truce, perhaps they had sent them out on purpose, quite different from the last wretched looking wan creatures we saw at the truce before, However, we will have their town yet. We should get on much better if we had not our Camp full of our Spies who tell everything that is, or is going to happen. We have been rather strict about them lately, and daily catch and nearly hang some unfortunate artist or amateur that may be wandering about.

Letter 61

Camp before Sebastopol, 28 June

I am afraid there is but small chance of our 'taking the field', and the summer is slipping by so rapidly that we are all somewhat gloomily looking forward to another winter in these our dreary Quarters. I have been taking advantage of the very lovely weather that we have been enjoying lately by taking long rides into the new territory that we have got in the direction of 'Baidar'. Arthur Wombwell and I got to Baidar the day before yesterday, and a more delightful ride you cannot conceive. All the road is thro' the midst of beautiful scenery, and the trees are looking their best. The village of Baidar was a very interesting sight, all the inhabitants being there. They were glad to see us and explained by signs that the Cossacks had taken away all they could carry of their possessions. It is in the midst of a very fertile smiling valley, not so highly cultivated as I expected to find it, but probably they have been unable to pay much attention to their fields, having to furnish labor, and bullocks, and all they had, to support the Russian Army in the Winter. The inhabitants were much more Eastern looking than any Tartars I have yet seen, and quantities of the jolliest little children I ever saw were running about. They had, the girls, a very pretty head-dress like a fez, with a sort of felt coronet round it, and their hair (very light colored generally) in thousands of tiny braids down their backs. We got some milk there which we enjoyed, the first milk, by the way, that I have tasted for 9 or 10 months. The last mile or two of the ride there was most pretty, winding down a hill to the valley and overlooking it through a beautiful forest and constant 'vedettes' of Turkish dancers here and there amongst the trees. Altogether, these little excursions form the bright spots of one's life here, and we all rush away whenever we have no duty to perform here.

We hear constantly of new 'Siege Trains' and big guns & mortars that we are going to put to somewhere or other to destroy the Russians, but you are probably as sick of hearing of them as I am of seeing them go by our Camp, so that I will not weary you by a long account of them. I believe we are going soon to recommence the old story, and now we are getting so skilful at dragging up shot and guns that we can have a Siege about once a fortnight, and I think we probably shall have them throughout the Winter at that rate. As to whether, by this process, we shall arrive at any termination of our business I don't know, but I fear that but few of us will last many years here. It is sad on visiting any Regiment here to see how few of those whom I recollect landing here are to be found now. However, I cannot complain: I have never had a day's illness since I landed.

Sir George Brown is ill on board ship and is going home, I hear. Ld. Raglan has been very ill these last few days but is rather better today.[66] Codrington is, I am happy to say, come or coming up to take the 2nd. Division, and is, I conclude, well again. Charles Molyneux of the 4th. is going to sell out and I think is quite right, only foolish in having come out at all. I think the days of Romance and Chivalry are gone by, and always think unfortunate married men quite right to think more of their wretched wives and families than of 'what people will say'. I cannot say that I regret the days when wives used to button up their husbands' iron clothes and pack them off so cheerfully to fight – and were quite contented to hear (about once a year) from a dreary old Palmer with a shell in his hat,[67] that they were not yet killed. Besides, I don't fancy knights bought their commission in those days, and my friend Charley has not ever much money to live on. There are lots of young fellows to take his place and they'll fight all

---

[66] As Dallas records at the end of this letter, Raglan died on 28 June 1855.

[67] Palmers or pilgrims traditionally wore cockleshells on their hats.

the better for not thinking of poor little pale women dependant on them at home.

I am going out this afternoon to pay a round of visits! First of all, Ld. Rokeby and Sir Colin [Campbell], who live close together. Then on to Col. McDougall who is living at Head Quarters. (He called on me yesterday: what is he doing out here? I thought he was a swell at Sandhurst. However, I shall know what he is doing before you can tell me). Then just beyond Head Quarters are the 'Imperial Guards' and I must call on an old 'Commandant', a most gorgeous old acquaintance of mine with a variety of long names, the last and most useful of which is 'du Holbec'. I made acquaintance with him on the 18th. June just as I had come back from our very unfortunate assault. I found a very 'dishevilled' looking old gentleman in the Imperial Guard uniform sitting on a stone near my tent looking very sorry for himself. I gave him a glass of some exceedingly valuable and very fiery sherry that we have got, which revived him much. He then disclosed to me that he had been down in the trenches during the 'unfortunate affair' and that he had come away with both a stomach and a headache, and that he was a stout man, and had missed his servant and horses and did not think he could walk home, on which I lent him my horse, which he got on, having first asked me if he was '*vif*'. He did not tell me what I have since heard: that the Imperial Guard ran away so fast from the Malakoff Tower that it is a wonder they have not all got stomach-aches! Nevertheless, he is a good old Bloke and called on me a day or two ago, having cured himself of his ailments he said by 35 pills and drinking nothing but 'Absinthe' (such filth!). I shall have to drink some today with him.

Most melancholy news has just come from Hd. Quarters. Poor Lord Raglan died last night at 9 P.M. and Simpson *pro tem* is our Chief. It is a very sad thing, poor old man: would that he had been spared till some moment of victory, instead of after our first defeat. All who knew him loved him much.[68]

---

[68] Officially Lord Raglan died of cholera. There was a widespread assumption, however, that he died of a broken heart, brought about by the failure of the assault of 18 June, and of the death a few days earlier of General Estcourt.

Letter 62

Camp before Sebastopol, 2 July

Today we escort poor old Lord Raglan's Remains to a ship for England. Who reigns in his stead we know not; for the time being, General Simpson. All those good qualities he possessed, his charming manners, his kindness, and his long reign in the hearts of all those who personally knew him, have made him as much and as sincerely regretted as if we had lost a great General. All his Staff are broken up and most of them go home with him I believe – if fame speaks truly of them, a more perfectly gentlemanly, useless crew never burdened an army.

Letter 63

Camp before Sebastopol, 5 July

We conducted our poor old Commander in Chief's [Raglan] Remains to be embarked at Kazatch Bay, for England, the day before yesterday & a more imposing and magnificent Military Spectacle you cannot conceive than the Procession on the occasion. I saw it all most satisfactorily as I was acting as the Brigadier's [Garrett] A.D.C. We lined the road with Infantry all the way, about five miles. Where we ended, the French took it up, & the Gun-Carriage bearing the old Lord's Remains was accompanied on each side (as Pall Bearers) by Pelissier, de la Marmora, Omar Pacha, & Simpson; after them, the whole of the French & English Staff, & then one or two Officers from every Regiment out here, the whole Cavalry of the Allies, (who by the way looked magnificent), accompanying the Procession all the way.

The Day was lovely, & to my mind no Military Pageant could possibly be conceived more exquisitely beautiful & affecting than the whole affair. At short intervals all the way were stationed Bands who each played sacred music as the Procession passed, & on each height Artillery fired constant, solemn salutes. I was stationed with the Brigadier [Garrett] who commanded the 4th. Division as the Procession passed, & on the height opposite to us was stationed a beautiful Sardinian Band, which played the simplest, grandest hymn, as the sad cortege went by.

Hardened & accustomed as we all are to death and horrors out here, I shall never forget my feelings as we uncovered our heads to honour the good Old Man's Remains – the simplicity of the gun carriage that bore his coffin, covered with a Union Jack & on it his cocked hat & a little wreath of Eternelles (placed there by old Pelissier) formed the most touching contrast to the magnificence of the Pall Bearers' dress & that of the numberless Staff who followed. There was a feeling of Reality about it all, that the Great Duke's [Wellington] funeral must have lacked. One felt that all this magnificent spectacle was a labor of love, not costing a farthing, a whole Army just turning out, as they were, from their Camps to do honor to one whom, whatever his shortcomings, all loved who knew. Apart from any feelings one might have on the occasion, the mere sight of the very *élite* of 4 Armies, in their '*grande tenue*' & all soldiers whom we are fighting and struggling side by side with, was a most grand spectacle.

After the Procession had passed us, the Brigadier (& I) rode on across the country to Kazatch Bay to see its arrival there. As the procession came up to the shore, the Cavalry defiled on each side and formed up on the sea shore, a long line. The coffin was put on a barge which was towed slowly along by some eight or ten Man of War's boats to the *Caradoc* who takes him home.

While waiting on the shore I had a good view of our Celebrities here. Omar Pacha looked splendid. He is a most intelligent looking old man with a most noble head, & his dress was more gorgeous and beautiful than I can describe: one blaze of gold, & on his Fez was one great Diamond like a star. On any other man one would only have seen the dress. Marmora is a most soldier-like looking man, dressed in the Sardinian pale grey uniform, a most becoming colour by the way, & looked every inch a gentleman. Simpson looked like a dear old English General somewhat scared at being made Commander-in-Chief. Pelissier was splendidly got up, but is a vulgar looking man & a bad horseman. However he was, they say, very fond of Ld. Raglan, & won my heart by bringing a simple little yellow wreath which he put on the coffin before starting, rather '*touchant*' I thought, perhaps a little 'French'. He has published a General Order to his troops on the subject of our late Chief's death. It is short &, I think, fine. However, you will see all these things much better told in the Papers & as soon as you get this.

I went with the Brigadier to call on General Simpson, our new Chief. He was very civil, but I fancy neither he himself nor anybody out here seems to think him much fitted for such an appointment. Who knows? Perhaps he may be the man?

I dined with our General Bentinck yesterday. He seemed a very pleasant gentlemanly man & I should not wonder if he was a really good man. He is very quiet & seems to know what he is about.

Some promotions that have lately come out here have (some of them) excited universal disgust. 1st Lord George Paget gets 100 a year for 'good service'. He has been a bad officer for something about 18 years, & except here, has never seen any service. There are heaps of old fellows who have been 30 or more years in the service & have fought everywhere! Then there is an Honble, one Percy Herbert, who has been 15 years in the service, who was a Captain when he came out here, has led an easy life on the Staff here all the time, & now is made Queen's A.D.C. and full Colonel! These are the two promotions that have excited most disgust.

Letter 64

Camp before Sebastopol, 12 July

As you may perhaps suspect we are all come to rather a full-stop here, & except 'Camp-gossip' I have but little to tell. First of all, in my last letter I think I said that the '£100 *per an.* rewards' or rather the distribution of the some of them, had excited some disgust, (as well as some other rewards). But certainly 'the Brigadier's' [Garrett] obtaining it could not but meet with everybody's approbation. He has been nearly 40 years in the service, had been in 4 general actions & got clasps for them, in about 20 'minor affairs' & had been severely wounded 3 times. If he does not deserve some reward, God knows who does! but I think you perhaps understood that the £100 pensions were for Crimean affairs, which is not the case. Those pensions have always been given at intervals to old officers who have seen service, & when given to men like Ld. George Paget who has been (if I mistake not) under 20 years in the service, cause, as you can understand, some dissatisfaction.

I can well understand your anxiety about us here, from reports you get at home. Another thing that I think most unwarrantable is the habit Doctors have got of returning everybody who is even touched, as 'severely wounded'. *Entre nous*, I think some of them are not disinclined to have their names returned in that form. Perhaps it may give them some claim hereafter, but is perfectly inexcusable when one thinks of their wretched friends' anxiety.[69]

Osten Sacken sent in a pocket-book of poor Sir J. Campbell's with a message, 'condoling with Lord Raglan on having lost so gallant an Officer' very courteous of him, was it not? It was found close to the 'Redan' (our point of attack). What curious Electro-plated Barbarians these Russians are. Nothing could exceed the splendid behaviour of our Officers in that affair, a great many of them went up almost by themselves. The men could not be got to follow them. The men of one or two Regiments whom I will not name, behaved very badly. The fire they had to advance against was certainly dreadful, and they were most of them young soldiers, & perhaps may do better next time. It is extraordinary what education & breeding will do. Old Pennefather could not have paid a more glorious compliment to us, than when he said (as is reported of him) that our two companies at Inkermann 'fought like gentlemen'. A Frenchman the other day asked me quite seriously if our first storming party 'was not entirely composed of Officers'. It was the 1st. Brigade of the 4th. Division that stormed, & the 2nd. (mine) supported them, in the same way as the Guards & Highlanders supported the 2nd. and Light, & owing to the hopeless confusion & crowding in the trenches where we lay, or perhaps to some feeling on the part of our Chiefs that it would only add to the slaughter to call upon us, we never came into action at all.

As you say, every mail from here brings grief to some one, & this prolonged siege, the most harassing of a soldier's duties, has only the gloom & none of the excitement of a Campaign for us out here. A night or two ago, an acquaintance of mine was killed, Maunsell by name, of the 39th. I had just been talking to him as he was starting. The next time I saw him, or rather his body, was a few hours after-

---

[69] Officers wounded in the Napoleonic Wars were later granted pensions, hence this comment. The practice of recording all wounds as 'severe' was not universal: one cavalry officer who had suffered seventeen lance wounds in the battle of Balaklava was returned as 'Wounded Slightly'.

wards brought up from the trenches, poor fellow! A shell fell into the trench & wounded a number of men. It took his leg off, & he sat up, as they wanted to carry him off, & said 'If there is anybody worse hit than me, he had better be taken first' (there being only one stretcher at hand). When he found there was not anyone 'worse hit', he allowed them to take him up, and died in a few minutes of loss of blood. The men ought to follow these sort of leaders!

I saw a rather interesting note from an Engineer Officer yesterday. He was taken prisoner, some nights ago (at least he went out to look at some ground in front of our trenches & never came back). His brother officer got a note from him. He told him that he suddenly came upon a party of Russes, who secured him, & warned his friends never to go out in front without an escort. They took him through the 'Redan' works, over the bridge of boats into the Town and treated him very well. He was taken before Osten Sacken, who asked him no questions except 'whether the report of Lord Raglan's death was true'; & then came a part of the letter deeply crossed over by the Russes, but with lime juice[70] 'we deciphered' that he was also taken before General Todleben, the great Engineer who was in bed, severely wounded with a 'musquet ball in the hip'. We could make out no more. His name was James, a good Officer.

Letter 65

Camp before Sebastopol, 16 July

I had a pleasant Picnic a few days ago, with a party of 10, all 'picked men', to 'the Monastery'. This is one of our ways, nearly the only one, of passing a holiday here. We start about 12 or 1 & each takes his share of food and drink & when we arrive, we put the Hock & other pleasant drinks, into a well to cool, & wander about, having tethered our horses, where they can get their 'Pic' of grass, & then we dine under a tree, & talk about 'the Russ' & horses & our old quarters at home, in fact about anything but the dreary old Siege. After feeding, we light our pipes & sit on the Cliff to stare at the beautiful sea, the more energetic ones occasionally throwing stones, & watching

---

[70] Lime juice (i.e., citric acid) was used to remove the Russian censor's crossing-out.

them hop down on to the beach, many hundreds of feet below us. Of course it would be pleasanter having some pretty girls to walk about with, but then as an exceedingly shy young 'Plunger' said the other day, 'Gals are all very well, but then a Fellah can't eat and drink as much as he does when they're away' & there is something in that.

I do not think we have ever been so completely without a rumour of any change, any expedition, any attack, any sort of movement in fact. The wise ones are beginning to dig holes and make huts for the Winter. Even Wombwell (who is a worthy rival of mine in energy!) & I are thinking of going on with the 6 stones that we commenced a hut with for last Winter. It is all very well tho' trying to joke about it, but God grant that we may not spend another Winter in this dreadful Plateau, but few of us, I fancy, could stand two Winters here. You would be surprised to see how old the healthiest of us look now.

Letter 66

Camp before Sebastopol, 20 July

As our poor old Chief [Raglan] would have said 'I have the honor to inform you that the Weather still continues favorable' & further than that, I don't know what to tell you. I always forget to answer question or remarks in your letters & I will this time for once. You have in one or two letters told me that we have been getting on so much better since 'Indian Officers' have come to put us to rights. As you did not mention any names until this last letter, I could not exactly understand to whom you referred, tho' I could guess from what quarter that news came to you, for whatever else has been said about a certain dear old General [Napier], no one ever accused him of being a lukewarm 'Partizan'. Now I have no sort of objection to Indian Officers, & would only be too delighted to see the 'Round' men in the round holes & the 'Square' men in the square ones, but I must tell you the truth about the 4 men you named.

1st., McMurdo,[71] at the head of a Corps, the expense of which seems almost fabulous, & with a Railway right up to the Camp, & the

---

[71] Col. McMurdo married the daughter of Sir Charles Napier, hence the 'Partizan' comment.

Roads in perfect order, does what the unfortunate 'Commissariat' failed to do in Winter, with no expensive Corps, no Railway, & roads impassable, & I can tell you with all this, he barely does it. One or two rainy days throw him back considerably, & the inefficiency of this splendid Transport Corps, I know to be one of the principal objections to our making any move. So much for him. I do not say anything against him, but I mean to say that with all the advantages I have enumerated, no one could do less.

2nd., Harding went to Balaklava to relieve Haines (my friend) with unlimited powers just at the end of Winter, & naturally put things to rights to a certain extent, (not much, I can tell you). He remained there some little time & then went into the Quarter Master General's Department, where he has been ever since. Nobody ever supposed him to be the least a clever man, nor is he, and Balaklava gets on just as well (or as badly) without him.

3rd., Simpson, good old man, nobody could ever have accused of doing anything for good or evil, for, except for the change of signature at the bottom of all orders, nobody saw him ever, or heard of him out here. He may be a most clever man, I only pray that he may prove himself so, but as yet no one may say what he is.

4th., Jones is a most energetic man, but has done nothing yet here to make himself talked of. The only change in our works since he came has been since the taking of 'The Quarries', a place concerning the importance of which opinions differ, as the possession of them hung upon the 'Mamelon' which completely commands them. What I mean is, whatever side had the 'Mamelon' must have the Quarry. The French having taken the Mamelon rendered the Quarry perfectly untenable for the Enemy. We have as yet done no good with the Quarry & one may reasonably doubt the judiciousness of holding a place where we have lost at the rate of one man every hour, since we have taken it: this is not exaggeration, as our loss has averaged between 20 & 30 men a day there! I forget when we took them, but you can look back and see, and then calculate the price we pay for them.

Now, these are the 4 Indian officers (you say, & have probably been told so) to whom we may attribute any improvement in affairs here: this is not at all fair on their Predecessors. The Commissariat & McMurdo's Transport Corps in fine weather with good roads & Railway, of course do better than the wretched Commissariat without a Transport Corps, without a railway, & last not least in Winter. Harding, perfectly independent, with unlimited powers, & the worst times over, of course does more than Haines with no powers, & with the dreadful state of things he found at Balaklava, much improved (by the way) under him, before Harding came. Jones has just followed Burgoyne's steps, tho' more energetic personally, & dear old Simpson as I sit writing here, I'll swear, has done as yet nothing. I fear you will think all this very tedious, but I have no news, and I should like you to know about the 'Wise men of the East'. Heaven knows we should gladly welcome any 'Great Man', if he came from the South Sea Islands, but one ordinary man is like another, tho' he may have been in India.

Markham has arrived here, I believe a really good man. He gets the 2nd. Division. I must now say Adieu & must ('appologize') 'beg your pardon' (I always put two p's in the other word) for such a prosy, stupid, letter. However, you may perhaps while away a quarter of an hour under the jolly tree on your lawn, trying to decipher it. I look vainly for a tree. Out of my tent door, I see only bones & dust & soldiers, all of which things I should like never to see again.

The Brigadier [Garrett] has just been in & sends his love. We were talking of Chobham & poor Old Yea: how many of those whom I laughed with & lunched with there, not long ago have I seen buried here.[72] God forgive any man, who having once seen it, wishes to take a part in, or see, another War!

Letter 67

Camp before Sebastopol, 23 July

An Engineer I met yesterday told me that they had got another letter from 'James' who was taken Prisoner. He said, amongst other things, that he had the *Times* lent him to read every day, either the

---

[72] The 46th Regiment did not take part in the first large-scale manoeuvres ever carried out by the British Army, at Chobham, in 1853. Dallas must have attended (as did many others) out of personal interest.

same date or I think a day later than we get it here! Some A.D.C. of Osten Sacken lent it him. Just conceive the infinite mischief the ample accounts in it from here must do us! They must know exactly where our batteries are going to be made, where we lost most men, & by the most careless journal of the Siege, can always refer back to dates, & see where, how & when we lost men! Tho' one of course knew that they got the *Times*, yet few of us knew how late a one they have in Sebastopol, & yet the *Times* & the *Vox Populi*, one and the same thing in England, will persist that their minute revelations can do no harm! I don't wonder at the French being indignant with our allowing the presence of 'Special Correspondents' during such operations as these in our Camp!

I am sorry to say I have never heard anything of my poor pony, but I have got still a very good horse that I have had most of the Winter & that, with a very good & frightful old French mule, complete my stud. 'Deary me'! (as the lamented Mrs. Gamp would say[73]) how cheerfully I would give anyone my horse and my mule & everything I had, to escape from this hole, with one suit of rags! I must say I am sometimes tempted to envy some of my brother Officers out here, with good cadaverous faces. They keep going home, one or two in general orders, I see, every day, some of them, I know, in the rudest health, & all because they have such jolly wretched faces. I'm afraid the most docile 'Medical Board' would reject me if I really was ill. And really, you may believe me when I say, that if I saw any prospect of advancement, any chance of an active life, any hopes of an approach to the end of the War, any energy or plan on the part of our Leaders, I would willingly stop here, & if I was offered a chance of going home would refuse it, as long as I had health, but in the place of any or all of these, I find here a more hopeless oppressive life of idleness than that I thought to escape from at home. I can assure you that the most remote out-quarters in England or Ireland offer a much more exciting life than that we lead here. Day after day, we get up and sit perspiring in our reeking tents with no chance or hope of any change, or doing anything, and if an opportunity does come of any active measure, we all have the most perfect confidence in its being badly done.

---

[73] Mrs Gamp was a Dickens' character famous for her umbrella.

However, growling will do me no good, & does not probably amuse you. There is a rumour of officers being given 3 months Leave, this Winter, from our Winter Quarters wherever they may be, probably here, whether we take the place or not. I don't think it can be true. The Authorities must be aware of how few they would ever get back if they let us escape once.

In the mean time I can tell you nothing about our prospects of taking the Town. If we had not those poor old men that the Russians mercifully thought were merely under the temporary influence of wine instead of being in their usual state of imbecility on the 18th.- if we had not them, like logs about our necks, I honestly believe the place might be ours in a fortnight. Of course we should lose men, thousands if necessary, but is it not better to lose men & gain our object, than lose them as we now do, & be the laughing stock of the World? I can assure you that our miserable plans, & their Originators are a theme of jest to the lowest Private in the Army. I have heard, in the trenches at night, common soldiers, whose simple good sense would make our poor old Generals shudder, talking of our 18th. failure.

Letter 68

Camp before Sebastopol, 30 July

Many thanks for your letter of the 15th which I received this morning whilst playing a cricket match on our hill against the Cavalry, who, by the way, managed to beat us most sadly. I was glad to hear that you had seen poor Brummell. I was sure you would like him. He is a thorough good soldier, which, like everything else good of its kind, is pleasant to meet with.

I believe that we are getting up some Batteries, & shot & shell into them, but nobody seems to take much interest, and I really think that under the new 'Régime' we have less purpose, energy or plan than ever.

The 'C.B.s'[74] have of course been much canvassed here, and I think that – with a few exceptions – they are dealt out as fairly as can be

---

[74] CB: Companion of the Most Honourable Order of the Bath.

expected. Of course Colonels and Staff people are those who get these sort of rewards, as '*Ex Officio*' (from their position) they are more likely to be noticed; & on reflection, I do not think it would be possible to do else than give them these rewards, for it is perfectly impossible to find out the merits & worth of those in humbler positions – with some few brilliant exceptions, of course.

The misfortune of the system is that perhaps nine out of ten Colonels do well enough, & the 10th is in every way incapable & unworthy, and this is only known to those who have the misfortune to be under him, & this 10th man is made a C.B. in the crowd. One striking example of this is the case of the Colonel of the 63rd, who, by his utter mismanagement completely destroyed his Regiment & we all expected to hear of his being tried by Court Martial at home, instead of which he is one of the first 'Companions' installed![75] Again, there are occasional accidents, such as men without interest or anything else getting things 'in the row'. This goes in favour of my theory of the names being sometimes put into a hat & drawn out on chance. But when I think of the many good fellows out here who have never missed a day's duty since the Army came out, who have on every occasion behaved splendidly, whose self devotion, whose bravery, and whose talents those only who have known & associated with them (and the private soldiers who adore them) could bear witness to – when I look at many of these sort of men, still Captains and Subalterns as they came out, and then at the Hon[ble] Percy Herbert, Queen's A.D.C., C.B., and I know that he came out here at the same time as they did, a Captain, & that instead of risking his life twice a week in the trenches & freezing 'on Picquets' for numberless days and nights all through the horrid Winter, he has led a comparatively easy life on the Staff, and has perhaps been 'under fire' as it is called 5 or 6 times for all these honours – when I look on cases of this kind, (& thank God such very disgusting cases are rare) I begin to think with some character of Dickens (I forget who) that all human institutions and laws are in 'a great muddle' & I don't see how it can be put to rights.

---

[75] The unfounded rumour of the impending Court Martial of Lt. Col. Dalzell is first noted in a letter written by Captain Hawley on 18 March 1855, 'I believe the colonel of the 63rd is to be tried for the novel offence of losing his regiment.'

Even for us out here on the spot, it is almost impossible to get at the truth of things that take place out here. We hear one day that 'A. behaved very well in the Sortie last night'. Next day it appears that 'A. couldn't be found on that occasion' & that B. was the man, & perhaps next day we find that B. was not there at all! Just conceive of the difficulty of 'an authority' getting at the truth of anything. I could give you 50 illustrations of this: perhaps one or two will do.

For at least 3 or 4 weeks after 'Balaklava' I heard of nothing but the gallant behaviour of Lord Cardigan & I can assure you that since I have heard from men on the spot (as were my first informants) that he did little short of running away! Now what is the truth? I can't say.

To this day I don't know, & cannot find out, who was the Officer of Artillery who at 'Inkermann' brought up two large guns that helped materially to gain the day. I ought to know for they fired away within 20 yards of me for some hours, & I positively cannot say who it was. 4 or 5 Officers all claim the honor of it. Where is the truth there?

There is another affair of the same kind, the last I will bore you with. You have probably heard of a certain Lieutenant Maxse, Naval A.D.C. to Lord Raglan. He is supposed to have carried certain orders from Ld. Raglan to the Fleet, on our march here, & to have ridden alone many miles through a country full of the enemy's cavalry. All this he did do & was made a Commander over perhaps 100 other men's heads, but I positively know for a fact that the man who took the orders two hours before him, & was sitting in Admiral Dundas' cabin having delivered the message some two hours, when Maxse arrived – this was Col Windham, Q.M. of our Brigade. He never heard anything more about it, & I recollect his telling me he had had an uncomfortable ride! Yet a few weeks afterwards the papers were full of this extraordinary feat of young Maxse & he was made a Commander![76] He has gone home, by the way, with our poor old Chief's Remains & will be one of your London Heroes! – isn't it all 'a muddle'?

---

[76] Dallas reports the plain facts here. Windham's services were ignored, and Maxse's treated as greatly daring.

How utterly valueless history, tho' written by the most eloquent & truthful men, will always seem to me, when on the spot where events daily are taking place, I can't tell you the whole truth of them, do what I can to fish it out.

I am sorry to say that Colin Campbell of ours got hit in the trenches the other night. He escaped wonderfully: a grape shot (about the size of an orange) ran, as it were, along his back, tearing all his clothes, shirt and all to little shreds, & inflicting merely a very large bruise or contusion. He was stooping at the time, or of course it would have killed him. I was in bed when I heard he was wounded & got up & on my horse to see him. He is living with the Engineers (acting Engineer himself) about a mile off, & I found him quietly sitting up drinking some chocolate, thinking no more of his hurt than many would of a mosquito bite. I hope they will oblige him to join his Regiment soon. He must get killed if he stops there. He is the most perfectly fearless fellow in the world, & his work is most dangerous. I trust that his wound will keep him away from the Trenches for some time.

Fortunately for us (the 4th. Division), altho' we had the most dangerous work in the Winter, now we cannot, (owing to the nature of the ground in front of us) get any nearer to the Town; whilst on the right, where Campbell is working, they are advancing slowly to the Redan & lose frightfully. I will not vouch for the accuracy of the numbers altho' I am convinced they are not exaggerated, but we calculated (Campbell & one or two of us) the other day, that the loss of French & English in the Trenches not including sick, was daily about 150 on average. Our share of that is about 30 or 40. Conceive what that drain is, per month, on our Armies. And as the nearer they get the greater of course is the loss, you may conceive our anxiety for a fellow like Campbell, whose complete contempt of danger only adds to his risks. He is very hard worked too, every other night in the advanced trenches!

Letter 69

Camp before Sebastopol, 7 August
I see the French on our right are grubbing away all about the detestable Malakoff Tower but no one seems to have a notion of what

our next operation is to be. Canrobert went away a day or two ago, to take some appointment 'near to the person of the Emperor' [Napoleon III], not at all in disgrace. One knows so little of people's private motives particularly of 'Generals', that I should not be at all surprised to hear some day, that he was a great General and that some disagreement with Ld. Raglan was the cause of his resignation. I have heard such, & that he altogether & thoroughly disapproved of the Siege. Of course, his asking for, and receiving a Division in the Army which he had just commanded, was in keeping with his theatrical manners, & was altogether French. He is much liked by all French Officers & is considered an *homme de coeur*. Pelissier, 'they say' will disclose nothing of his projects to any one, if he has any. I think he is quite right as regards us, as we should probably publish them in the *Times* which would somewhat affect the result, but it seems odd, his not having hinted at his plan even to his own Engineer Officers &c if the story is true, doesn't it?

Forde, the Brigadier's [Garrett] A.D.C., has gone away for a little change of air, not at all well. They wanted the M.D.s to send him on board ship, but as he truly observed, 'It makes me very ill to look at a ship when in rude health', & he doubted its making him well when ill. So they sent him to a place by Balaklava, on a hill called the 'Sanatorium'. The chief and I went to see him yesterday. It seemed a very healthy place with good air, but found him rather wretched, as he was living in a long room, with a lot of other poor fellows, very much more ill than himself.

We have had as you know, considerable changes among our Generals here, some good ones. Markham is we believe, a very good man, then Richard of England, as he is called, goes, which is a capital thing, altho' the Division falls to Eyre whose conduct on the 18th.[77] ought to have stamped him as a most blundering reckless General, reckless by the bye of other's lives, for he disappeared, on that occasion, very early with a most lucky little wound; this, added to his brutal demeanor to all under him, makes him sufficiently unpopular. His Brigadiers are Barlow, who is almost imbecile, & Trollope, who is

---

[77] See Letters 58 and 59 for details.

a perfectly empty-headed donkey, so that the poor 3rd. Division is not to be envied.[78,79]

Letter 70

Camp before Sebastopol, 10 August

I have been living with the Brigadier [Garrett] a good deal lately, doing A.D.C. for him, Forde having gone away for a few days for a change of air. I cannot exactly understand what they mean to do with the Brigadier. I cannot conceive for a moment that they intend to pass him over in any way, as he is one of the most efficient officers out here, and my notion is that they intend to make him a Major General & give him some command either in the Mediterranean or elsewhere. I hope he will get something of this sort, for I fear another Winter here for him, and secondly I dare say he might have something to give me. However I am a little sick of building '*Châteaux en Espagne*' & with a continuance of my present health, can go grumbling on with the rest, come what may.

I really think that nothing that McDougall can say of the sad state of things here is in the least exaggerated. We live like spendthrifts from day to day, with no apparent thought of tomorrow. I foresee, (& it is merely the prophecy of any one not an idiot looking around him), that if we have to stop the Winter here, that with some very few alleviations, our suffering will be a sad repetition of last year's. We are rapidly approaching the end of Summer, & unless our Leaders feel perfectly certain of our being in the Town by the Autumn, nothing can excuse their want of preparation & miserable supineness. We have made and are making no sort of road to Balaklava, no intermediate stations or Depots for provisions. The railway is just laid on the surface

---

[78] The names of the two Brigadiers have been deliberately omitted from the transcript. Whilst it is certain that the Brigadiers were Barlow and Trollope, it is not clear which was the imbecile and which the donkey.

[79] An interesting entry appears in the diary of Captain Savage, 68th Regiment for 31 July 1855. 'Dallas and Wombwell came in and played a rubber' i.e., presumably, of whist. Dallas does not mention this evening's entertainment in this, or in his next letter, and in fact never mentions playing cards in any of his letters: one must assume that he was keeping the dreadful fact of his gaming a secret from his family!

of the baked ground, & the bad weather will find us much as it found us last year.

McMurdo's Transport Corps is the most costly failure ever undertaken. We are still in the same sieves of tents that we lived & died in last Winter, & I really think that we shall live on biscuit, & our horses on each others tails, as usual. I look forward to such an outcry in England when the Winter comes, and again catches us unprepared, as will astonish those that are so grossly to blame.

With such a prospect as this, in addition to the utter & complete want of confidence on all our sides in our Chiefs, the miserable way in which an order comes one day & is directly counter-ordered the next, Batteries built that can hit nothing and nobody, (those not in power showing where the guns should be placed getting snubbed), hot old Sir Colin quarrelling with & now not speaking to Barnard, the Head of the Staff, Airey still Q.M.G., Filder still head of the Commissariat, Hall Chief Medico – with these, & they are but a small portion of the long list of hopeless messes, that we do, and are likely to continue to, suffer from – can you wonder at me, or anyone else, wishing to get out of the row?

The Russians seem to have got a new stock of powder and shot, & fire constantly & heavily on us. They do but little harm [on] our side [Left Attack], but on the right the casualties are great. Our approaches are almost come to a stop, as are the French, & our only hope seems now to rest on the favourable 'accouchement' of the mysterious project that people say Pelissier's brain has been some time 'big with'. I only hope to be able to write some day that the 'Infant & Payrient' are doing well.[80]

Now with all this dreary prospect – in a patriotic point of view – I must tell you that personally I am about as happy & comfortable as anyone could possibly be under the circumstances. We have got up a cricket club & when not in the trenches play matches, & live luxuriously, in a small way. I cannot describe how pleasant it is out here so far away from home, meeting old cricket antagonists whom one met last time at 'Lords'. By the way, I am going to look up Ewen Macpherson today. We are going to play a Match of Etonians v. Harrovians next week. I think he was at Harrow.

---

[80] Infant and parent: i.e., the scheme and its originator.

Letter 71

Camp before Sebastopol, 13 August

We had information last night of a general attack to be on our trenches & lines, & were consequently 'under arms' last night to repel it, but as is usually the case with those sort of preconcerted affairs, it did not come off, and after spending most of the night laying down on the side of a hill, we came home: no great hardship by the bye, during such weather as this, as it is just as pleasant 'out of doors' as in (if we call one's tent 'indoors'). I really think that the Russes did mean to do something, but probably heard of our being so well prepared.

Beyond the everlasting shooting of big guns on both sides, there is but little doing 'along of' the Siege. The Russes seem to have more ammunition than ever, if one may judge by the quantity they waste, & it has these last few days appeared to be quite new. On picking up & examining their balls, we have found them to be quite newly made. Where they come from, Heaven knows! We have had the Duke of Newcastle stopping with us lately. When I say with us, I mean with the 4th. Division, at Sir H. Bentinck's. He is a 'great big man', in a shooting coat with a short stubbly red beard, & if I was not told he was a Duke, should have mistaken him for a Grocer.

Today has been fearfully hot, 98 in one's tent. I must say I hope it won't get any warmer, for it is quite as much as I can stand now, tho' except that one's face is nearly black & one is in a constant state of moisture, I don't know that we suffer in health from it as yet. Forde has come back quite recovered & has resumed his duties, & I mine.

Letter 72

Camp before Sebastopol, 17 August

I am so full of my good news that I must deliver myself of it at once. The Russians had the temerity, poor creatures, to come on against our lines in the Valley of the Tchernaya, where the French and Sardinians are camped, and got so tremendous a beating that I don't think they will attempt anything more for some time. The only way one can account for the frightful lesson they received is the fact of the French having received good information of their intentions. We have known for some little time of the arrival of large reinforcements in the Enemy's Camp, & have been on the look-out for some attack on our trenches for the last few days, but they did not come on till yesterday, Thursday Morning at about 3 or 4 A.M. & then they attacked along the whole line of the Tchernaya, about a distance of two miles. Their numbers are estimated at about 60,000, & about 30,000 were engaged. The French let them come on quite close and then literally mowed them from the face of the Earth with Artillery and Musquetry. The Russians lost about 5,000, and the French about as many hundreds. They retreated then back to somewhere about Mackenzie's Farm. The Sardinians whom they attacked about Tchergorun behaved splendidly & altogether it has been the most gallant affair. Of course we were not there, as we were under arms all day ready to repel any simultaneous attack on our trenches which was naturally expected.

I went down to the field of battle this morning early, & from the immense extent of ground over which it was fought it was impossible to estimate the numbers I saw all over the plain, but their loss, I should say, was by no means overrated at 5,000. They appeared very ill clad & looked thin and haggard, altogether a worse sort than our foes at 'Alma' & 'Inkermann'. They (the wounded) said that they had come from Moscow, poor creatures. They looked very sad, and wretched as they always do, more like the Peasantry of a Country than soldiers. They must have come on very gallantly & have been nobly led, to have ever got to where I saw hundreds of them lying. The French were paying every attention to them (the wounded) & the beastly Enemy who ought to be swept from any civilised part of the world, were, when I was there, firing shells from their distant Batteries, in amongst their own wounded, and the French who were tending them!

We [i.e. The British] had nothing engaged but 1 or 2 Batteries of Artillery who did capital execution. The Russes as they always do, retired in good order & got away their guns, (with the exception of one Battalion who ran like a flock of sheep). The affair could not be followed up as they got under cover of their heavy Batteries on the opposite hills, a short way from the Tchernaya, & of course could not be followed. We took some 4 or 500 Prisoners. Altogether it is to my thinking the completest thing that has been done yet. The French were so thoroughly prepared & let them come on so close that they had no escape, the perfection of their arrangements proved by the comparatively trifling loss they sustained. The French lost a good many Artillery by the heavy guns of the Enemy. A man who was there and saw it all said, nothing could exceed the splendid way in which the Artillery, principally '*Artillerie de la Garde*', fought their guns, under the heavy fire of the Enemy. I went to a small spot where they lost 60 horses while working the guns. They made the most frightful havoc among the dense columns of the Enemy tho'! To my thinking nothing can exceed the French Artillery. I saw so much of them at 'Inkermann', as I & my party were for a long time 'supporting' the guns, and nothing could surpass the devotion with which they came up Battery after Battery & were mown down by the heavy firing of the Russes. Every Battery that came up (one after another) had barely horses enough to slowly crawl away when it had fired its ammunition off, but they all came up '*ventre à terre*' & fired as coolly as on a parade ground. We are all much delighted at the Sardines having had an 'opening'. I don't exactly know what their share of the victory was, but all hands agree as to their gallant behaviour. I have no other news I hope you will say that the 'Battle of the Tchernaya' is enough for one note.

We have been firing all day very heavily on the town, not with, I fancy, any view to an assault, but to relieve the French, who are so close to the Malakoff that they cannot move for the terrific fire kept up on them.

Letter 73

Camp before Sebastopol, 19 August

The Ruskis have been quiet since their attack, & we have been sending a most terrific fire into their works & town ever since. Why, I don't exactly know, but I believe it has been by desire of old Pelissier, who wants to take advantage of their being engaged to push on towards the Malakoff Tower. On the person of a Russian General Officer who was killed on the Tchernaya, 'Wrede' by name, we found most important dispatches containing a full account of the intentions of the Russes. They had about 60,000 men for the attack of the plain and if successful, were to have come out with 40,000 on our trenches. '*L'homme propose &c*'. The Generals were, we hear, Gortchakoff Commander in Chief, Liprandi one wing, & Wrede (killed) the other. The brutal Enemy – would you believe it? – after the fighting was all over, kept up a constant fire of shells &c on their own wounded & the French who were paying them all attention! They were even firing next day when I was there: such are our Foes! Yesterday there was a flag of Truce & they came down into the plain to help to bury their dead. They say the French alone found 1700 dead & took 1500 Prisoners. The Prisoners all say that they had come immense distances & only halted one day before they attacked. They were all young soldiers, and very different from those I saw at 'Alma' & 'Inkermann'. They must suffer dreadfully for want of water. There is none nearer than the Belbec River, a weary march from the heights over the Tchernaya. In fact the precipitate way in which they attacked without resting to recover from their fearful march, proves how hard pressed they must have been.

Talking of being hard up makes me think of a little mouse that came quietly whilst Arthur [Wombwell] & I were at dinner today, & after jumping onto the table, climbed onto a potato in a dish & sat there eating it, & then tried to drink water out of a tumbler, which he, from his small stature, could not accomplish. He went away & we poured out some water on the table for him in case he came back, which he soon did & lapped it all up. Wasn't it nice of him? He is getting quite tame & came just now & sat by my inkstand. He is very pretty, with large eyes like little Jenny Johnston. By the way, I think he is a 'she' and from her very stout figure, is going to have a family. Perhaps after all she may be a modest little unmarried mouse & would perhaps be horrified if she knew what 'shocking stories' I am telling about her! I will tell you more about her in my next (if I see anything more of her). Do you think potato is a good thing for a mouse in her situation, in case my suspicions are true? I will have some Porter on the table tomorrow.

We had 3 new Ensigns join yesterday, two youths nice looking enough & one very old man, from his appearance about 50. He came from some Militia Regiment, & without he has good luck, is not likely to ever be a young General.[81]

---

[81] The three Ensigns who joined the 46th Regiment in August were Foster, Kelson and Marsack. The eldest, Marsack, was born in 1822 – five years older than Fred Dallas, and thirteen years older than the other two Ensigns. He did not make a young General: he retired by the sale of his Captain's commission in 1863.

The Brigadier [Garrett] has got his appointment officially as Brigadier. As I supposed, it was a mistake his name being omitted from the former list. However, it annoyed him, naturally, & now he is all right and happy again. I have not seen Lord Rokeby lately, nor have I met him about, but I don't think that he is ill, for he was quarrelling with Sir Colin the other day, & Sir Colin with General Barnard, & (I hear) Barnard with Eyre, & Eyre with everybody, which must make a meeting of our Generals rather a pleasant 'Reunion'.

The Camp is at present overrun with the new 'Army Works Corps' whose principal work seems to consist in getting drunk as yet, tho' they will settle down of course, they have only just arrived. A great many of the 'Land Transport Men' are Cabmen from London, & I occasionally meet an old friend. I found one out near Baidar, the other day. He was looking rather dismal & I asked him how he was getting on, when he astonished me by saying 'Pretty well, thank you, Sir, but I'd sooner by a long way, be waiting at the "Rag" for you, Sir'.[82] I then recognised him as a well known old 'Hansom' Driver. His principal grievance appeared to be the humiliation of having to drive 'Mokes' instead of 'the little mare with the neat 'ed, as you may recollect, Sir', & having to wear such a very absurd hat. I gave him a shilling to comfort himself at a French Canteen with, & the pleasant associations that he stirred up were 'cheap at the money'.

Letter 74

Camp before Sebastopol, 24 August

We have nothing to write about from here now since 'the fight', which, by the way, from all I hear seems to have been even more successful than I had at first imagined. The Russian loss is supposed to amount to nearly 10,000! The Russian Army, outside, are still hovering about, & we all expect that they will make some further attempt, for it is evident that they cannot support so large a force for nothing, & they must either fight or go away. The consequence is that we are constantly 'under arms'. I cannot conceive where they are to

---

[82] The 'Rag and Famish' was Punch's nickname for the Army and Navy Club in London, a popular hangout for young officers-about-town. It would appear that Dallas was a member.

make their attempt but trust it will be soon, as the result can only be their utter defeat & then we shall 'be rid' of them. The French have a most immense force along the Tchernaya, & that is the only point, or rather Line, on which they could come.

I saw the day before yesterday two letters to Pelissier from the Emperor & our Queen who dated from Paris. I hope the victory that they congratulated Pelissier on, will be a pleasant addition to the Fetes.

As regards my having any chance or opportunity of seeing you this Winter, I think we had better not indulge any thoughts of it, as I fear that it is utterly out of the question, & indeed while I enjoy such good health I would not wish to go until the affair is over. The few who have gone away on 'urgent private affairs' have been, in most instances, men that by some death in their families, have come into properties & intend selling out when they get home & I think them quite right. But in my position I could not at present think of it. Of course we are all weary & disgusted of this Campaign, which has probably never had its equal in danger, monotony, & hardship, so that whatever I might desire, I have made up my mind to struggle on, & do not attempt to indulge in dreams of what I feel I cannot expect. Do not think me unkind or unfeeling in saying this, Heaven knows! I would sooner be at [sic.] with you two, than commanding a Regiment here or anywhere else, but being out here & enjoying perfect health, I feel that I must see it out. I have no intention of, & I am sure even the best and dearest of Mothers would not wish me to do, as so many do, sham being ill & sneak home.

Letter 75

Camp before Sebastopol, 31 August
We had previously got the news about Sweaborg,[83] but until I hear further accounts, I don't think so much of the affair, as I have always my suspicions about 'the utter destruction &c of Public Buildings' & we have no detailed accounts of the Fortifications being destroyed; I

---

[83] Sweaborg, on the shores of the Baltic, had been successfully bombarded by the French and the British Baltic Fleets. Dallas here is being cautious about reading too much into initial reports.

only hope it may be completely done. In papers we got yesterday of the 18th. we see a telegraphic message about the affair of the 16th. I am pleased to see, underrating it as regards the numbers & its importance. It is always pleasant to find the reality surpassing one's anticipation (not a common affair by the way) & I see they say that the Allies only took 400 Prisoners – their number is over 2,000. The Russes are still 'poking about' the mountains somewhere & all preparations are made for them, wherever they may choose to attack, & attack (I think) they must, or else go away.

The Siege goes on much the same as usual, with the usual sad loss on our right attack, of course, as we advance, increasing. The French had a mishap on their 'Mamelon Vert' a few nights ago: a shell – quite an accident – from the Russes blew up their principal magazine & of course with it, everybody in the neighbourhood. The French who are always 'Pooh-poohing' their misfortunes, placed the loss of killed & wounded at 150. From the extent of the explosion we all surmise it to be about 3 times that number. We had, in our trenches a long way off, 20 men wounded by the falling stones and timber. It is the largest explosion that I have yet heard & actually woke me! It took place at about 12.30 A.M., & all I saw on getting out of bed was one immense cloud hovering over the trenches. This, tho' a sad business, does not affect the siege importantly, as they will make another magazine & the works were in no way injured. The French have got on wonderfully towards the Malakoff & are now grubbing away at about 60 yards from it. They have just got to what is called 'the Abattis', a defence made of immense logs of wood and trees; this they are now going through! The Russes have just completed a bridge of rafts & boats right across the harbour & have been going backwards & forwards over it for the last day or two. It seems well made and strong. I only hope that the Ruskis will march over there some day and blow up this side, of which there are occasional rumours here.

We had a grand installation of the Bath at Head Quarters the other day, Lord Stratford [de Redcliffe] having come over to invest the new K.C.B.s. We were all kept in Camp on that day, with the exception of a portion of each Regiment engaged in the Show. It seemed that they rather expected the Russes would attack us, knowing from their numerous spies, that all the Generals were away from their Divisions. However the Russes wisely kept away, thinking probably with me, that we should do much better without the good old Creatures than with them, in case of any attack.

After the ceremony, Soyer who has set up here, showed the Generals & Staff &c how to make their 'rations' into delicious dishes. I was there & he certainly made very nice ragouts & soups – he said – of our ordinary rations, but I fear it will be a very long time before we can do it for ourselves. His dishes had the additional advantage of being washed down with iced Champagne. Pelissier was there; it was the first time I had ever had a good look at him, & a more detestable Ruffian in appearance I never saw, very short with a large head, no neck, a stupid cruel face, immensely fat, with very short arms & very tight clothes that he appeared to be bursting out of. He never rides, but drives about in a filthy old broken down open carriage with four Artillery horses. It was quite a relief to take ones eyes off him & look at dear old Simpson by his side, looking completely a gentleman, (tho' rather haggard looking). By the way, I suspect, poor old Gent, that he would be much happier at home with lots of porridge & no Frenchmen or Russians to annoy him.

I have just seen Campbell [46th] who told me of a little row they had in the right attack last night. The Russes came on against a working party of ours, who all ran away & behaved exceedingly badly. A friend of mine, Wolseley (90th.), was badly wounded.[84] No man can stand this dreadful work going every 24 hours for nearly 12 months to the trenches knowing with the certainty of 30 or 40 being disposed of – they run away constantly now in the trenches. God knows how it will end! I see in the Gazette McDougall promoted for distinguished service in the Field. What does it mean? He was here a fortnight about, as an amateur!

Letter 76

Camp before Sebastopol, 7 September

I am only just recovering (or rather have only just recovered) from a rather smart attack of the *Mal d'Estomac* of this country, a few hours

---

[84] Later to become perhaps the most famous soldier of the Victorian age – Field-Marshal Viscount Wolseley.

attack of which disorder leaves the victim 'limp' & good for nothing for many days after, & tho' I had it for about a day & a half, & am quite free from it now, I feel a 'poor creature' & am some pounds lighter than I was before. I attribute it to the rather sudden change in the weather that we have had here. Autumn announces itself by a most marked alteration in the evenings & nights. A fortnight ago one never thought of taking a coat to the Trenches, now one would be frozen without one. These changes of weather are a great cause of the increase of the class of complaint to which mine belonged. The days are, or rather were until I shut up, lovely, tho' the last two or three have been blowy and dusty.

I trust our troubles here are approaching their end. As I can by no means take any part or share in it, I don't mind telling you (tho' of course the telegraph will tell you all) that the Grand Assault is tomorrow; the French at the Malakoff, & we at the Redan, & French again everywhere else. I see no reason to anticipate anything but success, even granting that the Enemy know all about it. The French have only about 30, or 40 yards to go, & as they will be sent in, in masses, I don't see how they can help getting in; this will give us, either tomorrow or (supposing they go no further than the Malakoff tomorrow) in a few weeks I should say at the furthest, the south side of Sebastopol, & then we have done with the horrid trenches which were getting too dreadful. Every night some acquaintance or friend was killed on the right attack, & the poor French have been losing 500 men a night lately!

I have so fiendish a pen I can write no more, &, as I am lying down, the ink is gently distilling itself over my fingers.

Letter 77

The Camp, In and before Sebastopol, 10 September
You may recollect that I told you in my last that we assaulted next day; this was by way of being a great secret, & from the surprise of the Russes must have been kept pretty quiet.

At about one the French jumped up & went in like hounds into cover, into the Malakoff, at all points. They had but a short distance to go and apparently met with no resistance until they had been in some time, when very heavy musquetry began which lasted for about 4 hours with no intermission. Our Second & Light Divisions were sent, as soon as the Malakoff showed the Tricolor Flag, at the Redan. They went out most gallantly & then when on the parapet of the Redan, nothing could get them on. In vain the officers got on the parapet & jumped in (about 90 men got in & lots of officers & the rest of the men nothing could induce to come). There were hardly any Russians there at first, but of course when they found our people did not come on & there were so few English there, their Reinforcements came up and drove them out. Our loss was frightful, over 100 Officers. This is very disgusting, as we all know and knew that whoever had the Malakoff must command the Redan and that there was no necessity in any possible point of view for our going at it. This, & the bad behaviour of the men & the shocking loss in consequence of Officers, tempers our joy at the fall of the place.

Whilst this was going on, the French had also attacked on the left, towards the sea, and were repulsed with great slaughter. On the night of that day we heard a succession of explosions & then fires broke out at all points in the Town, and we then saw that the Russes were evacuating & destroying their works.

On Sunday morning, the 9th., there was not a Russian to be seen, & frightful explosions at intervals taking place in their Batteries &c, & the whole town in flames. There are occasional explosions even now. The more I hear of what is to be found in the Town, and of the strength of their works, & of its state, the more I congratulate myself on the termination of the Siege. The place is full of all sorts of ammunition, thousands of guns that have never been used, all sorts of provisions & stores in profusion, and if they had not been completely surprised at the Malakoff, I don't know how we should ever have taken the place.

The French took them so utterly by surprise in the Malakoff that they came upon & took prisoner the General of that part, eating lunch under the Tower in a bombproof hut! When they had recovered from their surprise tho' they made the most frantic attacks to retake it. Fortunately, 'Francee' was there in immense numbers & fought them for about 4 or 5 hours. Their loss (the Russes) must be something awful! Campbell [46th] who has been down there tells me that he saw 'acres' of them! & heaps of French too, The French lost tremendously where they were repulsed on the Left – but if we had lost half of each of our Armies it would have been cheaper than another winter in the open trenches. The Russes have sunk their remaining ships all except the Steamers & have of course destroyed their bridge across. They have made, I imagine, the most glorious defence in the history of war, & their end was worthy of it, for knowing that the loss of the Malakoff must lead sooner or later to the capture of the whole place, they went away, having repulsed us at two, out of three, of the points of attack, & having fought at the other for nearly 5 hours, leaving us the smoking ruins of the Town.

I hope you will now make Peace for us at home. Of war I am quite sick. This last 'Butcher's Bill' has very nearly finished my list of old friends and acquaintances, & now it is all over I may confess to you that nothing could exceed the horror of our Duties during the Siege. Our first question every morning was 'Well, who was killed last night?' & only too often one heard the name of some 'old friend' – the four last days of the Siege I lost 4 old Allies of mine. It was perfectly impossible for a life with such incidents as these daily occurring to be made either pleasant or gay. Thank God, it is all now over, & I only pray I may never see another Siege.

They say the Russes are burning their Establishment on the North Side. I wonder what it means? & where they can be going? I hope you may be able to read this, for I have written it in bed, & I have lately had a most filthy stock of spiky pens and rough paper.

Letter 78

The Camp at Sebastopol, 12 September

The Russes must have lost most frightfully before they evacuated, & we have discovered one or two of the Hospitals in the most dreadful state. They had escaped the flames, but the fire would have done them but little harm. The one we last found contained 800 dead men and 1 live one! I have no idea what our further intentions may be. I am so sick and weary of war & sickness, and all one's friends being killed and mutilated, that I should prefer resting after our success. I think we are certain to make a mess of any more that we attempt. Windham is made Commandant of our quarter of the Town. I shall try all that I can to get home this winter & perhaps I may manage it. I am very tired of the whole business, having had all the work, and none of the Loaves and Fishes. I suppose I ought to be grateful for being alive at all.

Letter 79

Camp at Sebastopol, 21 September

I took advantage of a glimpse of sun a few days ago, to go down on a pony to the town and as you may suppose found it the most interesting sight, having looked at it so long from a distance that I hardly expected ever to see the inside of it. It is utterly knocked to pieces by our shot & I can't conceive how 'Ruski' ever managed to live at all in it. I went as far as the water by the Dock in the 'Karabelnaia' quarter of the Town (our part) & I certainly could hardly find a space of 1 yard square, without one of our shot & a lot of our shells on it, the houses either utterly knocked to pieces, or riddled with holes, guns in position & Batteries in every street nearly, and preparations made for defending the place inch by inch, which either were intended to give confidence to the Russe Soldiery, or else, that they could not be induced to hold, for everywhere are there are signs of the most hasty flight: long galleries of Barracks with all their knapsacks and possessions lying about.

The works are extraordinarily strong, & on going over the ground, I am scarcely surprised at our not getting the Redan. We had such a long way to go under such a galling fire. The French at the Malakoff, on the other hand, had only a few yards to go before they were in. We had 250 yards with guns of all sorts sweeping the approach, & after all we lost 1700, out of 2 or 3000 who went at it. The great mistake was sending the tired Light & Second Division at it, who had been beaten before there. I have no doubt that fresh troops would have taken it, but we all know & feel how wanton a waste of life it was going at it at all, as it is utterly at the mercy of the Malakoff & would be perfectly untenable by any troops, with an Enemy in the Malakoff. The Russes knew this well from their deserting it, tho' they had beaten us back at it.

The struggle about the Malakoff must have been something fearful; they fought so close to each other, for so many hours. Campbell [46th], who was there the day after counted in one place above (I think he said) 1500 dead Frenchmen & the Russes, two to their one!

The amount of soldier clothing & stores we found is immense & over 2000 guns in one part of the town alone. It must have been a most lovely town: such quantities of magnificent houses, and such beautifully built Public Buildings. The Docks are splendid & will take, odd to say, 2 months' hard work to destroy them! The Russes have nothing but a few small sailing boats, as they sunk all their ships of war the night they bolted, and next day, burnt all their Steamers. The sun is shining so jollily, that I must go out for a little ride & will finish this tonight.

There are constant rumours of some or all of us moving to take the field before the Winter comes on. I don't, & have never believed in it. It is too late in the year & our Transport is so insufficient. The honest truth is, and a very melancholy truth it is, (that with all our exultation at the fall of Sebastopol & our successes generally) we have completely used up our Army. The miserable mobs of Recruits that we now have in all Regiments are a very sad lot compared to the Army that we landed with, (wasted as those men were by disease). There are no old soldiers left in the Army, excepting perhaps in the Highlanders, who have as yet had an easy time of it, having lost but few in the fights or hospital since we arrived. The general run of our men now are almost children in years & barely know how to load their guns. As to their fighting an 'Alma' or 'Inkermann'!, I sincerely trust that they will not have a chance of so doing for some years at any rate, and I don't quite see how we can recover from this, for of course, if the war continues and we remain in the field, these poor creatures will never become 'old soldiers' for with all good fortune and care they cannot be expected to live more than two or three years. Between you and me, the sooner, as far as our fame is concerned, you make peace the better, for little as we have done, we shall never do anything as good again.

My poor little mouse, I am sorry to say, comes now very seldom, & is looking pale and ill. She takes sometimes a little piece of biscuit out of my hand! but she is evidently watched and can only get out but rarely.

Letter 80

Camp at Sebastopol, 28 September

I have just got your letter full of the fall of this Stronghold of which you have just heard. I am still more confirmed in my former opinion that we shall not 'take the field' this season. Now I think it is out of the question, and I personally am very glad of it, for various reasons: 1st. I do not think I could stand much more roughing it for some little time to come, and I also think that we have a better chance of surviving another Winter here, having dug out holes and stables, & having our last year's winter clothes at hand than if we were to march away for a week or two with our strict amount of baggage, & then be put down somewhere to fight the cold as naked as we were last year. The Russians, I think, will get sick of keeping an immense Army at such an expense 'eating its head off' all the Winter & will probably 'crope' away somewhere themselves.

The North side consists of nothing but a green hill sloping down to the water with various Forts and Earthworks all about it. They have no town of any sort there, & I fancy their great Camp, to my eyes, seems diminishing. They fire now at us in the town whenever they see large parties of 'Foragers' together, but they do very little harm & we are making batteries on our side, which will at any rate knock down their beautiful Stone Forts: Constantine & others. The more I see of the place the more I admire it. The Public Buildings are so beautifully situated, and are themselves so handsome, I don't think that there is a single house that is not completely destroyed, excepting the mere outward shell, and most of them with great shot holes through them. Menshikoff's Palace must have been a charming house, now quite gutted, but not much so injured by shot, as it was a long way from our Batteries. I saw the French packing up some beautiful marble 'Sphynxes,' I suppose to send to Paris, from Menshikoff's house. Gortchakoff, whose dispatches are generally truthful, tells a very wanton falsehood about the numbers he lost. Good judges of those matters, who were all over the ground the day after, place the Russian loss at from 20 to 25,000. Gortchakoff says he 'lost 100 on this occasion'.

Letter 81

Sebastopol Camp, 30 September

We are quite in the same place that we have occupied now, for so many months & that we are likely to occupy for many more, with the great advantage of having no dreadful Trenches for our men to die in, as they did last year. We are now showing some little energy in the way of road-making, & the plunder from the Town gives us so much wood and material for making huts that we do not look forward so gloomily to the approaching season, as we otherwise should. As regards Government Huts, they (for us at least) only exist in the imagination of the Contractor, for we have not got any given us as yet and this is the last Month that we can expect decent weather.

I have been various times over the Town and the Russian works & the more I see, the more delighted I am to think that they are now ours. The works towards the sea (the opposite end of the line to the Malakoff) are extraordinary for their strength and I really think utterly impregnable. I am not surprised at the French failing at the '*Bastion du Centre*', the Malakoff for strength and the difficulties opposed to them was nothing to it.

I think I may safely say that we shall not have any field operations this season and notwithstanding the gabble of the Papers about following up our success with our troops 'elated by victory', I greatly question in my own mind the advantage of it. The French have been advancing and reconnoitring about, and the Russian Positions are all very strong & difficult to approach and a victory, where we were beaten at 3 points out of 4, and where we all suffered such tremendous loss, has not, as you may imagine, caused that triumphant feeling of elation that the Press, who are always crying out for blood, would lead you to suppose. They forget how weary and worn with Trench work, and death & disease, our Army is. We are in an almost impregnable position now, & if we live without great loss through the Winter we shall have done pretty well, & then we may take the field with our wretched boys somewhat more seasoned and soldierly.

We have rumours of successes from Eupatoria where General D'Autemarre,[85] with some French Cavalry, went lately. I don't know

---

[85] In the next letter Dallas corrects his error. The French Cavalry General was D'Allonville.

the truth of them, also of a 'brush' between some of our Light Cavalry at Kertch and the Enemy.

Our Cavalry from here by the way are wisely going to be withdrawn to the Bosphorus and Scutari in a few weeks with the exception of one or two Regiments.

General Markham, you will be surprised to see, has been obliged from ill health to resign, and our Brigadier [Garrett] gets his (the 2nd.) Division. I shall probably be on his Staff, but I am so accustomed to the proverbial slip that takes place between the cup & lip that I shall not believe it till I see my name in orders. Markham is one of those strong wiry men, who being a great sportsman and priding himself in his extraordinary endurance & physical powers, overdid the thing in India. The consequence is, that tho' his celebrated feats in India are familiar to us all, there is now nothing left of him and he goes home with his health utterly broken. He is not expected back.

The Highlanders are still out at Kamara, which is an excuse for Sir Colin [Campbell] having them under arms at daybreak altho' the French are at least 10 miles in advance nearer the Enemy on every side of them.

I don't hear much talk now of Simpson going home. Poor old chap! He was so very angry with Pelissier who embraced him when the place fell. He said he knew it was their custom, but that it was a 'vera disgusting habit'. He has received the 'Grand Cross of the Legion of Honour' & was I hear very unhappy as someone told him that he ought to go and kiss Pelissier in return.

We are all very busy building homes for the Winter and sending down all our available horses & ponies & mules for doors and windows & planks to the Town. Wombwell, Campbell [46th] & I are going to build a Mansion & have collected a good store of 'Material'.

We are rapidly gutting the Town, a work by the way not unaccompanied by danger, for there are such quantities of magazines and stores of powder about that constant explosions take place & 'frightful accidents', as they would be called in the papers, take place daily. There were 90 men killed & wounded the day before yesterday just at the entrance of the Town, & yesterday I believe there was a still more serious one. The Russians, outside all their works, have Machines, our men call them 'Man traps', which explode when you touch, or rather tread upon them, and they are a frightful source of accidents. The Russes shoot into the Town tho' without much serious result & the French have some Mortars that shoot back at them. We were building a great Battery to silence their guns, but it was suddenly countermanded last night.

Letter 82

Camp Sebastopol, 5 October

I am duly installed as A.D.C. to the Brigadier [Garrett], or rather General (as he now commands the 2nd. Division) and as I partly expected this piece of good fortune I waited to see if this long lane of ill luck that I have pursued out here would take a turn before I asked you to send me various things that I want for the approaching season, & please understand that I really consider them commissions as, when I get over the first few expenses of my new dignity, my pay & allowances make me quite a rich man.[86] This appointment has fallen to me most opportunely as, in addition to its being in every light a good thing, it provides me with a comfortable home for the winter, capital stables & allowances for self and horses, & next spring I shall commence a campaign somewhere, certainly in a better position, & I trust a campaign of a more stirring & less harassing nature than the one which we have just terminated. As it is, I have done what comparatively few could boast of: my duty as a regimental officer with no intermission from the day that this expedition landed until now, and until my late attack (Thank God) without a day's ill health.

---

[86] The pay of a staff officer on active service was made up of several different elements. Maxwell Earle explained all in a letter of 9 February 1855, 'You are mistaken in supposing that every officer receives 4/6 field allowance on service. Subalterns 1/6, Captains 2/6, Field Officers 4/6 a day, 9/6 staff pay + 11/7 (Captain's pay) making a total of £1.5.7 a day [in his case, as a Captain doing duty as a Major], from which Income Tax and Mess Quarterly subscriptions are to be deducted.' Earle further explained, in a letter dated 11 February 1855, that these deductions meant that his nett pay, as a Major of Brigade on active service, was 'about £400 a year'. The initial expenses mentioned by Dallas included such things as a cocked hat and a frock coat. His comment about being 'quite a rich man' reflects the 67% pay rise he has just received (an increase of 9/6 on his previous pay and allowances of 14/1 per day).

I am now, by the bye, quite recovered though somewhat pulled down, which, though it would have utterly prevented my doing such work as last winter's again, does not interfere with my light and pleasant duties, which consist principally in riding about with the Chief, who, dear old man! as you may conceive, is delighted at his new honors, which indeed he has earned, for though by accident in no engagement here, he has steadily & well performed his duties ever since he came & is certainly one of the best men here. When Simpson gave him (provisionally until he heard from home) Markham's Division, the reply to his telegraphic message on the subject was 'very highly approved'. He told me, & I believe him, that his pleasure at his promotion was enhanced by being able to take me on his Staff, which he always intended me to be, but on the arrival of the Regiment was not allowed to do so, as they said they could not allow him to take a Captain from his duties with so strong a Regiment. Now perhaps you will be thinking (with me) that that is nearly enough about myself and my fortunes.

The first Brigade, Spencer's, of the 4th. Division embarked yesterday for I don't know where, Rumour says to form part of an expedition to a 'Fort Kinborn' which is situated somewhere on a spit of land at the mouth of the Bug. I have my doubts about their destination. There are only 8000 French & English going & this Fort Kinborn being taken would I suppose form the first step towards Nicolaieff, a place they say as strong a Sebastopol & if to be attacked would hardly be commenced so late. I should not be at all astonished to hear of the Expedition going to Eupatoria, where D'Allonville (I said by mistake D'Autemarre in my last) with the French Cavalry have been doing a good business – Maxwell Earle went with them of course. I hope it will turn out well, & that we shall see them all back. They expected to winter somewhere away from here (also, I think, unlikely).

The French are poking about out towards the Belbec River & we hear constant rumours of their having effected a lodgement on the heights there, to use a military phrase, turning the flank of the Russian Army on the North side. I fear that it is too late for much to be done, but if they had got them it would be a most splendid thing for us. I can perhaps explain this thing to you. The Russian Army at present is on a plateau which hangs over the Tchernaya on this side & extends to the Belbec on the other, & is naturally protected by steep heights & further by strong works thrown up by the Russes at every weaker point – it is unapproachable this side, also by the road we came (Mackenzie's Farm) & if the French have (which I doubt) got round & up into the Plateau on the Belbec side, we have (granting the weather continuing favourable for Field operations) to follow the French & there meet the Russian Army on even terms on the Plateau without the frightful slaughter that even a successful forcing of any of the defended approaches would entail. The utter defeat & destruction of the Enemy would of course follow, but I doubt the French being there & I am sure the season is too far advanced to, as it were, commence such a campaign. So that I expect to winter here & do not expect to see the Russe much nearer than we are at present. As it is, I conclude poor old Jamie Simpson & Pelissier will have some unpleasant leading articles to swallow along of their supineness.

I shall take the first opportunity of sending you & dear Puss one or two small souvenirs taken in the town. There are heaps of things about, but few that are characteristic or interesting, great French clocks & prints one can get better in France. One thing I have got is a small painting on wood (not without merit) found in some lady's bedroom. Puss will make a pretty frame for it & forgive its being somewhat damaged. The young lady's bonnet (I trust not her best) was presented me with it, but I did not think you would care about it. It was considerably injured by being brought up from the town partly on a sailor's head & subsequently, it having refused to stay on, in the sailor's pocket. Another thing is a rather better specimen than usual of the little religious tablets in brass & enamel. I think it one of the best I have seen. I do not quite understand their purpose, as they are too large to carry on the neck. It looks ancient. Another thing I have is a Russ child's book which will perhaps delight some of your little nephews and nieces: why not my nephew? He will be surprised & pleased to see that in Russian A is an Ostrich! I believe some men are sending home boxes of things, but in the first place I do not think that musquets made at Liege, Clocks made in France and prints from Ackerman, altho' found in Sebastopol, would delight you much, & secondly I was so unwell that I could not even visit the town till some days after it had been given over to plunder. So you must excuse my meagre share of plunder. My little offerings are at any rate Russian '*pur sang*'.

I am glad to say by the way, that Campbell [46th] has rejoined us so that Wombwell will have a companion. If I had left him alone my heart would rather have reproached me at deserting so dear & true an ally & messmate (the filth that we have eaten together by the bye!!).

Letter 83

Camp Sebastopol, 9 October

You need not be uneasy any more about my health for I have got quite well. I think the change of air, even of moving from one camp to another, has done me good. I am now as you know in the 2nd. Division, not such a well situated camp as the old one, but in very comfortable quarters.

We have heard nothing about the expedition yet. It started the day before yesterday & I still think it not at all certain that their destination is Fort Kinborn, tho' everybody appears to think that there is no doubt about it. The weather still continues quite perfect altho' the days are getting sadly shorter. There are heaps of rumours of moves in every direction for us, flying about the camp, but one cannot but feel that we only have about 3 or 4 weeks at the outside of campaigning weather. We are now taking furiously to road making & I think are running into the extreme of making too many & on too large a scale so that they not only will not be finished before winter, but will take more labor keeping them in order than we can well afford to give them.

There is a good article in the *Times* of the 24th. about the 8th. affair – very true I think, but not having waited for the facts of the case they do not, & of course cannot, seize on many disgraceful points of the business. What do you think they will say to the Engineers & the wonderful Jones when they know that we opened fire on the 8th. September with rather fewer guns on the right attack (*the* attack!) than on the 18th. June & the assaulting party started from the same place as on the former occasion! & that we had regularly lost from 20 to 40 men a day doing nothing in those trenches!

Letter 84

The Camp, Sebastopol, 12 October

I have a very jolly little 'Marquee' which is a square tent, like a tent 'in a play', all double so that no rain or wind comes in, & live & feed in the General's [Garrett] hut which is a most comfortable one, very like a barn in England, but here a Palazzo.

Windham has got, as you know, his promotion & we are all delighted. Our General showed me yesterday a most gratifying letter that he got (private) from Lord Hardinge stating how pleased he had been to appoint him & how highly he approved of his commanding the 2nd. Division, giving him the local rank of Major General, & promising him to take the earliest opportunity of further promotion & explaining how Windham, who was promoted over Garrett's head, would in no way interfere with him as he is to have the 4th. Division. This has naturally pleased the good old chief immensely as it was quite private & uncalled for – he, the General, is in great force & as well as ever I remember to have seen him in health & I think is pleased to have me on his Staff. Lord W. Paulet gets my General's old Brigade.

I have just been reading a most disgusting & scurrilous article in the *Times* of Saturday 29th. abusing wretched old Simpkins [i.e., Simpson] and endeavouring to make our army and its name despicable in the eyes of all the world. There is no doubt of our ill success on the 8th., but why they should try to make it much worse than it was, we here can't make out, & are all furious at it. I hope you are.

We have as yet but scanty news, in fact only rumours, about the expedition that Earle went with. I heard, & from good authority, today that it had completely succeeded, but won't answer for its truth.

Old Barnard has gone away. I think him an old sneak. He comes out here & stops, doing nothing, during the fine weather & then scuttles home when the winter comes on in perfect health. They say Airey is going home. I hope he is, as he is a miserable impostor. I should not wonder if Windham was made Q.M.G.. He would make a capital one.

We are busy now making roads which are getting on well. I was talking to the Engineer (Civil) who has charge of the work & he told me that they will be done in time & well, so that I am only too happy to change my gloomy opinion on the subject of their being too grand & begun too late.

Part of our Cavalry have [sic] gone to Eupatoria & more are going, but the weather is rather rough for embarking horses. The rest will go to the Bosphorus for the Winter except perhaps one Regiment or so to be left here.

We have heaps of Huts come out of various patterns, but unfortunately no one who knows how to put them together. I believe they have telegraphed home for the necessary conjurer, but until his arrival, they are lying about like melancholy Chinese puzzles!

We hear every day of the French who are dodging about getting further & further into the country, but they never seem to find any Russians & I rather doubt their doing much. We are going out to their outposts someday. It is a beautiful ride tho' rather a long one, about 30 miles out, & as we have got an Interpreter to talk to the nations it will be very jolly. The weather is fine autumn, still not at all cold yet. My duties are not at all onerous & consist in dining at the General's table, riding about with him, helping to entertain his Guests at dinner & going to Church with him in a cocked hat, so that I do not expect to die of overwork this winter.

Letter 85

Camp at Sebastopol, 15 October

We are still here & here we shall remain. The French are coming in from their expedition towards the Belbec & I suppose have found the passes impracticable in that direction. We have heard nothing of the 'Kinborn' Expedition, which caused great surprise here as they expected at Head Quarters to hear some time ago. The Highlanders were under orders to embark immediately for Eupatoria but tonight will be countermanded, the result of a Council of War held today, where all the Division Generals attended, & where the A.D.C.s smoked cigars outside & decided on the total destruction of the Russian Army somewhere & somehow. The truth is that Simkins had received information (telegraph) from Berlin (which proved a true quarter for news before) that the Russes meditate some insane attack on our position & therefore the Highlanders are not to go.

Ewen [Macpherson], by the way, I saw in the distance a day or two ago. My Chief was calling on Sir Colin [Campbell], & I went to dig out Ewen & found that he was out, cutting wood on an adjacent hill, with a 'Fatigue Party' of Soldiers & the little speck that I saw I believe to have been him, & conclude from his employment that he was not in bad health.

I cannot tell you much about the attack on the 8th. It is almost impossible to get at the truth of things here & the *Times* has settled it its own way at home. Windham behaved most gallantly. By the way, tell dear Puss, who is so kind and warm a 'Partizan', that I was riding with him today & he told me that he had intended me to be his second A.D.C. if I had not 'got a place' as it was, & I dare say he would. Failing so distinguished a man as me, he has, I am happy to say, appointed a young Earle (49th.), a very nice boy indeed. To resume about the 8th., it is most difficult to lay one's hand on the man to blame in any affair, but if I was to say who was in fault I should say the Engineer, who had not made the trenches half large enough for the men to be put into them & had lost three months not making any new Batteries, altho' there were guns lying out everywhere, & lots of places to make batteries in. I also, as I said before, think it was a mistake sending in the tired Divisions at the place. I do not say it jealously, but we out here are rather sick of having the 'Guards & Highlanders' so continually stuffed down our throats. The truth is, I believe, the Highlanders would do anything if they had the chance but they never have had yet, except at Alma where between you and me they had but little to do, and have never served in the trenches at all. The Guards never served in the trenches having scuttled down to Balaklava for the winter (a fatal mistake of old Lord Raglan's by the bye) & when they did come up a day or two ago they behaved on no occasion at all well. I believe they are nearly all recruits. You need not repeat this, though it is notorious in the army here. I certainly think that it would have been better to send troops that had not been beaten before, & the Guards & Highlanders might as well have gone as the 4th. & 3rd. Divisions, which latter have, justly, a certain reputation in the trenches. But it is certainly tiresome for us to be so constantly told that the two Divisions who in the Siege have done the least, would have taken the Redan so easily. The energetic Sir Harry Jones is the man to blame for all the engineering faults. He never would listen, I hear, to any suggestion, & for personal energy & obstinacy is certainly without a rival.

Letter 86

Camp at Sebastopol, 19 October

After a long & unaccountable delay we have news from Kinborn. The place is taken, 1300 prisoners, 100 odd Russes killed & wounded, & 70 guns, a General too taken, no loss on our side to speak of. We have no particulars & I conclude it was done by the ships.

We are here awaiting an imaginary attack from the Russians on our Lines. Why I don't exactly know, as they could only come to their utter destruction. But telegraphic news of it came from Berlin (a good quarter generally) consequently we get up half an hour before daylight every morning & have our horses saddled. It is rather a bore, but probably healthy.

The General [Garrett], Colonel Wilbraham our Q.M.G., & Colonel Herbert, A.A.G & I went for a most charming ride a day or two ago to the French outposts, about 23 miles off through the loveliest country to the eye but a dreadful unpracticable one for military operations. The French have now withdrawn from a rambling expedition they have been taking for some time and now their '*Postes Avancés*' occupy hills that overlook the beautiful valley of the Belbeck. The day was, fortunately, perfect, & the views were extraordinarily wild & beautiful. We found a most agreeable old French General Pâté (I don't know if he spells his name so) who made friends with our General & they found out that they had been alternately in Valladolid during the same year (the years 1813 & 14 I think). They had naturally not met there, for whenever Pâté went into the place, Garrett went out & vice versa, owing to their not having (as the Frenchman mildly expressed it) 'the same views', at that time. The scene was quite perfect, the French Piquets lying about on the hill we were on, the beautiful valley at our feet & a most abrupt mountain close on our left, with Cossacks watching our manoeuvres with great apparent interest from the top of it.

Our Quarter-M-General is a most superior man; talks every language under the Sun, & has been everywhere. He is a man of very strict ideas about religion accompanied by the most dreadful whining voice, that at first, until one knows him, is very disagreeable, but as he is by no means a Humbug & is full of information & good nature, I like him much. The other man [Herbert] is one of those not born only with a silver but a golden spoon in his mouth, a full Colonel, a C.B. &

a Queen's A.D.C. Why I cannot tell you, except that he is an Honourable & has always been on the Staff.

I lead a very pleasant life now. In the first place, the weather is quite perfect, half the battle with me always – then I have no tiresome Regimental Duty, & nothing can be more jolly and kind than the Old Chief. We generally have somebody to Dinner every day. Altogether, I think I have found the employment suited to my energetic disposition, good pay, good food, & good company & no walking, & lots of forage for one's horses. I generally go after breakfast & sit for an hour or so with a very jolly young friend of mine who was wounded on the 8th. His name is Swire. He was Windham's A.D.C. & was 3 times in & out of the Redan. He was shot very high up in the leg & in spite of all the Doctors, who said he would never recover, is getting on splendidly. I never saw such a good plucky boy. I think anyone else would have certainly died. He looks better & brighter every day & is always cheery. If he had not a good many visitors, I don't know what he would do. His Regiment, the 17th., is gone away to Kinborn & he here in a hut all alone.

Lord William Paulet is come & has the Chief's old Brigade under Windham. He dined here a night or two ago. He is a pleasant man, & I fancy popular enough. We have a very pleasant French Colonel coming to feed tonight; he commands a neighbouring French Regiment (49th.), a Baron de Mallet. He married an English Lady & comes to our Church Parade every Sunday. He is a very pleasant fellow, talks English, & affects Englishmen.

I must now be going to bed, the dear old French Colonel having kept us up rather late considering our early hour of rising. By the way, he is one of the most agreeable pleasant fellows I ever met & we had a very cheerful little party. He was much struck by a gooseberry tart we gave him & told us in confidence that he would have asked a second help of it, if we had only asked him! So he promised to come some day again & have two goes at another.

Letter 87

Camp at Sebastopol, 24 October

Our roads are getting on wonderfully, & I really think that with ordinary foresight & care there ought to be no difficulty about feeding the army this winter. What we should have done if the siege had not ended, I can't conceive. It is only by having the whole of the army released from all military duties, that we are able to make our preparations. I was talking to a French Engineer (a General). He told me that the amount of guns taken came to 5000, & I think he said 3000 not including the unserviceable ones! and the amount of powder something enormous. There are two or three Yankee Officers here sent by their Government (I think them, privately, Spies). Two of them dined with us last night & seemed shrewd vulgar men looking like 'Old Clo' men. By the way one of their names was Mordecai, whose parents must at any rate have been Old Clo men and women.[87]

Letter 88

Camp at Sebastopol, 26 October

We have had one or two pretty Reviews lately; one, that of the Imperial Guard (they say, preparatory to their going home). They looked exceedingly well & were inspected by General MacMahon, a most soldier-like looking man & I believe a good soldier too. His dress, horse & seat on it were the most beautiful I ever saw. Ld. Rokeby was there in great force. He affects the French Generals very much & with all due respect be it said, and only speaking of him as a General, is the greatest old Donkey I ever saw. We had yesterday a Review of our Cavalry who looked splendid, about 2000 in number. Scarlett reviewed them, accompanied by Morris, the French General of Cavalry here, who, they say, admired them much. Whatever their value in the field (& in their Campaign there has been no opportunity of showing it) there is not the slightest comparison between the English & French; our Horses, Equipments &c being so infinitely

---

[87] 'Old Clo' is Dallas' way of expressing 'Old Clo(thes) Dealer', i.e., a Jew. The term, Dealer in Old Clothes, crops up in his description of Sir Moses Mainchance in R.S. Surtees' novel *Ask Mamma* which appeared around 1850 and is probably where Dallas got it from. Dallas was quite strongly anti-American, but this observation does not necessarily mean he was anti-Semitic too. The members of the American Commission were Captain A. Mordecai, Major R. Delafield and Captain G.B. McClellan.

superior. The *Chasseurs d'Afrique* are, they say, first rate Cavalry troops, but not to be compared to our 10th. or 12th., who are also mounted on Eastern horses, in appearance.

Letter 89

Camp at Sebastopol, 1 November

We are I fear approaching to the end of our fine weather, having enjoyed tho' a most charming second summer: today it is cloudy and blowing hard & who knows what tomorrow may be? The Expedition for Kimbourn has at last returned, some of the ships and a part of the Brigade that we (the English) sent. We have rumours, & of rather good authority, of another expedition being made to Kaffa before the weather breaks up. I think it is too late. We ought to have done all that was wanted there long before this.

We are still busy roadmaking, & I believe that they will be done in time, but, as I always thought, they are on far too large a scale. We don't require roads to be shewn in future times as monuments of our visits, merely as a means of bringing up the necessaries of life for a few months, and I fancy that, muffs tho' they are, military engineers would have made roads good enough with a tenth of the labour that the civil Engineers (accustomed to make roads at home to last for ages) have been employing here. I was dining with General Windham last night & was pleased to find that he agreed with me about it.

In the course of making these roads a certain Colonel Munro (39th), who happens to be a great antiquarian & Geologist (a very good fellow too), was in charge of a number of men who were digging up stones to lay down in the road, & he came across a most curious Greek Temple full of urns, Amphoroi, coins etc. and now about 100 men are employed under him making further excavations & clearings. I went to see it the day before yesterday and it is certainly a curious old place, but I fear my bump of veneration is very small for I am but little impressed by old pots without handles, which they told me were very striking Amphoroi and bits of tiles exceedingly like British ones: the great curiosity seeming to consist in their all being smashed into very small pieces. Altogether, altho' they affect to make a great fuss about their curious discoveries, I am Goth enough to think that he and his 100 men would be much better employed in making themselves huts for the winter than in raking up old bones. It was a curious thing, however, that Munro, probably the only Antiquarian in the service here, should have come across these remains. Anybody else would have made the precious old temple into road metal with no compunction.

We hear constant reports of Simpson going, & of other changes, but they all come from you at home. I don't think anyone expects him to go & I am quite sure nobody wishes him to do so, at any rate until 'the man' is found. He is by no means unpopular & I, in common with many others, think him as good a man as any. The man you seem at home rather to look to, Eyre, would be most dangerous & utterly unfit man in the world for us, a man of ungovernable temper, most unpopular with the whole army & the miserable massacre that he led or rather drove his Division into, on the 18th of June, would for ever settle his pretensions as a Leader, notwithstanding the trash that it pleased the *Times* to say about him at that time. I really can form no idea of who is likely to succeed Simpson, supposing him removed. The disgusting & scurrilous tone of the *Times* towards him has excited the most universal indignation amongst us all. I have heard no two opinions about it. We all know that to many, the abuse or attacks on any in authority over them is at any rate amusing, but on this occasion so gross & personal & low has been the language & tone about him, that there is only one feeling of disgust in the whole army from highest to lowest. Even Russell, 'our own correspondent', has the decency to avow (with I don't know what amount of truth) that the low personalities about Simpson, Airey & others in the trenches on the 8th were written in a private letter & not intended for publication.

We took a pleasant ride a day or two ago, to the pass of 'Phoros' beyond Baidar. Dunkellin joined in on the road & was most amusing about his Captivity. They were very civil to him he said, & he saw lots of 'company'. The Russian ladies talked indifferent English & professed to be great admirers of English writers. Odd to say their favorites were 'Dickens & Thackeray'. They were very angry with Dunkellin telling them 'that he was surprised at that, as few not English could understand great portions of Dickens's writings'. Fancy a person not familiar with English enjoying Pickwick!

We are busy fortifying & strengthening our (or rather the General's) hut. It is at first a very thin wooden house, but we have built stone walls to it lengthwise up to the roof about 6 foot from the ground & built a Porch at each end, & have completed a fire place which burns frantically, until a certain malevolent wind blows, when not a single spark, or puff of smoke, or flake of ash pretends or tries to go up the chimney. It all comes straight into the room, & there is nothing for it but putting the fire out & lighting, if necessary, a little stove that we fortunately possess at the other corner of the room, which does not smoke but gets perfectly red hot in ten minutes, which will be very delightful in about 6 weeks. There is an Irish bricklayer (now a soldier) who is breaking his heart about our chimney. Every day he comes & either knocks part of it down or builds more up, but as yet the wretch has beaten all his Efforts. He is now singing on our roof like an immense Irish bird; I trust he won't come through. I of course have not seen my little mouse since I left my old tent & I much fear that she will not get on well with the new proprietor. I saw a wall being made round the interior of the tent which I am afraid will not suit her.

The French withdrew their force from the advanced post over the valley of the Upper Balbec yesterday, & I think wisely, for they had much toil in getting supplies there, and as regards the enemy, we are quite sufficiently protected from them by nature not to apprehend their coming over such a country.

Letter 90

Camp at Sebastopol, 9 November

Our energetic chiefs are still undecided about an expedition to Kaffa & in consequence they do not disembark Maxwell Earle's Brigade, which has been for some days at anchor off Kamiesch, returned from Kinborn. I do not believe in the expedition at all but rumours of all sorts are rife concerning it here.

I wrote so far, and then went out riding with my Chief [Garrett]. While out we heard news that Codrington is to be 'Simkins' successor as Commander in Chief.[88] I must own I thought that Simpson would

---

[88] By General Order of 10 November 1855, Simpson resigned the Command-in-chief in favour of Codrington, who assumed it formally by General Order of 12 November 1855.

not go home, but lately it has been generally known that he was going. Codrington is a pleasant, gentlemanly man & very popular. It is perhaps an unfortunate moment to elevate him, as the miscarriage of our portion of the assault on the 18th. is generally attributed to him in a great measure. It relieves my mind as regards Eyre, a man I think much to be dreaded as Chief. This accounts for Sir Colin [Campbell] going away in such a hurry, he being senior to Codrington & having probably had a hint about the affair. He (Sir Colin) has never been happy, poor man since they gave him the command at Malta (which he refused), a somewhat uncalled-for insult to a man like him when serving in the field; at least he so considered it. He is a great loss to his Division altho' he is occasionally fussy & a dreadful hand at drill. All the Cavalry expect to go away to Scutari or thereabouts, except the unfortunate 11th., who having had the hardest work & been here the longest, are doomed to stop still longer! The first almost to go were the 1st. King's Dragoon Guards who came here about 2 or 3 months ago! Isn't it disgusting?

Letter 91

Camp at Sebastopol, 12 November

Yesterday the General [Garrett] & our party went to a review of the Sardinian Army under La Marmora in the plain, and a more lovely scene you cannot conceive. They commenced with a High Mass which was performed by their beautiful bands and afterwards we rode up and down their lines. They were about 12000 in number & looked splendid; to my mind, the most complete & soldierlike little army conceivable.

We are all in a great state of excitement about what we appro-priately call here, the '*Coup d'Etat*', the particulars of which you will of course know before this. Codrington's appointment was unexpected out here but is popular enough, as he is associated with Windham as Chief of the Staff, and it generally understood that Windham will not allow his office to be the mere dead letter that his predecessor Barnard allowed it to be; so that we may now look upon the firm as 'Codrington & Windham'. Airey goes & is a good riddance, as he was a sort of log about poor old Simkin's neck & did what he liked & what nobody else liked. The new Quarter Master General is, they say, Herbert, of this Division, to my thinking a most wretched appointment. He is a most overrated man but has a reputation I believe 'at home' and *'par dessus le marche'* is an Honble & has interest in the House. His appointment, if it comes off, is, I think, a job, & a bad one.[89] The man I fancy is Wetherall, a capital man, but odd to say, rumour gives out that they are afraid to give it to him as it would look like a job!! I wonder what the Herbert will look like? However, the appointment is not quite certain. We, I mean Garrett & Co., go back to the 4th. Division, which I am glad of as it is the best Division in the Army & we know everybody in it & our General has always wished to command it. Barnard, late Chief of Staff, comes & takes the 2nd. Division. The army is to be divided into two *Corps d'Armées* (after the French), one of which is to be offered to Sir Colin [Campbell] who will, it is pretty well known, refuse it, & Barnard be here, in the way to take it, & the other to Markham, who is pretty well known to be too ill to do anything, & failing him, Sir R. Eyre. The *Corps d'Armée* plan we all dislike as it will only complicate our system & make an additional gate for everything to have to pass through. I am very glad to get back to our old original Division and we find a capital house there ready made by Windham, who of course is loath enough to leave it, but of course must go to Head Quarters to live.

Maxwell Earle's Brigade has landed & as I always fancied the expedition to Kaffa will not come off this season.

The Russians had a great review a day or two ago on their Heights & we could see a carriage & 4 horses & a tremendous Staff inspecting them. They say here it was the Emperor.[90] It is a curious state of things for so long a time having looked on at each others Reviews & goings on. I think the Russians are diminishing on their heights, and should not be surprised if they left them altogether. They will have bad times in the winter if they don't. The Crimea is not a country to support an immense army for a long time. Our force alone here, I mean the allies, outnumber the whole of the inhabitants of the Crimea, who only amount to 200,000. There is a great sale of the last Administration's effects at Head Quarters today, horses, clothing &c. I have got two

---

[89] It did.

[90] It was; Czar Alexander II.

horses that suit me well: one I was very lucky in getting, an Arab from an officer of the 10th. Hussars, who was ordered home. He is a most charming little horse & never tires. They are most beautiful little horses, they can only canter, gallop & walk & hardly ever trot, & though quite ponies, carry any weight any distance. Mine is a great beauty, white with a blackish mane & tail & as tame and quiet as a big dog. My other horse is a good strong old English hunter & between them they do my work well. I have a good deal of riding to do which suits me, as you may guess, better than walking.

Letter 92

Camp at Sebastopol, 16 November

The last mail brought the Brevet which as usual pleases the fortunate ones & does not improve the temper of the disappointed, among which you need not include me for I knew that I had no chance. My only claims I had already been told were altogether too old to expect anything from them, & indeed when I see Thesiger, Markham's A.D.C., promoted for about 3 months service out here, about 10 visits to the trenches & no clasps – when I see his name in the list, I begin to think my claim must be 'rococo' altogether. However, he is a right good fellow & I am glad at his good fortune. There are many others, I dare say also good fellows, in the list with him. I am glad to see Wombwell & Algey get it.[91] They have both had lots of hard work & are old soldiers. Campbell [46th] gets a Lt. Colonelcy, which he deserves if ever a man did anything.

The Sebastopol clasp crowns everything that our people have ever done in the way of folly and injustice. It gives the clasp to every man who was present for one day, the 8th., in the Crimea, (thousands at Balaklava &c), and to a man who had very likely been month after month in the trenches & who from sickness was obliged to be away (& there are hundreds such) for that day, to that man they refuse it. Can you really believe the disgusting idiocy of such a system? I know many men who served from the begin-

---

[91] Arthur Wombwell and Algernon Garrett were promoted Brevet Major on 2 November 1855.

ning of the war & who never missed a day's duty for 10, 11 or 12 weary months & who broke down at the end of August, or even the beginning of September, & not one of them by the accursed order get the clasp. I, again, know a whole Regiment who had been a short time at Balaklava & had never seen Sebastopol, who were in the Crimea on the 8th. & they will get it. I shall be ashamed to wear it as indeed I am to wear any of them, when I see the way in which they are dealt out. By the way, I have not got mine & certainly shall not wear it in the Crimea when I do.[92]

I have been so busy writing about Brevets, clasps, &c that I have not yet told you our only news here & that I grieve to say is a disaster, which I will relate to you as I saw it. I had been to a review of our Artillery in the morning & had come home by myself, the Chief [Garrett] having gone to pay a visit somewhere. I had come home & changed my cocked hat for a cap, & proceeded to take a great ride among the French Camp to look for a band to listen to, & was riding along, looking by accident, towards the camp of our 'Siege Train' when suddenly the whole earth seemed to open & one great flame rushed up into the sky. My horse, an English one & a very nervous one, wheeled round, but suddenly a succession of the most tremendous explosions in the air took place, many hundreds of yards up in the heavens & lasting like constant musquetry for about 2 or 3 minutes. My horse, whom I fully expected to become perfectly unmanageable, was so dreadfully frightened that he almost lay down on the ground trembling all over & covered with sweat until it was over. Directly I saw where this extraordinary volume of smoke arose from, I knew that the French & English Siege Train had exploded. Many thousand shells were sent up into the air & killed & wounded people to the distance of a mile. I owed my safety to my being too near, most of them going over me completely. Houses were levelled & showers of bits of shells fell not far from me, but I was quite safe. An immense conflagration then commenced in the camp where the explosion took place & I rode home as hard as I could, & found the General. We went to the scene of action & found that the entire French Siege Train had blown up &

---

[92] There was an outcry against these award criteria, and they were altered to include anyone who served in the siege at any time from its beginning to its end.

destroyed their own & our adjoining camp, & a fire raging within 200 yards of a Windmill containing powder, compared to the amount of which, what had previously gone up was as nothing! All our efforts were directed to covering the windmill with wet blankets & tearing away everything that would feed the fire. The men worked magnificently, perfectly regardless of the constant minor explosions that were constantly taking place, & by 9 P.M. the fire was got under control and all was safe.

This morning I went with the General at daylight to the spot & a more melancholy sight you cannot conceive. All the adjoining camps laid quite flat; huts, tents, stables, everything destroyed. The loss of life & casualties were great, tho' wonderfully small considering the thousands upon thousands of shells that exploded in the air — it is impossible to tell as yet the numbers, but ours are supposed to amount to 150. An entire French Guard of about 20 men that were in charge of the powder have totally disappeared – not a button or rag of any of them can be found! I saw many dead horses lying about but comparatively few human remains, but the French I fear have lost many tho' they say not. It was entirely the French's accident, our Siege trains join each other, but we do not keep ammunition or loaded shells there. It is not known how it originated. It was the most beautiful & horrid sight I ever dreamt of. The whole Heavens for minutes seemed filled with extraordinary explosions. Men were killed nearly a mile off. My horse, in the intensity of his fear, laid quite still & I saw it from the first spark going up. Fortunately, the Siege is over, or else we should be in a bad way.

Letter 93

Camp at Sebastopol, 23 November

We are come up, as you know, to the 4th. Division, our old one, & I am very glad to get back for I know everybody in it, & I knew but few in the Second. We have got a very well built house with three rooms: one sitting room, & a bedroom for the General [Garrett], & one for us A.D.C.s. The dear old General, who had taken a great fancy to our Second Division's House, tho' he prefers commanding this Division, has taken a most furious dislike to our new one, which is certainly not quite finished, but will be in a few days (& the bedrooms are already). We dine in a cave that was found & inhabited by Sir John Campbell, which is pretty comfortable with a large fire, but is shared with us by a large force of rats. We have got a very good stable & if we can only sneak through a few more weeks of this lovely weather the winter after all will not be so very dreadful, tho' I must say I sometimes long to see my name in general orders 'to proceed to England on urgent private affairs'; however, I must not think of that now.

Where we shall go next spring I can form no idea, but my great theory is that we ought to have a totally different field of operations from the French, tho' I fear that they will never consent to that. They find us much too useful, and it is not to be wondered at if they do object to separating, for it is very pleasant for them to have us with them &, ably assisted by our beastly 'Press', to affect to consider us as auxiliaries. I only trust we may get divided from them for the next Campaign.

You will ask me what we think about Codrington. I fancy on the whole that his appointment is popular enough, & I think him a good man. As to his youth, tho' he is I believe under fifty, his appearance is that of a man of sixty, his hair quite snow white, very nice looking & clean, the same style of looking man as 'Simpkins' tho' of course younger looking, with a clean shaved reddish 'rasped-looking' face with small white whiskers. He is a man of no military reputation & came out here as a Captain in the Guards. I myself think him much to blame in the Redan affair, though perhaps no one could have done much there. By the way, it suited the *'Times'* to tell everyone that poor Simpkins was an utterly infirm man unable to get on his horse – the most absurd lie you can well imagine, as he was riding about everywhere & all day. Pelissier on the other hand, whom it suits them to call a miracle of vigor for his years, really can hardly get on his horse & tumbles off when he does, & constantly goes about in a most absurd old carriage & 4 old artillery horses.

Today is the clearest day I ever saw & I am taking advantage of it to stare through my telescope at the Ruskis, whom I still think are gradually disappearing. This morning I saw 3 or 4 Battalions march away from the north side with all their baggage. There is very little firing between the North and South sides now, which is a good thing

as they did no good & occasionally killed a poor wretch. It is extraordinary how little importance is attached to life in scenes like these.
At the explosion the other day there were at least 500 killed &
wounded of French & English & no one ever seems to think or talk of
it now!

Letter 94

Camp at Sebastopol, 26 November

Our fine weather has, I fear, departed & now we have some rain &
some wind & cold, but nothing very bad. We certainly have had a
most splendid season, and I look with contempt at rain & wind now,
for I and Forde have got a very snug little room with a fireplace in it
that burns frantically. This is the first time that I have slept under a
roof since I left England, having endeavoured more or less to keep out
the elements with canvass until a few days ago, & very pleasant it is
not to hear the canvass flapping over one's head, even if it kept the wet
out. The men, generally speaking, are hutted & their health good. The
road making has now come to an end which relieves the men from a
good deal of labor, which, however, did them no harm and kept them
from getting drunk (I am sorry to say the only real pleasure the British
Lion seems to enjoy). They get now an extra sixpence a day, the result
of which is an immense increase of crime & trouble. Our house is not
quite finished and the General [Garrett] consequently not reconciled
to it yet, & we still have to dine in the cave, after all the more comfort
one has, the more exigeant one becomes – last year the cave was
considered a Palazzo.

I have been riding about with our General & the Commander-
in-Chief today, poking about the men's huts & camps, & rather
cold it was. He is a very pleasant gentlemanlike man (Sir W.
Codrington) and I should say would do well in his present place.
Whether he will be a good General or not who knows? Today we
heard & with much sorrow of poor Markham's death. We had no
idea of his being in immediate danger. How sad an end to all his
hopes & brilliant prospects! Poor fellow, I suppose he was completely worn out. I wonder whether he would have distinguished
himself. He was, as all are, very unfairly treated by the Press. It

suited them to make him a reputation by no means warranted by his antecedents, and he might or might not have come up to the reputation formed of him in consequence; but it is very unfair to cry up a man, for if he does not do wonders, he is immediately called an Impostor – he felt this, I know. Windham's name has been used the same way by the *Times*. I, and the 4th. Division in general, know how energetic a Q.M.General he was, but he is looked forward to by the people at home as the future C-in-Chief, who is to do such wonders, not for the merits the 4th. Division know him to possess, but because he was fortunate to escape unscathed from the Redan and behaved with a gallantry that cost poor Sir John Campbell, on a similar occasion, his life and somewhat of his reputation as a General. All this is very disgusting & we all know it out here, no one better than Windham. I only trust, & from what I know of him think, that Windham will do well, but it will not be from the only reasons that the 'Times' cries him up for, viz: for his being 43 years old & behaving gallantly under fire. If that was all that was wanted, there could not be much difficulty in finding a Commander in Chief out here.

You ask me if I was not disappointed at the Brevet. I told you, I think, in a former letter that I expected nothing & got it. I knew, as I think I once told you, the exact value of having ones name favourably marked for promotion at the Horse Guards.

I am rather amused at your fear about one's sitting up late here, for no one in the country is out of bed except on duty at 11 P.M. & I am glad that you refrained, as you told him, from giving the General a lecture on the subject, as I don't think old gentlemen, especially Generals, are over-fond of advice about their domestic habits. Forde and I, of course, live with the General but have private little lunch parties in our room when our intimates come to see & we eat very rich little things from Kamiesch, *Pâtés de Foie Gras* & Cherry Brandy, very nice this weather.

The Russians' Camp over the way looks somewhat smaller than it did. The Russians have been shooting rather more than usual today, partly at a boatload of their own people who deserted to the French, I hear, this morning, as the Harbour is about 3/4 of a mile across & the deserters were in a slow 'lighter'. They must have had good shooting at them, but odd to say did not hit them.

Letter 95

Camp at Sebastopol, 29 November

I dare say you will smile when I tell you that we have none of us heard of Ld. Rokeby's going home, which you talk of as settled. I was calling on him yesterday & he did not at all talk of going home & abused [sic.] for having gone. I dare say he will go someday (his daughter's marriage will be a good excuse). He was very pleasant and agreeable, as he always is, but will be no great loss in a military point of view.

Now about Sir Colin [Campbell]. I do not quite understand your sentiments about his not serving under a Junior Officer [i.e., Codrington]. As a personal friend, you may regret that such should be the case, but in a public point of view I don't quite see what you want. You all agree that the old plan of Seniority has failed & should be relinquished. Then, when such is done & the Government appoint the man they consider the best, you say that you think that those who happen to be Senior to him in age & rank are quite right in refusing to serve under the man! I don't quite see how to please you: you want the best man to be chosen, whatever his age & rank, & then consider that the ones who are older than him are right & justified in leaving their commands, for which they may be ever so well suited, as in the instance of Sir Colin, a great loss as a General of Division. I think, on reflection, that you will agree with me in condemning the principle, however much you may admire & like Sir Colin – fancy if all the Engineers, Senior to him, were to have refused to serve under Todleben, a name by the way we are always having crammed down our throats. My own impression is that Sir Colin will come out & command one of the new absurd *Corps d'Armées* (if that plan be carried out & if our system was not complicated enough already).

The papers are all full I see of our drunkenness out here. As they always do everything, they are hunting the subject to death, & talking dreadful nonsense, about our 'losing by our own vices &c. &c. &c. as we did last year men by the enemy's fire and disease'. There is not the least doubt that the men drink inordinately, as English soldiers do & will when they get overpaid and underworked, but unfortunately for their argument about our expected frightful losses from that source, nothing can exceed the good health of the men. The French who, fortunately for them, are not dogged about by newspaper correspondents, drink in proportion to their means much more than our soldiers, & before the ill-judged 6d. a day was given to our men (with only one means of spending it) I had often remarked how much more drunkenness I always saw in the French camp than in the English one. They do not take the same notice of it that we do, and have not the disgusting publicity given to their punishment that we have. Saying that the French don't drink because there is not so much notice taken of it is the same as if a man were to read a French and English newspaper for a month & at the end of the time say how much more faithful French wives seemed to be than English ones. I hate a drunkard, and I have a not very splendid opinion of the British Soldier (at least of the present sort) but I don't think the way to improve them is to exaggerate all their faults & hold them & their affairs up to public execration. The attack of the Redan was not certainly a pleasant affair to be engaged in, but I really believe there are few of us all, who wouldn't go at it pretty cheerfully with the Editor of the *Times* [Delane] on one side of him and 'Jacob Omnium'. or some of the crew on the other. I only wish we had them out here doing something more perilous than sitting at home writing at us.

I had not heard of any very recent quarrel between 'the Baron' (as Ld. Rokeby is called) and Sir Colin, but I cannot conceive their agreeing, Sir Colin being, as you know, very *'Vif'* and the Baron very touchy 'along of' his dignity & position. Yesterday, by the way, he was just recovering from, & full of, a triumphant squabble that he had been holding with the principal Officer of Artillery (I forget his name). He had just defeated him on some point & was very happy.

Today is the 30th. November & we have sneaked through it without much winter weather. The ground is today more beastly than I think I ever saw it.

I heard, by the way, the other day from a friend in Liverpool to whom I had written to try & get my friend Brummell some sort of situation. He tells me that he went to see him & found him very well & just going to enter upon the duties of some place that Col. Greg, the head Policeman there, had got him: 15/- a week, a house, and coals & candles, which will help him on. I was so glad to hear of it.

Letter 96

Camp at Sebastopol, 3 December

We lead much the same sort of life as usual here, varied today by an extremely good steeplechase & Race-meeting at which the Allies mustered in great force. The first race was nearly won by General Lawrenson (17th.) but he unfortunately got a very severe fall at the last fence & it was won by an Artillery man. The French were much astounded at seeing a General risk his neck, and a very funny little French General, fired by our General's noble example, rode & won a French race, tho' he wisely confined himself to a flat race. Lawrenson was not hurt & is a splendid rider. The weather was beautiful which is a great piece of luck as we have had a very indifferent 10 days of weather lately. La Marmora & Pelissier were there & much enjoyed apparently the races, especially the ones with what they generally call 'obstacles'.

I agree with you about Sterling's letter concerning Sir Colin [Campbell] in as much as it is a manly defence of a patron & friend, but although the expression 'laid up in lavender' is no doubt an offensive one, the truth is that the Highlanders did have but a very small portion of the fatigue and dangers of the Siege & the good ones amongst them always regretted it. Even in Sterling's rather laboured account of their performances, he only can make out that they had trench & outpost duty until the 6th. of December, & Heaven knows we have had a good deal of sieging since then. Besides, a day & night's duty in the trenches of Balaklava must have differed somewhat from one in our attack. Nobody wants to cry down the Highlanders, who have always done splendidly what they have had to do, & the little trench duty they had in the front, they did right well. But they happened not to be engaged in the trenches & the siege & it is nonsense comparing their labors with those of the troops who were so engaged, and the most satisfactory proof of it is that they alone of any Brigade in the army have any old soldiers left: would that we had many Divisions like them! Of Sir Colin's energy, pluck and merits as a Division General no one entertains the slightest doubt. On the whole I don't think that Sterling's letter is thought much of here. Sir Colin's reputation as a Soldier is much too high to require his Adjutant General's writing about it, and we all know out here exactly what the Brigade did & did not do, without his telling us at such length.

Our people are now really pretty comfortable. Heaps of little private huts to be seen about all our Camps and in each, perhaps the last animal you would expect to see, the cat!! The town was full of very jolly tame cats & all our men have their cats in their huts & very useful they are for the amounts of rats & mice is something awful. We have a particularly nice female cat who presented us with 8 tiny little sketches of herself but, feeling the responsibility too great, she wisely sat down upon 3 of them, whom we found in the morning after the event, quite flat like little fluffy crumpets. As the Yankees would say the 'Balance' are doing well. They appear to me to be quite blind, but I am told that is the right thing. We have also a very nice kitten, half-grown, a most delightful puss, the result of a former marriage. She lives in my room as she is not on good terms with her mother.

Letter 97

Camp at Sebastopol, 9 December

I am afraid I cannot write you a very cheery letter, for the weather is so dreary, rain, rain, rain, & one great scene of mud all round us; no want & no suffering, as in last wretched winter, but oh, such dullness. Fortunately I do not like the taste of strong drinks, or I might be tempted to seek a relief from ennui by the same excesses that the wise *Times* is just discovering that the 'Anglo-Saxon race' (as they call our Recruits) do, when a judicious Government gives them, in addition to all they can possibly want, 6d. a day, nothing to do, & no shop to spend it in but Grog-shops. I am just beginning to be satisfied that of all the idiots who have ever had anything to do with us, Ld. Panmure is the greatest. Will you believe that a day or two ago at Head Quarters they got notice that 'they wanted immediate accommodation' for what do you think? 200 Schoolmasters!! who are coming out immediately. Doing all we can, we have not accommodation for half this army, as it is, & in the midst of it 'every accommodation is to be afforded to 200 Schoolmasters'. How any man can be found to take the command I can't conceive! Oh what a blessing it will be when we get away from the Telegraph & the poor C-in-Chief not paralyzed by Idiots dictating to him from home, & not suggesting, but ordering, their ridiculous plans to be carried out 3000 miles from the seat of their ignorance &

stupidity. Poor Windham told me that it is quite heartbreaking trying to do anything: the Schoolmasters affair is only one in fifty of the absurdities that they have to contend against. What with our costly failure of a Transport Corps, our Army Works Corps, our Civil Artificers paid somewhat more than Officers, and the Staff Corps (happily died a natural death), I don't wonder at the tax-payers being somewhat sick of us. It will be a happy day for the army when we take the field and shake off all their encumbrances. Some little time ago we had a 'Pathologist', a Deputy do. & a Deputy Assistant do., all with high pay & allowances, and after much enquiry I have at last found out that their business is to discover, when we are dead, what we died of! It only wants the carrying out of the *Corps d'Armée* plan to make a Commander-in-Chief of the Army the most complete Cypher.

10th. We have rumours of bad doings at Kars. I hope to Heavens that they are not true. We hear that the whole of that gallant Army (the Garrison) have been reduced to capitulate. The knowing people here have been looking with a most anxious eye for some time there, & if it is not true at present, it is highly probable. I cannot but think that we ought to have helped that Force. We are told that it is 'too far' & 'great difficulties'. I wish to Heaven that instead of humbugging about Kinborn we had tried at any rate to relieve that gallant garrison, who, if not relieved, must inevitably be starved out. In my thinking there is only one great man and Soldier in the whole business of this war & that one is Omar Pacha, even he (if it has not yet fallen) can hardly be in time to save Kars, supposing he is able to get there at all.

I am at home by myself tonight, a thing I don't dislike & have been having tea instead of dinner, fancy that! The General {Garrett} is dining out in one direction & Forde in another. The truth is we live here a sort of exceedingly stupid & muddy garrison life. The General happily hates going out to dinner thro' the mud when he can help it, & when we are by ourselves we dine at 6.30 and sit over the fire reading & smoking sundry weeds until 10.30 or 11 P.M., when we generally turn in. This week will be rather a dissipated one for tomorrow we dine at General Barnard's (close by); the next day, at a dinner given by the Staff of the Division to a Colonel Wood R.A. who is leaving us, & next day I dine with my old mess Wombwell & Campbell [46th], & I know well that I shall get a leg of mutton at each gentleman's house, that being the 'piece of resistance' in the Camp.

Letter 98

Camp at Sebastopol, 15 December

I do not want anything in the way of warm clothes this winter, as my last year's lot are still to the front and a certain pair of warm waterproof boots that you sent me – though a little late for last year's snow & cold – come in most splendidly now & the Zumarra is a splendid coat & quite like uniform enough to wear on any occasion.

We have a pleasant neighbour commanding (our late) 2nd. Division: Barnard. I dined there a night or two ago & had a very pleasant party. If you had seen the style (it began to rain about 1/2 an hour before dinner) you would have pitied us, but we had not very far to go and the exceedingly absurd appearance of the dear old General [Garrett] in fishing boots, a long waterproof coat, a red woolly nightcap, with a very tall indiarubber extinguisher on it (which by the way he insisted on wearing with the curtain over his face, instead of his neck & then wondered he couldn't see!) kept up our spirits & we had a very merry party. Instead of a 'Brougham', I have a most amiable & hairy old mule.

By the bye, I believe Pelissier is going home and (I think it is a secret, so don't mention it) Sir Edmond Lyons & Marmora also, for some great 'Council of War' at Paris. Codrington does not go I hear. MacMahon is in command of the French Army when Pelissier goes – poor 'Bruat' is dead. (I dare say you will be inclined to say 'so also is Queen Anne' as you probably had the news of it as soon as we did). He was a good old fellow, not much dash in him they say, but immense admiration & friendship for the English Navy.

The French had rather a brilliant 'affair of outposts' the other day. A small outpost of theirs was surrounded by the Enemy in force but fortunately the Russes' hearts were not big enough, & instead of rushing on their little enemy & annihilating them, they began shooting at them and a French Reserve had time to come up & kill about 130, & take 40 live ones. I saw some of the prisoners; they seemed poor creatures.

Letter 99

Camp at Sebastopol, 21 December

We are now in the midst of a furious frost, everything white and hard as iron, tho' not so cold now as it has been. Two days ago the thermometer in a much warmer place (our Head Quarters) than here, was at 2. I think that is 30 below freezing point Fahrenheit isn't it? The consequence was that it was the most beastly day I ever felt, actually taking one's breath away. Our house is comparatively warm, averaging by day about 36, cold enough in all conscience, I think. Today is what is called a fine seasonable day, with a pink thing supposed to be the sun, in the sky. We kept ourselves pretty warm at first going about having frightful combats with snowballs, but now the snow is like flour and will not make into snowballs. I must say I should be quite content to get back the good old warm mud tho' I did abuse it when it was here. The General [Garrett] and I think alike about weather: Spring and Summer are the only seasons worth living in.

I don't quite know what to think about Peace. I don't quite believe in its probability yet, and as far as I myself am concerned I should not be averse to a Summer Campaign in some other country than this. As I am now placed, it would be almost certain promotion for me, and a regular campaign I have not yet seen. Fighting, tho', at the best is sad enough.

I am glad to hear that Sir Colin [Campbell] has been well received at the Palace. He is a fine old Soldier, I think probably the best General of Division in the Army. You know I don't quite agree with you about his being 'shamefully used'. I think that he was and is, either fit or not fit, for Commander in Chief − if the Government thought him not fit, I think they were quite right not to make him such, merely because he is a fine old Soldier.

We have been amusing ourselves papering the drawing-room with pictures from the *Illustrated News*,[93] & anything else pictorial that we

---

[93] These decorations were later to cause consternation amongst General Veselitskii's ADCs, who accompanied their General to dine with Garrett, Dallas and Alexis Soyer, the Reform Club chef. Soyer reports that they were

much taken with the engravings from the Illustrated News *pasted round the walls of the General's dining-room. They could not make out how it was that General Pelissier wore a Russian uniform, and Prince Menschikoff the French military order − that General Canrobert was dressed like the Emperor Alexander II while His Majesty was dressed in the French general's costume. Count Orloff wore the French imperial uniform; and, above all, their general-in-chief, Prince Gortschikoff appeared attired as a Highlander, while the Grand Duke Constantine was rigged out as a Zouave.*

Soyer had to explain that a pair of scissors was responsible for these anomalies.

can lay our hands on, and it makes the room very cheerful. We did not get our pictures this time, as we only received the mails of Sunday and Monday, and they always come by Saturday's mail.

By the bye, you ask me why some man who went onto the 'Mill' at the explosion was not promoted. I did not know anything about who went onto the building, and I have no doubt that whoever did it did it well, but as regards the danger I do not suppose there was any more danger there than round about the bottom of it where we all were, as in the event of its catching fire, nobody, they say, could have escaped for 1/4 of a mile all round.

Letter 100

Camp at Sebastopol, 24 December

I was glad to hear that you had seen Sir Colin [Campbell] and that he was in good spirits and had been well received at home. I agree with you in every respect as to his goodness, and as to our especially valuing him and his friendship, and I know that you will quite understand that anything I have ever written to you about him only referred to him as a Commander-in-Chief.

A very limited number of Crosses of the Legion of Honour have been given by the Emperor to be distributed amongst the British Army. There are only two given to Regiments which have been out from the beginning, and one to all other Regiments to be given to one Individual officer or Private. My Regiment has only one, and my name has been sent home for it. The reason it will be valued is that the names have been selected by Commanding Officers and then revised, if not approved by Generals of Division. Consequently, one may naturally conclude that they will not be given to the worst men. I do not at all mean to say it vaingloriously, but I value a thing of this kind much more than a C.B. which is always given to Commanding Officers and others who can't help themselves. I can't imagine why such a mystery has been made of it all, but as nobody, perhaps except myself, knows of his own name having gone in for it, I would rather, until it is settled, that you said nothing about it, for the dear old General [Garrett] told it me as an 'immense secret' over a cigar one night. What makes it pleasanter for me is that he had nothing to do with it, as Windham commanded the 4th Division at the time, and consequently it was he that sent in my name, and I suppose told the General. If our General had commanded the Division at the time, there would have been lots of kind friends to say 'Of course he recommended his own A.D.C.'. As it is, they can't say so.

We have got up some Theatricals in our Division which are great fun, as there are some good actors. The ladies have to be done by the tiniest of the boys that now come out as Lieutenants and Captains, and it is great fun altogether. The Commander-in-Chief [Codrington] is coming tonight. We have not room for many people, and there is immense trouble & interest to get a ticket, quite as much as to get to Almacks in former days. I don't act myself, but it is great fun. The most amusing part of the performance is 'getting up' the ladies. We cannot make them look even decently respectable. There is one boy in the 68th., with lots of light hair that is frizzled back and two little curls at the side *à l'Impératrice*, and ordinarily he is very pretty, shy, modest-looking little boy, but when dressed up for his part, tho' in very quiet looking clothes, his appearance is anything but correct.[94] Another boy of ours has to act a very stout lady, and just as his turn came to go on the last night he came in great affliction to the manager to tell him, that 'his bosom was slipping gradually down to his knees'. However, he got very well through his part, his bosom having been cunningly secured to his neck.

Tell dear mother not to be at all alarmed about the Steeple Chases here as I had nothing to do with them, except looking on, also that I am not the least annoyed at her 'express' on the subject, altho' if I had entertained any notions of self-destruction on the occasion, I'm afraid her dear little note would have been too late.

I am very sorry for poor Col. McMurdo's bad health, but between you and me, (tell it not in Gath or Clapham) I think it difficult to say which is the greatest failure: he, or the Land Transport Corps. The present man (Wetherall) (who ought to have been Q.M.G.) is a first rate man, and will do all that can be done, with such hopeless materials. There was actually – when a sort of census, after McMurdo went home, was taken of the animals of the L.T.Corps – a deficiency to the amount of 4000! of whom no possible account can be given was

94 Lt. Saunderson.

found; that was not including some 1500 that were known of, & accounted for as dead. These 4000 have disappeared, Heaven knows where, or how; this does not say much for McMurdo's system of accounts, supposing himself to have 4000 more horse and mules than he actually had! And they were known to have landed in the Crimea.

I don't know of anything more to tell you or any question of yours to answer, so will wish you all a happy Xmas. We have a turkey tomorrow but he is I fear thin. We have two left, out of a flock, and have eaten all the family except these two, who have been fretting about the eaten ones I think, and over exert themselves. They are usually on the roof of our house, which can't be a good thing for them.

Letter 101

Camp at Sebastopol, 28 December

I don't think the Russians will consent yet, and if we could only manage to campaign in a Christian sort of way, I shouldn't mind it: fighting and marching about in Summer and spending the Winter in some decent place with shops and houses, and somebody to speak to. But another Winter like the two we have had, I do dread: one Winter worked and starved to death, and this other one ennuyed, almost to death. We have lots of dinings out at one hut or another, but I hate males and their society & always long to go to bed. For those who enjoy those sort of festivities, the time must pass pretty well. The theatricals are rather fun, and go off well, and occasionally one has pleasant enough dinner parties at Windham's, or Barnard's, or any place where one meets clever or original people: after all, mortals are poor discontented creatures. I live now in the best house in the country, with the best food to be got, and get well paid for doing nothing and wearing a 'cockit hat'; and after all, I really think I never was so bored in my life, and that is a great deal for me to say. I don't see why I should bore you tho'; you will be suspecting me of suffering from what our Allies call 'the *vin triste*', after our Xmas dinner, perhaps I am.

Our little family of cats are, you will be pleased to hear, flourishing and big enough to be amusing. They are the greatest darlings, 4 tiny ones and the mother, and they all live in a box, which the tinies can just climb up and tumble out of. I have invented a most successful plan for warming them this cold weather which consists in heating a little log on the stove, and then putting it into their box, upon which they all cuddle about it, and go fast asleep. You will also be glad to hear that a reconciliation has taken place between the mother and an elder daughter (by a former marriage) who used to be on very bad terms, and the daughter now comes in and sits in the box with them all. In the absence of the real mother, we see the 'tinies' trying to obtain refreshment from their elder sister, which I should say must be a rather light meal as she is 'quite a young person' and not married. The dear old General [Garrett], who is the strangest *mélange* of soldier and child, spends most of his leisure time in pulling them away from the stove, and if he could, I am certain, would suckle them himself. One of them is mine and has got blue eyes. My servant calls her 'Betsy-Jane'. I am not sure that I think it either a pretty or lady-like name. Excuse my writing to you this history of cats, but they really are so much more pleasant and amusing than anybody else that I usually see, that I pass a good deal of my time with them.

I'm afraid that Omar Pacha must be in a bad way in Asia, and now that he is so, our Grand Military Authorities affect to say that he ought never to have gone there at all and that he is paying for his rashness. Heaven knows! no one can accuse them of rashness. If we had tried to do something *there*, instead of sending such a ridiculous Armada against Kinborn, we might have saved all this. I should not be at all astonished if we yet have to try there under fifty times worse circumstances than if we had boldly done it three months ago.

I don't at all wonder at your not understanding the 'promotion' question. Our General is a local M-General and, until his rank is made what is called permanent, actually commands the 46th., tho' of course only in name. Such is our absurd system, it is impossible to tell exactly what a man is out here. One of the most strange examples is Wetherall (who ought to be, I think Q.M.General). When he was Q.M.General of the Turkish Contingent, he was Lieutenant in the Guards – Colonel 'in the Army' – Q.M.General of the Contingent – Major General 'in Turkey' – and a Colonel 'on the Staff', all these things at once. Of course, this is unintelligible to you, and is in every way ridiculous. I think that now Codrington has been made a 'General', but before he was made so, Barnard told me that one day at

Head Quarters, they were looking over the names, promotions &c., and quite accidentally discovered that if Codrington were to die, the Command devolved upon Vivian (who is at Kertch), a man who is not with, or in this army, but who had got rank as General 'in the East' and as such would, until someone was appointed, legally be Commander-in-Chief! Conceive the absurdity of all this nonsense. Wetherall joining his Regiment, would be, and do duty as, a Sub-altern.

Letter 102

Camp at Sebastopol, 31 December

I really don't know what to tell you except that I am very well, & the General [Garrett] is very well & wishes you many happy new years & the Cats are very well. The mother of the Cats ate, yesterday, half a *Pâté de Perigord* while we were out but seems none the worse. It cannot be good for a cat nursing! I am suffering somewhat from want of exercise, too much to eat, and the general 'dulth' of life here (it only affects me mentally) and as you may guess from this letter, I really think that a general softening of the brain is coming on.

What do think of Peace? I heard from a very good source today that we shall soon know what it is to be, that there will be no 'Negotiating', merely an answer 'Yes' or 'No' from Russia, as we won't listen to anything else.

Part Three
1856

'They appear to be as sick of the Crimea as we are.'

Letter 103

Camp at Sebastopol, 4 January

I have just been outside the house looking through a glass at a rather interesting sight, a large sailing vessel had unwarily gone in rather too near the fork on the North side & every gun opened on her. She did not appear to be hit and when they left off shooting at her I came in.

The roads are in capital order but it is very cold riding; except on business, I don't often try it. On New Year's Day we went over to Head Quarters & from thence went a cavalcade to Pelissier's. The Commander-in-Chief [Codrington], Windham & my Chief [Garrett] went in to see him, & all the wretched Aides waited outside, which was not amusing. The French believe in peace, more than we do, and a French 'Aide' with a tiny waist and a large bustle, told me he thought it was settled. As he looked very wretched & cold, & had a very thin sky-blue jacket on & very thin pink trousers & nose, he probably believed in what he must earnestly have desired.

I do not exactly know when Sir Colin [Campbell] is expected out, but I believe it is settled that he (& he alone) is to have a *Corps d'Armée* of two Divisions, and that the plan of dividing us into regular Corps is relinquished, a good thing, I think. I rather fancy that if, as supposed, Sir Colin were to command one, & Eyre the other, in the field, poor Codrington would soon be left to command Windham & the Transport Corps.

We have no news about Omar Pacha, towards whom all eyes have been lately anxiously turned. I trust he is holding his own.

We have been blowing up & destroying the Docks in Sebastopol this last week & they are not yet done. I saw the last one done, & a singular spectacle it is to see a man with a single wire utterly destroy a beautiful mass of masonry that took so many thousands of money, men's lives, & days to make. The floors are first blown up, then the sides & all with very little noise & danger. The whole floor appeared to rise about 20 or 30 feet, & when one went afterwards to look at it, it had the appearance of a quarry – a great hopeless looking hole full of stones. It was fired by a galvanised wire.

Letter 104

4th. Division Camp, 14 January

The General [Garrett] and I dine at Barnard's tonight, at the 2nd. Division, & a pleasant walk there we shall have. Forde & I generally go out to 'parties' on a mule of mine, a very dear creature with a long back who in an emergency can carry 3. We have had some very good theatricals which are very popular & everybody who can get a ticket comes from all sorts of distances. I always ask somebody to come & dine & then give him a 'shake-down': there are some goodish actors among them. Ld. A. Russell is good, & Maxwell Earle, and there is a young fellow named Lacy who acts women's parts wonderfully & is very clever. I myself usually detest amateur Theatricals & never think Amateurs good actors. I don't much affect a real play with real actors but out here it is good fun.

What think you of the Peace question? I was reading a French Pamphlet that I hear is making some stir at home about the urgency of a '*Congrès*' I was not much struck by it and did not see much new light thrown on the subject in it. I should not say it was half clever enough to have been written by Louis N. as is thought.

Thank Heaven this winter is slipping by wonderfully, for I am very weary of this kind of existence. One gets so sick of seeing the same people & hearing the same conversations every day. Nothing can be kinder than the good old General (Chief) but after all I am afraid I should get tired of even an old angel, having to sit every night from 6 till 10.30 knowing exactly what he is going to say and patiently awaiting dear bedtime. He is a capital soldier & General, one of the best we have, & I am happy to say is well known to be such & is very highly thought of at Head Quarters, I know. But I am a *little* weary of his old jokes, and lately he has been telling me *my* old jokes, which is rather too bad. One of his peculiarities, you must well know, which is the extraordinary mania he has of thinking nobody knows his own business so well as he does. The consequence is that one day he shows a groom how to clean a horse, another day an Engineer how to blow up the Docks, & really yesterday he got quite annoyed with a cat whom he was endeavouring to show how to suckle her kittens. He told me quite seriously that he really did not know how the cat could ever expect to rear her kittens if she continued her present stupid method of suckling them! I think if I was a rich man I should regularly hire clever amusing people to stop with me & directly they got tiresome I should change them, as you do flowers in London.

By the way, I got my medal & clasps sent me yesterday. Such a frightful thing it is, with Albert's filthy Coburg colours on the ribbon, have you seen any? They say that the colour of the ribbon is going to be changed. It is too frightful now. The only decent ones I see are little ones, I don't know where they come from; there is at any rate less of them than the Government ones, with the four clasps. They hang down all over one's coat. I have heard nothing more of the 'Legion of Honour'. I believe they have to go through all sorts of hands from here to London. & eventually they will come, I conclude, out here.[95]

Our Quartermaster General, Colonel Hallewell, was showing me today a splendid pencil-case he received, a present from the Queen in return for some beautiful sketches he had sent home for her. He is such a jolly frank good fellow & was as delighted with it as a child. It was like all that description of presents, very gorgeous, covered with jewels, & curiously frightful & vulgar. I always wonder where those things can be made so expensive & so ugly. It was nice of the Queen sending it though. She had before sent him another which never reached him & he of course couldn't say anything & was very wretched, but someone told the Queen that he had never got it & she immediately sent him another. He is a first rate Staff Officer & a good artist. We are altogether very lucky in this Division having capital Staff officers all through – Hallewell has Windham's old place here.[96]

---

[95] By and large officers affected great contempt for the Crimea medal and its clasps; Lord George Paget wrote, 'Our medals have come, and I think the man whose taste the clasps were ought to be obliged to wear one. They already call them here "Port", "Sherry" and "Claret"'.

[96] Dallas fails to mention in this letter that he had taken part in a paper chase two days previously, and although he had not won, had been amongst the leaders. The excitement was fully reported in the *Illustrated London News* of 9 February 1856.

Letter 105

Sebastopol, 18 January

My ship, the *Ossian*, has come but I cannot get my box until various things, such as huts, Horses & other trifles are removed from the top of it. I trust that it will have survived it all.

A poor young fellow of ours, one Messenger, lost his life in a very sad manner a few days ago. He was an 'acting Engineer' & was employed in superintending the road making & somehow, I suppose incautiously, approached a blast, the fuze of it being supposed to be out, when it blew up & must have destroyed him instantly. We regret him much. He was a most straightforward simple-minded fellow whom everybody liked much – one of those good creatures who seem mysteriously to be carried off so often when so many other less valuable lives are spared.

We all expect an early campaign & the Transport Corps is being altogether remodelled by Windham & Wetherall. I think Windham is a good appointment. He is a man of most original mind and a wonderful head for combination & for organising anything he sets himself to. I have great hopes of his doing wonders: an earnest, original man with opportunity & energy must do well. After all, I fancy that is what we want. I know nearly everybody out here & he is the only man I see with a single original idea about him.

Letter 106

Sebastopol, 21 January

People here are much excited about some very important news that is supposed to have come to Head Quarters, and are full of speculations as to its purport. Windham & Codrington are the only two who know it and of course don't tell, but I know that Windham said at dinner the day the news was supposed to have come (the 18th.), that when the news was known that had come, the 18th. would be one of the 'most memorable days in the Campaign', and the company present all wrote down on slips of paper their prophecies, one saying 'Peace', another 'that Austria had declared for us', another 'a Campaign in Asia' and so on. I do not think that he was joking, and must own myself as curious as any dear woman about it. If there is anything, I suppose you all know it in England ere this. I hardly believe in Peace, but cannot conceive any news but that important enough to justify Windham's remark, supposing him to have said it in earnest.[97]

Letter 107

Sebastopol, 24 January

We are all so full of the extraordinary news that we have received that one can hardly set oneself down to write or do anything except wonder. The French Ambassador sent a special express to Pelissier the day before yesterday, telling that the Emperor Alexander has signed and accepted all our propositions for Peace unconditionally. I believe myself that there is no doubt at all of its being the case, altho' our C.-in-Chief [Codrington] has not received his announcement of the same. What an extraordinary & unexpected thing it is! It is implicitly credited by everybody with a few exceptions here. With what delight I should have heard the news some months ago! and indeed as it is, tho' I see my little coachful of hopes and prospects upset, I look, I must own, with indescribable pleasure, to getting home and being with you all again. I don't expect, by the way, that if peace were proclaimed tomorrow, that we should all go home immediately, as there will be a great deal to be done here, and in all probability, an army of occupation somewhere. An event of this kind always stirs up the stock (more or less large) of selfishness in everybody, and one's first question, I fear, is usually, what's to become of me? Consequently, there is a rather ludicrous expression of blankness in the faces of the Hd. Quarter & other 'Staffs' here at present. My Chief [Garrett] looks on pretty calmly and will in all probability find employment. Your son Frederick smokes his cigar of peace and endeavours as clearly as the fragrant mist will allow him, to look on both sides of the question: on one side, a Campaign with promotion and honours and glory, with perhaps disappointment and a wooden leg; on the other, every prospect of getting home with his legs, without the promotion, and seeing you all again, & but small chance of earning so good a livelihood as at present. The blessing of peace, to mankind and the 'balance

---

[97] Russia had accepted the Austrian proposals for peace.

of power' &c. &c. don't appear to trouble us much out here, and I am quite sure that all our dear Mothers, with a holier selfishness than ours, are delighted, and are of 'the Peace at all price' party.

Letter 108

Sebastopol, 28 January

I wonder what you think about Peace at home? Here we have not any doubt altho' as yet we, the English, have no official accounts of it, but there is a new mail in, I have just heard, tho' we have not had our letters yet. I dare say the ship has brought some news to our Generals from Constantinople. Some Prisoners, English, who were released from Odessa arrived here a day or two ago, say they fully believed in peace at Odessa and were proportionately happy. I can't fancy any person more likely, by the way, to be rejoiced than an Odessan at peace, for they must have daily expected their Town to be destroyed for the last two years. I think it is very creditable to us, not having done so, as it would only take a few hours doing.

Now that the weather is practicable, the amount of soldiering and drill that is going on, would, if I had anything to do with it, drive me distracted. As it is, I have nothing to do with it, but smoke a cigar and look on. I spent yesterday afternoon very pleasantly, listening to a very good French band and basking in the sun. The poor French, by the bye, are sick and wretched. They look ill-fed, and I know are suffering a good deal from hunger, scurvy and all sorts of miseries. They are good contented creatures, and one never hears a complaint from them.

Letter 109

Camp at Sebastopol, 1 February

Peace here is looked upon — as regards its likelihood — by different people, in proportion to the good or harm it will do them. The 'Staff' generally 'don't think it a certainty by any means', the French, who are very sick and wretched and half-starved, have no doubt of it. I believe in it, but should not be at all surprised if the Russes were to make a squabble about some point or other. I think that as usual the *Times* does as much harm as it can. I am quite certain that the way to make Peace is not to assault, and affect to look with suspicion on, all Russian offers. The French who desire peace much more than we do pursue a better course in their Press to obtain their object.

The General [Garrett] and I had a pleasant dinner at Windham's a few nights ago, rather a long way to get through the mud and back, but the night was fine. He always gets pleasant people to meet. His second A.D.C. by the way is not a very lively chap – a nephew of his; a heavy youth [Ennismore]. He (Windham) did not seem confident about peace. He is a man who has everything to lose by it. I was happy to hear that peace or not, all our preparations for war go on just the same. We shall have a most splendid Army by April or the end of March, much larger than I imagined: among the items, 9000 Cavalry, English, and 120 guns with 9000 Artillery. Indeed such an Army (independent of Contingents of all kinds) of English, as has never been heard of before.

Letter 110

Sebastopol, 4 February

We are now again in the midst of snow and frost, tho' I must own that today was a perfect day for doing what I unfortunately don't enjoy, walking. However, I did walk down to Sebastopol and saw a splendid sight: the destruction of Fort Nicholas by our Allies. It was done at 1.00 P.M. and very well done too. There was one great cloud of dense smoke, then a roar, repeated, I think, 8 times in about one minute, and where an immense casemented Fort stood before, as the smoke cleared away, there was nothing but a long ridge of stones by the water side. If you have a map of Sebastopol you will see where it stood. I never saw anything so utter and complete as the destruction of it. It seemed like a dream, where we had our eyes fixed on a beautiful white building about a quarter of a mile long awaiting the explosions. When over, there was not the faintest outlines or trace of anything but a sort of beach (tho' of immense stones) sloping down into the water. The French, having received orders to do it in a great hurry, were obliged to resort to the simple plan of filling the lower 'casemates' with powder (110,000 lbs!) and letting it off, and in consequence did it much more successfully that if they had made all sorts of scientific mines under it.

We are waiting rather anxiously for news from home, and of course, the mail due today has not yet appeared, but very few here seem to doubt about Peace. How delighted I too should be with peace, if I had got my promotion, but as it is, it is rather a bore to think that I have spent, at any rate, an unpleasant and somewhat dangerous year and a half here, and all for nothing! I have gained nothing by it all. I should be in the same place in the Army if I had gone to Australia! where, by the way, I should perhaps have found a 'nugget' which I fear is not to be picked up here.

Letter 111

Camp at Sebastopol, 11 February

We are all employed at present, inspecting and being inspected. My share of it is a simple affair, consisting in riding round and round the regiments with the Chief [Garrett] accompanied by seven other Donkeys worse than myself, forming what is called the 'Staff of the Division', the whole affair being somewhat like what one imagines the ride in the old song 'To Banbury Cross' to have been.

Today we have been blowing up more Forts in the town; and a very singular looking town it seems likely to become, ere we have done with it. The weather has, I trust, broken up for good: today is mild enough & muddy underfoot, not very pleasant for riding or walking, but better than frost. I wonder where we shall pass the Summer. I should not be at all surprised in the event of peace if a considerable portion of the Army were kept somewhere, as an Army of occupation, and I think it more than probable that my Chief will be employed if anyone is wanted, as it is pretty well known at Head Quarters that he is about the best General out here, and would be more likely to take command than many others, five of whom, by the way, are supplied us from 'our less fortunate brethren of the Guards', three or four of our Generals are nearly 'Cretins', and having no interest either, of course will never be employed again anywhere.

I am quite sick of my promotion story. Windham told me the other day that he was disappointed that I didn't get it, as he expected I would, but told me that in the event of peace, he advised me to try again, and he would do all he could. He was very kind about it. The whole thing is a piece of ill-luck; we never know when we are well off. When I first came out I thought myself very lucky, and I hoped to get on. All I have to be thankful for is my being alive when so many more deserving have been miserably destroyed. As regards 'getting on' I am no great soldier, & hate the whole thing, & I don't quite see why I should expect to get on. If I had been in what is called an unlucky regiment, and not been out here I should be in just the same place in the Army, perhaps higher.

You will be sorry to hear that I am now, while writing, filthily dirty, having been all the morning assisting at 'Scene painting' for our new theatre,[98] and I am mass of paste, glue and dust: to see the horrid hands with which I am penning this affectionate and interesting letter would, I think, have a fatal effect on you, my dearest of sisters; as a stain, (so says the fable) on his little white coat, kills the Ermine. I do not think there is anything to tell you in the way of news. The Russians shoot a good deal at our half of Sebastopol, but do no harm. When I say 'our half', you must understand, what many at home don't seem to know, that we have the whole City of Sebastopol: there are nothing but two or three Forts on the North Side – not a single house.

Letter 112

Camp at Sebastopol, 15 February

We amuse ourselves as best we may with soldiering, riding about the country, and theatricals. The latter are flourishing in our Division as we have built a capital theatre holding about 300, and last night had our first performance in it, which went off capitally. Maxwell

---

[98] Dallas refers to the 'Theatre Royal' of the 4th Division. At the end of the campaign, Alexis Soyer described visiting the vandalised theatre, 'Nothing has been respected but her Majesty's royal arms, which ornamented the centre of the proscenium. These had been painted by Major Dallas.' Soyer goes on to explain how, 'by the aid of a ladder', he removed them, and added them to his personal collection of souvenirs.

Earle, who had most to do, acted extremely well, & tonight there is another 'go'. A very pleasant Frenchman dined & went with us last night, a Baron de Mallet, who was delighted. There were various French there; a dear old General, de la Motte-Rouge, who seemed quite enchanted, & laughed his old sides nearly off, which was very nice and festive of him, as he doesn't understand a word of English. Three of four of our Generals were there. It gets rid of a longish evening.

We had rather fun the other day at a 'shooting match'. Two men, (Guardsmen), Ponsonby & Blane (I think a brother in law of Codrington's) one day challenged the whole Army to shoot with a rife, and men from each Division accepted the challenge. The match came off a few days ago, and the joke was that the only people who hardly ever hit the target were the 'Appellants': Ponsonby hit it once, I think, & Blane never (or vice versa). We have a great laugh at them in consequence.

A Regiment is now passing the window, the 13th., headed by the most singular maniac, the Colonel Lord Mark Kerr, who always goes about without a hat, long red hair and moustaches, red fisherman's boots & no stirrups. He is perfectly insane & goes about in the height of summer with his frightful head bare.

Letter 113

Camp at Sebastopol, 18 February

More eccentric weather, yesterday was warm and mild like the two or three preceding it, and today we were to have a review of the whole Army at 10 A.M. but to our astonishment this morning on waking up, we found the ground white with snow and as hard as iron!. The Chief [Garrett] and I dined last night at Ld. W. Paulet's and met Ld. Rokeby and Windham. As we broke up in decent time it was pleasant enough, but I suppose three harder talkers never met before, and dear old Ld. R came off quite triumphant, possessing the great advantage of not hearing what the other two tried to say. The result was a mere 'canter over the course' for the Baron, the other two being for once in their lives completely shut up. He associates much with the French and consequently knows more of their internal economy than most men, and he told us that nothing could exceed their miserable state and the infamous way in which they are treated and looked after — dying by hundreds of fever and scurvy, and but few Doctors, no 'medical comforts', and when sent away, packed like sheep in the first ship at hand, such a thing as a Hospital Ship fitted up as such being quite unknown! I knew this to be the case but Ld. Rokeby's testimony of it, himself a most blind admirer of everything French, struck me much. He is great friends with most of the French Generals & talks most fluent & execrable '*parlez-vous*'. I like him very much & find him always most friendly. He was great fun last night, & is coming to dine with us and go to our Theatre on Thursday.

Some of the other Divisions are getting up theatricals & tonight the General & I dine with Gen. Lysons of the Lt. Division & go to his theatre & a nice ride there, and back, we seem likely to have, the air (at least at present) being filled with poudre snow and the ground like ice. My wonderful old Chief is a younger man now than I am, and goes everywhere. Certainly 'the sword has not worn out the scabbard' in his case.

Lord Rokeby, by the way, amused me last night: he told us that he is not a very good sleeper & goes to bed late, & his plan is to let his fire out an hour or so before bedtime, open his window, and put on a great coat, by which means he gets so exceedingly wretched that he is glad to go to bed! That does not sound cheerful?

I heard a capital story the other day showing what style of man Ld. Panmure, is and how utterly shameless he is about advancing his relations & friends. I thought it a mere 'good story' but have since found it to be true. Soon after Simpson came to command & before he had appointed his Staff, he got a telegraphic message from England from Ld. P. as follows: 'Keep well with the French — do something for Dowbiggin', Dowbiggin being a young nephew of Ld. P.s in the 4th. Foot. Poor old Jamie had to make him a Brevet Major & put him on his Staff, to his great disgust as he knows nothing about him. Could you believe anything so utterly disgusting? This I believe to be perfectly true.

Sir Colin [Campbell] has come back. I have not seen him, but I hear he is looking very fresh, & has shaved off his beard, & his hair instead of being white, is yellow! He can't have dyed it? I must go off directly to help paint a most Grand Scene for our theatre, a drop scene, that

Colonel Warre & I am engaged in. It is a beautiful 'Allegory' full of meaning, ('if one could only discover it'). There is a *Zouave* with a tricolor flag, & a 'crusher' with an English one, and six & twenty young ladies, with short clothes & salmon coloured legs, and a precipice behind them and a ship, and a blue sky, and two large columns, and over all a 'Queen's Arms', the whole forming a beautiful & intelligible work of art.

I hear they have scraped together a *Corps d'Armée* for Sir Colin consisting of the Scotch and the troops at Balaklava. Failing his being C.in-Chief, I fancy, it was difficult to know what to do with him, as he was much senior to Codrington.

Letter 114

Camp at Sebastopol, 25 February

We had a Grand Review of our Infantry yesterday on our Heights, every Regiment except about 8 or 9, and a more beautiful sight you cannot conceive. The day was cold but bright & nothing could exceed the wonderful appearance of our men, in all respects as clean, healthy & steady as a field day in England, in all about 22,000. The Guards were very strong & looked magnificent, as did the Highlanders. I should place the latter first in point of appearance, as they have so many old soldiers, not having lost men like all the Regiments in the Front. The French were much struck by the sight, and some Spaniards who are here *En amateur* were wild with delight. It was altogether a most beautiful sight. Odd to say, it is the first Review that has been had of our Infantry in the Crimea. We have had so much work, fighting, & digging, and dying, that we have had no time for parade soldiering. Codrington was delighted with them all. I saw Sir Colin [Campbell] looking very gay and juvenile without his beard, (but not to speak to) yesterday. I am glad to see in today's orders a warning to newspaper correspondents, officers & others to take care what they're about, which delights me. Codrington is the first man that has had the courage to allude to what everybody has felt long to be the most crying evil. The order is a trifle wordy, but better written than usual. I suppose you'll see it in the *Times*.

Our Theatricals go on most gaily, the Commander-in-chief dines with us on Thursday & goes in the evening, and other Divisions are getting up plays also, but I fancy that our establishment is grandest one. What do you think of the Peace, is it still a certainty ? I think so, I must say, but I fancy that if our ministers act with anything like their usual wisdom there'll be a row in America, failing the Rooshians. I would, I own, much sooner fight with Yankees than Russes. I have a great objection and dislike to the former who want much to be thrashed.

The new 'Order of Valour' seems to have quite set the minds of her Majesty's Ministers at ease in the distribution of C.B.s and K.C.B.s, having established an order with some pretensions to merit in its distribution. They appear to have lost any scruples left about 'Baths'.

Letter 115

Camp at Sebastopol, 29 February

Today is a rather memorable day to this Army as the Armistice was settled and arranged this morning by the various 'Chiefs of Staff'. They met at the Traktir Bridge over the Tchernaya & arranged it. Windham, our chief, Martimprey the French, & the Sardinian (name I don't know); I don't either know who the Russes sent. I conclude their Chief of the Staff. It lasts I hear to the 31st. of March & I don't quite see the use of it, as it interrupts nothing except active hostilities which in all probability could not take place until April, & all preparations and movements of troops, reinforcements arriving, even the completion of our work of destroying the South Side, go on as usual. On the whole we have somewhat the best of it as they sometimes killed one of us & we never fired at all at them.

Last night we had a dinner party and went to our Theatre afterwards. Sir W. Codrington dined with us, and Ld. W. Paulet, and various others, and appeared to have enjoyed themselves much when they started off for their various homes. Jasper Hall is Sir W.C.'s A.D.C. (some relation I think, of his). I have known him a long time. He is a good natured jolly fellow, but a trifle uncouth. I had read the extract you sent me about Airey & Co. & I think it very good, but exactly what everybody always knew. I think you are a little mistaken in fancying that nobody believed the *Times* when they abused those people '& that now they find out the truth of it'. Everybody knew perfectly well their incompetency and there were no two opinions on the subject; that they should be praised and rewarded when driven away from here is the usual course of things, and did not much surprise us out here, who are long tired of being surprised & disgusted.

I rode out today to pay my respects to Sir Colin [Campbell], found him at home, & sat some time with him. He was most kind and pleasant, sent heaps of messages to you both, and told me to say that he considers himself as owing Caroline a letter of thanks for her present and will pay his debt. He was very amusing about Paris, where he had not been since 1817, and naturally found it a good deal altered. He told me that from conversations with many French, and with the Emperor [Napoleon] himself, he found that the distribution of our Queen's medals has caused the greatest delight, and was most politic. One rather curious advantage of the affair, an old French General told him was, that all the old-fashioned people in the Provinces, when they saw the soldiers returning with the Queen's medal, will understand that we have been fighting on the same side; at present it being most difficult to persuade them that we are not fighting against one another. The Empress [Eugénie] he was charmed with. He said that she was, to his mind, the most perfectly unaffected ladylike person he ever met. He himself was looking very well, much improved by having removed a grizzly beard. I afterwards went on and found Ewen [Macpherson] who was looking exceedingly well. What a pretty boy he is! He confessed to me that he was dreadfully cold hanging about at last Sunday's Review which I could well believe. It was a bright day but cold and by no means a day for standing about without one's trousers.

The Highlanders are most amusing in trying to persuade one that they have had such dreadful work in the Rear during the Siege. Today I remarked to some of them how splendid they all looked on parade, adding 'You have so many fine old soldiers' upon which one of them said 'I'm sorry to say we (the 93rd.) have not much more than 200 of the men who landed'. I don't think we have in six Regiments in the front as many as that. This astonished them much and they said that they 'couldn't understand how it was'! Lord bless them, I could have explained it very easily, if I had not foreseen that they would have sounded their 'Slogan' and probably destroyed me. Ewen Macpherson is a very dear boy and I hear that there are some good fellows in the Regiment, but generally speaking, they are very ugly fellows and talk but poor English. He has a nice little corner of a Hut which he shares with another young Celt, whom he told me he didn't like at all, which must be unpleasant, as their feet almost touch when in bed. He promised to come up here and dine and sleep and go to our Theatre next week. I hope he will be able, but there is a dreadful 'Villain' named Cameron who commands the Scotch & seems to make everybody he can unhappy, and if he finds out that any of his young men are attempting to enjoy themselves he will pounce on them, so they told me!

Letter 116

Camp at Sebastopol, 9 March

Nothing has yet been settled about the armistice but, through a sort of tacit understanding, there is no shooting. In spite of all orders our precious Subalterns go down in hundreds to the Tchernaya and fraternize with the Russes, and until some poor wretch is caught and tried for it, will continue to do so. A quantity of books has come out for the Soldiers to read, a present from the Queen, and one of the Division A.D.C.s has charge of them in each Division. I am the Librarian for the 4th. Div: by which means I have had lots of books to read during the late filthy season. Tho' officers are not allowed to take them, I of course make an exception in favour of the Librarian. It is very good natured of the Queen and the books are capital ones, all the travels, Novels &c of the day. Have you read Mrs. Duberly's book? I hear that it is a very shady one, and have read one or two rather severe articles in the paper about it. It appears more a history of a dismal old horse she used to ride about on, than anything else. I must own I am rather pleased at her ill-success, for she is to my mind a nasty woman.[99]

We have of course had no more reviews or field-days on account of the weather, but I suppose soon shall resume them. Shervinton's

---

[99] Mrs. Duberly's Crimean Journal was published in 1855. Her horse 'Bob' may be said to be the hero of the book.

appointment to the L.T. Corps gets him out of my way but the man whom they had the effrontery to say must be promoted before me is Piper, who came out after me and has been absent from his duty for more than six months, besides having never been recommended by anyone, so that if I wait on him I am likely to do so for some time. I can't form any idea what will be done with my Regiment when this is over, some say India. We are still very weak and it is some comfort to hear, as we do from everybody, that our Depots both at Winchester and at Malta are the smartest and best conducted in both garrisons. Whatever may become of us, I of course shall try, and probably will be able, to get some leave before joining them wherever may be sent. There are rumours of an army of occupation being sent to Moldavia, or somewhere about there, and we should probably form a portion of it, (the 4th. Division). I should not dislike it as we should of course be withdrawn somewhere for the winter and I should prefer it much to going to Malta, which is from the intense heat (and General Penne-father being in command) a most disagreeable quarter.

Letter 117

Camp at Sebastopol, 14 March

I have been spending a peculiarly wretched morning sitting on my horse with my silly old employer [Garrett], watching a meeting between the Russe and ourselves and the French, the same affair as the last, with the same result I fancy. They cannot quite arrange some point or condition of the Armistice, and we are 'as we were'. I think Peace will be proclaimed before our stupid old Armistice is settled. I heard of its coming off and endeavoured to conceal it from R.G. [Garrett] but some villain told him about it & of course he must needs go and sit for three hours about 1/2 a mile off from the meeting, which took place in a tent, until he & we were frozen. Nobody (as I knew) was allowed to go near, and of course all we saw was a little body of English and French and then they got off their horses and trotted into a tent and stayed there about 2 hours and then came out and trotted away. This seen from 1/2 a mile off was not amusing, I must say. There were heaps of old donkeys there, but they all went away after a few minutes. Mine being stronger than the rest stopped till it was over. I saw dear old Lord Rokeby there. He came up very grandly and was snubbed by a sentry who wouldn't let him or anyone else pass, which of course made him frantic, but he wisely rode away.

Letter 118

Camp at Sebastopol

I don't exactly know the day of the month, but it is the festival of St. Patrick, for which, see your almanack [17th March]. I know this to be the case, from seeing a large proportion of the army going about with Shamrock in their caps, and generally having the appearance of having dined early and freely.

Yesterday we had an exceedingly filthy sort of *Promenade Militaire*. 3 Divisions, 1st., 2nd. & 4th. started at 7 A.M. to go to the top of a mountain near the Monastery of St. George's and there spend the day, taking fuel, uncooked food, &c &c. When we got there it was so dreadfully cold that we merely marched past the Commander-in-Chief [Codrington] and came home by about 2 P.M. Such an affair at Aldershot in very hot weather would have been excusable, but it does not require much sense to see the absurdity of this sort of thing with troops who have been campaigning so long, nor could anyone see the advantage of going, with the thermometer at 19 degrees in the sun, to the top of a cold mountain for the men to cook their dinners. Altogether it was so absurd that we were allowed to come home, and if at first a march there and back had been ordered, it would have been a wise thing but 'playing at soldiers and cooking and sham bivouacing', is childish with an army that has been nearly two years going thro' the realities of such things.

It is a sad thing that neither the C. in Chief nor his assistants can write English as of course the press are delighted at so legitimate an opportunity of laughing at them. I certainly never did see any dispatch or order of his that was good English, but the maudlin sentiment and utter bosh of two accounts of the explosion of Fort Nicholas was quite unpardonable. It is also an odd thing, for he appears to be a perfect gentleman, and sensible and dignified in his present extraordinary position: for mistakes in grammar, I think his Secretary must be somewhat to blame, as he surely might correct them. He (the Sec.),

Blane, I don't suspect of being very clever, but is connected by marriage with his Chief. Blane is a singular looking man, remarkable for having a snow white 'Imperial' about an inch square in the midst of a brown beard and hair which one can perceive 1/2 a mile distance from him.

Letter 119

Camp at Sebastopol, 24 March

Today we had a Grand Race Meeting on the Banks of the Tchernaya, which went off very successfully; a Frenchman, I am glad to say, having the good luck to win two races.[100] The Russian Commander-in-Chief, 'Luders', was invited, but did not come.

What a mess old Sir de Lacy [Evans] has been making. He always does whenever he tries to speak and consequently has to eat dirt or rather his own words (the same thing). The result is that the two men whose names he brought up have come brilliantly out of it and he more than amply apologizes to both Gordon and young Dowbiggin. Tho' all he said was true enough, he said it so stupid a way, and so brutally (in the French use of the word) that he has done them more good than harm. If ever I am in a scrape, I will try and get him for my prosecutor – his insulting manner of speaking of poor old Simpson (his contemporary) excites much disgust out here. By the way, what a sad spectacle we present to the World with all these criminations and recriminations between these old soldiers. The regular system seems to be 'if I'm attacked, I'll go in at somebody else', a very unworthy and peculiarly unsoldierlike plan.

We have the most agreeable rides about the Tchernaya, which has been under fire always until the 'Armistice'. I enjoy much wandering about there, and the ground where the Russians came at Inkermann is of course most interesting. From neither side (Russe or Allies) being able to get there, we found quantities of the bodies of men killed in the battle. They are now mostly buried, but a day or two ago I came

---

[100] Strictly speaking 'Frenchmen' won two races – Capitaine Cornat of the *Chasseurs d'Afrique* on 'Bignet' won the first race (half-a-mile, flat; 39 ran) and Viscomte Talon on 'Paddy Roy' (an Irish horse) won the second (two miles, hurdles; 6 ran).

across the remains (merely a skeleton) of a Russian soldier, poor creature! He had been shot in the act of biting off the end of a cartridge, (while loading) and singular to tell, the cartridge was still in his hand! and there he had fallen, and lain so many months undisturbed, his clothes almost perfect, himself a skeleton! It was a dreary sight on a lovely spring day, & looking round on the beautiful scene all about me, I honestly wished the Conferences good luck! How any man not insane, having seen a battle, can wish to see another, I cannot conceive.

I am going over some day to see some 'Scottish Games' this week at the Highland Camp, not that a Scottish game is a lively affair, for it generally consists in what is called 'putting a stone' and then getting drunk, but the General [Garrett] and I are going over to pay a visit to Sir Colin [Campbell], who of course takes a great interest in the savage sports (by the way one of the sports (?) is a match on their fearful bagpipes!!). The Colonel (at present) of the 93rd. is a very friendly blustering fellow; his surname Sebastian L.H. (we call him Sebastopol L.H.), and he invited us to a Scottish banquet on the occasion of the Games and promised us Sheep's Heads, and Intestines, called Haggis.

Letter 120

Camp at Sebastopol, 31 March

I enclose you a programme of a ball that is coming off tomorrow night, to which we are all invited. Fancy a Ball out here! Where the ladies are to come from, I don't quite know. The invitation and the picture will be the best part of it, the latter in colour, the two streams of 'Company' coming from Kamiesch, and Balaklava, are charming I think.

Our Armistice is prolonged until further orders, and I suppose that means until Peace is proclaimed.

I see, as I expected, in the *Times* a furious attack on Codrington (about the Correspondence out here) I was pleased to see the more than usual 'Pothouse' style of it. His ordinary dispatches &c are so bad, that it is easy to cut them up. In this case they can only resort to low abuse.

Letter 121

Camp at Sebastopol, 3 April

Today being (I believe) my birthday, the General [Garrett] having discovered it, wished me many happy returns of it, a felicitation, which however kindly intended, would not, taken literally, be worth much, for so horrid a day I never saw. A furious north wind blowing, and a heavy visitation of snow falling, it would altogether be a filthy December day. I do not exactly know how old I am, but what with rheumatism in my back, and irritation at the weather on my mind, I feel about 50 and by no means 'young of my years'.[101]

Yesterday, having received news of the Peace being concluded and signed, we fired a salute of 101 guns, which I went to see, for having seen the first shot of this war, and nearly all fired since, I thought I might as well see the last. And, dearest Pussy, you will hardly believe me for having a little 'squeeze' of regret, mixed up with pleasure at the thoughts of seeing you all again, when I saw the curtain as it were, drop on our Drama out here. For notwithstanding the thankfulness I ought to feel at being alive to write about it, this Campaign has been (as I dare say it has been to many a better man) a most bitter dis-appointment to me. I saw many round me yesterday who were at school when I was a soldier, and who have served weeks for my months in this Campaign, promoted and now senior to me in the Army. I should have been in the same position and rank, had my Regiment gone to Australia (where perhaps we may go now), and this war will have been merely an episode in my life in no way affecting my interests, a rough way tho' of spending one's time, and all gratis and for nothing! Altogether, the announcement of Peace in our orders, suited my temper; it was as follows – 'General orders No 1. Peace is concluded with Russia' – *voilà tout*!

I went to see Sir Colin [Campbell] yesterday with my General. He was, as he always is, most friendly and pleasant. He had just come back from a grand breakfast at Vinoy's (a French General), a great friend if his, and he seemed very full. While we were there, General Rose, our French Commissioner, called. He is a pleasant person, clever and amusing, but most effeminate in manner and appearance. The *malins* young French Staff call him Mlle. Rose, a good name.

---

[101] Dallas was 29 years old on this day.

My mother told me of Lady Pembroke's serious illness, poor old lady. She will be cheered by the news of peace, I hope: for tho' actually on her Brother's ground here we are no longer so as enemies (Guests, however, he will be glad enough to say Good bye to I think.)[102]

Letter 122

Camp at Sebastopol, 11 April

The French are going to have a Fête next week, consisting of races, and a 'Carousel' which is a sort of Batty's Circus, tilting and 'cur-vetting' about a ring. I went over to see the ground for a steeplechase and had a talk with a very pleasant Frenchman, Viscomte Talon, who was arranging it. He talks English! and when showing me a little stream that he was making into a water-jump, said 'She is small, but a nice jump, would you like to try her?' I happened to be on a capital Fencer, an English horse, and to please him, jumped 'her'. I suppose we make just the same sort of absurd mistakes in foreign languages, but I think our plan of genders certainly better than theirs. It always sounds so funny to me, if you ask a Frenchman, who some great hairy *Zouave* may be that you see standing about, to be told that 'she is a sentry', '*une Sentinelle*'.

Letter 123

Camp at Sebastopol, 16 April

General Luders gave a *Déjeuner* to our Chiefs a few days ago, & I went with mine [Garrett] there. It was a most beautiful spectacle. Luders came over the Traktir Bridge with an immense Staff and escort and met the Marechal [Pelissier] and Codrington and then we all went in a cavalcade to his Camp at the well known 'Mackenzie's Farm'. As we approached the heights, all the guns in their Batteries com-

---

[102] It is a curious fact that the lands around Sebastopol were owned by the uncle of a British Government minister. Lady Pembroke was the daughter of Count Worontzoff. Her brother owned the estates and the ground upon which the Crimean War was fought. Her son was Sidney Herbert, Secretary-at-War.

manding the approach thundered out a Salute, a specimen in blank powder of what would have met us had we attacked that point. The effect was very fine. Luders then gave us a Review of the troops that are left there, about 15,000, who marched past looking very well and soldierlike, and then there was a lunch, for the 'Swells' in a Marquee, and for the lesser fry A.D.C.s &c everywhere, with three or four good bands playing.

After lunch Luders escorted the Chiefs back to the foot of Mackenzie's Heights, and we all galloped along a plain about 3 miles of grass to the Traktir Bridge. The ride home was great fun, for Codrington and all the English being mounted on great English well-bred horses led our allies on their little 'chevaux de parade' a very weary time. Pelissier, as usual, was in his absurd old carriage, and looked like a highly *decoré* Butcher. He rode up the heights, and to my English eye, his ridiculous fat figure and so miserable a seat on his French horse formed a most charming contrast to Codrington, quite plainly dressed, on a thoroughbred English horse, looking a perfect Gentleman from his head to his boots. Luders is a good-looking stout man and rode in a green coat covered with gold and *assassiné* with orders, which he carried off better than our vulgar-looking ally.

Yesterday we went to a Fête the French gave, *Races à l'Anglaise*, and an absurd performance called a Carousel, which consisted of *Chasseurs d'Afrique* titupping about on little horses covered with ribbons. Luders was there & looked exceedingly weary of the Carousel which lasted about 2 hours. My friend Talon, I'm glad to say, won the steeplechase (the man who told me 'She was a nice little brook'), and very well he rode too.

Alexis Soyer is living up with our Division, and is great fun. He dined with us last night. He is a most pleasant amusing man, and great friends with my Chief [Garrett], with the power of whose stomach he is much struck. He has known and met such a variety of people, and tells his anecdotes so well, that he is capital company.

7th. Yesterday we had a most tremendous day of soldiering. Luders and Co. came over to see our two armies and began about 11 A.M. to ride down (with a most tremendous Staff of Russians and English – all our Generals and Staffs being there) the French lines. Their Army looked very well, but they had spread them out, so very palpably to increase their apparent numbers, that the effect was somewhat spoilt, tho' to the eyes of people not accustomed to see large bodies of men, their numbers would have appeared endless. We, and of course the Russians, could tell pretty well how many there were. They had about 30,000 bayonets (Infantry) & about 2000 Cavalry, and (we were rather surprised to find) 200 guns. They dragged out the affair to such a length that we could not get away until about 2.1/2 P.M. and then Luders and party came to our Head Quarters & lunched with Codrington. All his Staff, Russian A.D.C.s &c, lunched with us in an adjacent hut, and we made immense friends with them. They absorbed champagne wonderfully and we had to make violent promises to come and stop with them at Odessa where they hope soon to go, for they appear to be as sick of the Crimea as we are. We afterwards showed them our Army, when we showed them 35,000 Infantry in about a quarter of the time that the French took, as we had ours in dense masses, and they certainly looked magnificent. I think the Russes really were delighted. Our Artillery, about 100 Guns with wonderful horses, struck them much, and altogether I fancy our Allies, who evidently wanted to 'cut us out', defeated their own purpose, for they utterly wearied everybody with their long thin lines and the great intervals between their Battalions, whereas the Russians saw our men, incomparably finer in every way and more numerous, in about a quarter of the time, and with the great advantage of being full of our champagne instead of dust, which was most dense on the French ground.

Letter 124

Camp at Sebastopol, 25 April

We have been having a grand *Déjeuner* today entertaining a Russian General who has fraternized with my Chief [Garrett]. He came over today, and we entertained him. Fortunately Soyer is living with us and certainly cooked the most delightful breakfast '*à la fourchette*' I ever saw. His grand dish was a '*Macedoine Ludersienne à l'Alexandre*' & also a wild goose '*garni d'ortolans truffés*' and what with Champagne, Moselle, Hock, and Claret and the most enticing 'Cup' made especially for the occasion entitled '*Punch à la Marmora*'. We had a very lively

Déjeuner.[103] Afterwards the Russian General, Vasilefski [Veselitskii] by name, inspected various military details that he desired to see, and went away apparently delighted. He is a fine old man with one arm, and commands a *Corps d'Armée*, the only troops left on the North side, Luders having gone to Odessa.

Yesterday Codrington had out the whole of the Infantry and we performed a few manoeuvres. It was a fine sight, a Field Day with 30,000 men, but the numbers made any quick evolutions impossible.

Vasiliski's A.D.C.s are very civil youths. I took a long ride with one the other day and had very interesting conversation with him about the Siege, he having been in the Malakoff when it was taken. The Russian Officers (the swells) are very pleasant fellows, with the usual weaknesses of half civilized races, very lying and boasting absurdly.

Letter 125

Camp at Sebastopol, 28 April

As is always the case with the British Army, our country, having done with us, treats us like dogs. There is a general feeling among us of indignation: first of all, without any warning, or reward, or compensation, they suddenly place about 15 or 20 officers in each Corps on half pay, all young men. They will amount to about 800 young officers, who have all served out here, and they are all thrown on the world with all their prospects destroyed, as but few, and those only

---

[103] Soyer wrote,

General Garrett met with a very cordial reception from Major-General Vassilefsky, who commanded after the departure of General Luders. General Garrett, in return, invited him to the headquarters of the 4th Division, which invitation was graciously accepted by the Russian General. I was spending the evening with General Garrett, when he observed that he wished to give General Vassileffsky a lunch, but that it would a difficult matter, as he had no conveniences for that purpose.

"Never mind that, general" said I; "send out your invitations, and leave the rest to me. A lunch for twenty or thirty shall be upon your table in due time."

"They are coming tomorrow morning."

"Rather short notice, general; but never mind, it will be all right in spite of time: difficulties are common enough in time of war. Pray leave the matter to Major Dallas and myself – we will turn out a lunch worthy of yourself and your guests."

with interest, have any chance of getting back ever into the service. Next, an order came out a few days ago which will fall most heavily on us Staff, viz: 'that they will neither take home, nor give us compensation for our Chargers, and advising us to sell them to the Russians'! everybody knowing that the Russians (at least the few left here) will give next to nothing for horses & in case of anything happening to them such as 'Shot in Action', the Government price given in compensation is £45 for first, & £35 for 2nd chargers – the least anyone can do with is two – that would amount to £80. No one can buy Chargers for that amount, and one has to give whatever is the usual price & now, at the last moment, they tell us that they will neither take them home with us, nor give us anything for them. The consequence is that the average loss will be about £100 to every Staff Officer in the Army – isn't it a shame? Mine cost me £160, and unless I can sell them, of which I don't see any chance, or unless the order is rescinded, which from its gross injustice it may be perhaps, I shall lose it all, & other Staff officers the same. As to making money, that I never expected to do, but it is rather hard to have the good luck to be on the Staff, and positively lose by it.

I have made a final attempt to get my Brevet promotion, not that I expect it. I have written a letter about it 'earnestly recommended' by my Chief [Garrett], by Windham and the Commander-in-Chief [Codrington], and as it is no use leaving a stone unturned about a matter of such importance to me, I will ask you to see if you can get Mr Bruce to tell my tale to some of his friends in authority. He is the only person that I think might do. I will tell it as shortly as possible, & will get you or the kindest Mother to give it to him:

I have served from the first day of the Campaign in the Crimea till now. I have the Clasps for Alma, Inkermann, & Balaklava. I was the only Officer mentioned in Ld. Raglan's dispatch after Inkermann not promoted. I have been recommended for promotion by the late Sir John Campbell, by General Garrett, by General Windham & by Sir W. Codrington & was informed a few months ago that two captains Senior to me were not promoted. One, Captain Shervinton, has been promoted to a Majority in the Land Transport Corps since then, and the other, Captain Piper, has been in no engagement, has never been recommended by any General, and has been absent from his duty with his Regiment since August

1855. I served with my Regiment until the end of the Siege, & since, on General Garrett's Staff.

If it is not too much trouble just copy this story (as short as I can put it) & give it to Mr. Bruce, asking him to take it to General 'Anyone' at home. – It is not a bad case I think – I am not surprised at your thinking that the list of those out all the time might lead to something, but I happened to know the true story and am not disappointed. It was in consequence of a discussion at Head Quarters as to the numbers, & to settle the question, they called for a return of all this Great Army, the number of fighting officers (not Doctors or Quarter Masters) was a good deal under 100!! I, of course, was one.

If it were not for one's little private anxieties and troubles, the time would pass pleasantly enough here now. I see a good deal of my Russian friends, who are pleasant fellows. I was up at General Vassilefsky's the other day. It was the day after the (Greek Church) Careme and they were all very gay. They have one curious custom on that day, everyone meeting another says 'Christ has arisen' and you reply 'He is truly' and then they embrace on both cheeks. I thought it a rather touching custom, but the latter part of it to my English ideas, nasty. I was a good deal embraced, but was consoled by seeing the old General, who is a dear old man, solemnly kiss his coachman on both cheeks. I met there, a Prince (with a hopeless name), a very nice fellow, like an Englishman, on the General's Staff. He told me that he was so delighted at peace, as he could get away to his young wife and children whom he had not seen for three years. He, like many other Grandees, volunteered for the war, without being a regular soldier, & now goes home. He seemed very fond of the soldiers, who, having fasted for some time during Lent, were making up certainly for it, and told me they were '*braves gens*'. You should have seen them as I have, starving & never complaining. No one ever will know what they have suffered'. While I was there a Sardinian Soldier came to see him and seemed so delighted to speak to him, that I asked him his history. He said that during the war, he was going his rounds by night, with four Cossacks as escort, and came upon three Sardinians. The Cossacks were going to shoot them, but he would not let them. 'For', he said, quite simply, 'I thought of my wife and children, and that they too might have left wives and children at home', so they rushed upon them to take them prisoners. Two escaped and they caught the third man – whom I saw. I hope he'll tell his wife that story. I don't think she would like him any the worse for it. He is very ugly with long red hair and moustaches.

All our people go for excursions into the interior. I have not yet been, but the General talks of going soon. It is rather inconvenient not talking Turkish or Russian and not being able to say a single word. I heard a most absurd altercation at an Inn somewhere, between an Englishman and the Inn-keeper. The Englishman sat down to dinner and was brought a leg of mutton, which was very nasty, and he decided that it was dog, and not sheep. So when the man came in, he didn't at all know how to tell this, until a bright idea came across him. and he pointed to the joint and barked like a dog, which offended the Innkeeper dreadfully, and he talked violent Russian to him, but seeing that 'Ingleez' didn't understand a single word, he too pointed to the food and baa'd like a sheep – that was all they could say to each other, it must have been very funny.

Letter 126

Camp at Sebastopol, 4 May

I, in common with other Staff people, are in affliction about our horses, which we are told to sell! The Russians, who of course are the only people to buy them, offer prices varying from 7s. to £5 which will of course be a very great loss to us.[104] The weather here is fine, but the constant wind still keeps on and I shall be so delighted to escape from the brown hill on which I have spent so many months. 20 regiments are going to England, and I suppose you will have some great Military show. I am glad we are not one of them as many of them, (and of course we, if we went home) will have to go to some distant stations shortly.

---

[104] Dallas eventually managed to get free passage for his horses, which accompanied him home.

Letter 127

Camp Sebastopol, 18 May

The General [Garrett] had a bad fall off his horse a day or two ago, and fortunately escaped with severe bruises of both legs. His horse shied at something and then plunged and he was sitting carelessly on him and came on to his tail on very hard ground. I was much afraid that he was severely injured but he has luckily escaped with bruises. He can't move, however, yet from his bed and has suffered much pain. You can imagine the sort of Patient (if the word can at all be applied to him) that he makes! and beside being exceedingly sorry for him, and wishing him a speedy recovery for his own sake, I also hope he will soon be abroad again for all our sakes. He is a most extraordinary old man. Anybody else being kicked off a large horse onto a hard road, would probably never have got over it; as it is, he gets off with severe bruises of the muscles of both thighs, from which he has suffered much pain.

Tonight Soyer gives a grand dinner party at which I assist: Generals Barnard, Paulet and other noodles besides. Barnard has accepted Corfu and I think seems to like the appointment. I fancy by the way, that our Division will be the last to leave this country which, as it makes a difference, in all likelihood, of a week or two, does not so much signify.

The Russians are rapidly disappearing from the opposite side. The General Vassilefsky is gone, and sent a most charming little *cadeau* to my Chief: a case containing a knife, fork &c of enamel work (that I dare say you have seen on Russian snuff boxes), a most graceful pattern of black and white enamel on gold, exceedingly pretty and very Russian. My Chief had sent him an English mare and saddle as a present.

Letter 128

Sebastopol, 23 May

My Regiment went away on the 20th. for Corfu in the *Britannia*, a small Screw Steamer, and parting with them was very *triste*. The poor old Chief [Garrett], unable yet to move about except on crutches, had them up to our house to say Good bye to them, and made a little speech, which he did well as he always does when called upon to speak, and then they gave him three very hearty cheers. It was a *triste* scene altogether, and the old man was much cut up, I think at parting from so many old friends. Forde went with them, *en route* for England and the General and I are left alone. He is getting better but slowly and cannot get about yet. The 68th. are also gone. I had many friends among them and shall be delighted to meet them again at Corfu.

Lord Gough is expected out here to invest Pelissier and others with K.C.B.s. I cannot tell you how I admire the conduct of my Chief under treatment that makes me indignant. He never complains or lets anyone see how much he must feel at seeing men like Lord Rokeby and Barnard made K.C.B.s and himself still a Colonel! They have used him like a dog. He has done more service out here and better than any of them, (apart from older services), and they have used him and consulted him, and know him to be twice the soldier that Barnard and others are, and now seem likely to throw him aside. It really disgusts me to see Herbert, who a few months ago was a Captain in the Guards, who had only one opportunity of getting a name & then failed miserably; Windham I will say nothing against, tho' Pelissier when he heard he was made 'Chief of the Staff' briefly remarked, 'I should have tried him by Court Martial'; [sic.], a pleasant courtier who has never seen a shot fired; Rokeby & Barnard, both deaf and imbecile – all these men loaded with honours! I don't at all see when I am likely to get home, probably after everybody else, & a very dreary time I look forward to, but I couldn't leave my poor old General, tho' I somewhat envied Tom Forde.

Letter 129

Camp Sebastopol, 29 May

We had a wonderful *Soirée* a few nights ago at old Soyer's, about 40 of the *Crème* of the Army, 6 or 7 Generals, right good fellows too. A Glee Club of Guardsmen and others sang wonderfully well, and we had the most exquisite supper and passed a most joyous evening, or rather night, most of the company being intimates. Lord Rokeby proposed Alexis' health in a very cordial but not fluent speech, to which our host made a most capital reply in his funny English. Russell of the *Times*, who is a most amusing vulgar Irishman, was there and sang some very good Irish songs. As you may imagine, Soyer is a most popular man and gets on with everybody.[105] Someone introduced young Sefton to him the other night and he amused me much with a little speech to him entreating him to follow the steps of his ancestors who were always he said 'famous gourmets'.[106] He had a most successful dish that night, a Pasty '*à la Chasse du Renard*' which was a most glorious looking pie and when someone opened it, the dearest little tame fox was discovered sitting solemnly in the midst of it. I must add it came at the end of the supper. It says something for the viands, that I have met no one the worse the next day and I am sure we all ate to excess.

I am much afraid I shall not get home for some time, & expect to be among the last to leave this Country. My General [Garrett] I think will be left in command when the Head Quarters go, & finally I expect to place the General in a small boat & jump in myself having pushed the boat off, the last Englishman in the Crimea. The General by the way is getting better.

Letter 130

Sebastopol, 6 June (?)

You cannot conceive a more utterly desolate scene than a deserted Camp, and it is very sad riding past little huts where one has spent many a jolly hour, now empty & falling to pieces. Today, there is a great affair at Head Quarters: the Installation of the K.C.B.s &c by Lord Gough. I stayed at home having rather a stomach ache and also from taking no great delight in seeing Hall, Rokeby & Barnard made

---

[105] The party started at 9pm and according to Soyer, 'as the hour advanced, the company diminished; but at five in the morning there were still a few guests enquiring for their horses.' The guest-list included Windham, Rokeby, Lord William Paulet, Lord Alexander Russell, Lord Sefton and Barnard as well as many others, including Garrett and his staff.

[106] Lord Sefton was sitting down having a meal, which included 'a most relishing sauce', which Soyer tasted before exclaiming, 'Oh! Sefton! Sefton! May your noble ashes repose in peace in your tomb! The glory of your name has not faded: your grandson, the youthful Lord Sefton, is an epicure!'

K.C.B.s, and my old chief [Garrett] only a Spectator. However, as is often the case, one feels for one's friends on many occasions more than they do for themselves, & my General has gone off in his little trap to see the show quite cheerfully. The old gentleman is getting stronger on his legs & I hope will soon be able to ride again. Maxwell Earle dines with us always now, which is a great comfort for I find it hardish work living all alone with my sick General. I rather look forward to hearing how the installation has gone off, for dear old Lord Gough speaks nothing but the rankest Irish and has to make pretty French speeches to the French 'Knights'.

Two regiments of Guards have gone & the Fusiliers go tomorrow. We shall miss them dreadfully, for I and others spent much of our spare time playing cricket &c at their Camps, & they are with no exception & in every way, the pleasantest & best regiments in the Service. Lord Rokeby goes tomorrow. I met him at breakfast a day or two ago at the Commander-in-Chief's [Codrington], where we had, by the bye, the band that is playing today at Hd. Quarters. It consisted of all the Bands out here playing together under one master, & you cannot imagine anything so magnificent as 'God Save the Queen' played in the open air by 400 Performers, any slight discord there might have been being softened by the distance we were from them.

The only Individual that keeps us alive & merry at all now, is old Soyer, who constantly gives the most perfect little entertainments, either Breakfasts or Dinners.

Letter 131

Camp Sebastopol, 13 June

I am happy to say that there are some more ships in today & the Regiments are going away pretty fast. I shouldn't wonder if all the Army were away in a few weeks. We shall in all probability be the last. My General [Garrett] is able, I am happy to say, to ride a pony about, & will I trust soon be quite well again. Today a mail ought to have come but broke down somewhere. Of course it is a mail supposed to contain some interesting news & I was anxious to see if my Chief gets his promotion. For myself I expect nothing, & am so burned up by the constant hot wind & dust, that I only look forward to getting away. All the Guards are gone, & I expect soon that our Staff (4th. Division) will be sent down to Balaklava to look after the remnants of the Army, as we shall soon have no one up in the front.

Letter 132

Camp Sebastopol, 18 June

The dear old General [Garrett], wisely foreseeing that he & I alone would soon be found *asphyxié* with 'drear' on our Hill by ourselves, has just been over to Head Quarters, & has arranged that we are to go to live there for the remainder of our 'sojourn' (as the *Post* would call it) in this country, & in a day or two we move.

Lord Gough has gone away. He was great fun when here, & talked Irish with great fluency to 'Palliser', as he calls the Marshal. He brought out with him an old acquaintance of mine, J. Baillie of the Blues, & I should say they enjoyed themselves much.

Letter 133

Balaklava, 23 June

I saw in a paper, before I got your letter, my name in the Gazette, and I must thank you my dearest for all your pains & trouble on the subject. I did not much expect it as I was weary of expecting anything, so that it was a surprise. There are a great many names of friends &c which I was glad to read in the same list. One ought 'not to look a gift horse in the mouth', but between you and me, with a few exceptions, a more absurd list in the way of 'Services' I never read; one or two of my own friends whose names, tho', I rejoiced to see, among them. Maxwell Earle has done a great deal of duty very well & very constantly, & has never been away and has earned his honor well enough. I expected to see all the Generals' names in the Brevet, mine [Garrett] at the head, & I can't conceive why they are not. I have not the slightest doubt of my Chief's being made a General, but why they should insult a soldier of his standing as they do, I do not understand. However, it is our custom. Oh! if they would only believe in the truest of sayings, an old Latin one, 'Who gives quickly gives twice.'[107]

You will see by the date &c, that we have changed our home, & now we are at Balaklava, the few remaining troops being concentrated here and under my General, who came here yesterday. It is a most filthy place, but our house is a good one, with lofty cool rooms and overlooking the Harbour, with a charming verandah, in shade 3 parts of the day. It is very delightful having somebody to speak to, which we had not when in the front, & here our house is a general rendezvous. We have a boat too, and four boatmen who pull one about. I have the most delicious baths in the sea, & except when obliged to go out in the middle of the day, when the heat is perfectly awful, am comfortable enough.

The Commander-in-Chief has been calling here since I wrote & has told us some of the arrangements, viz: that Windham and the 'Head Quarters Staff' will probably go immediately, and that he (Codrington) will go as soon as his brother (Commanding some ship) arrives, and that my old man will be left in Command until everything is embarked and that a few Line of Battle Ships will wait to take away the remaining Regiments altogether.

Letter 134

Balaklava, 26 June

There is a Mail arrived at Kamiesch which will probably, when it comes here, bring me a letter from you or our Mother. As yet we have only a telegraphic message which brings notice of my General's [Garrett] appointment to command the troops at Gibraltar with the local rank of Major General. Fortunately, Gibraltar is the quarter of all others that he would choose, as he has been there, and is very fond of it. Otherwise, a Brigade anywhere with only local rank is a most shabby thing to give him, but as he is pleased, it is all right. I don't exactly see or know what I shall do, whether it will suit him to take me there or not. Of course, I should like it and its pay &c, but it would not break my heart if I did not go, as

---

[107] Publius Syrus (1st Century BC): *Bis dat qui cito dat.*

my Regiment is in so pleasant a quarter for me to join them in (this between ourselves).

We have a most pleasant house here, and my principal amusement is bathing and paddling in the jolly warm sea. Maxwell Earle is just come back from a most pleasant trip to Odessa where the whole party enjoyed themselves much and were most hospitably treated. I am so glad that he has got his promotion. He is one of the best hearted really good fellows alive. He is stopping on with us as 2nd A.D.C. for the time being, the Brigade to which he was attached being broken up.

It is an odd thing, by the bye, the Brevet in which I was, took in four of us who have always been most sworn allies: Maxwell, Blakeney (48th.), Oxenden (Rifles) and myself. We have fortunately on the Staff left here a most pleasant lot, all old friends, which makes it very jolly, most of them 4th. Division men.

We have some new pets at our present house, swallows. A couple of them are bringing up the most charming little family in the corner of the ceiling of the General's bed-room & they don't mind us in the least, but fly about the room catching flies & making themselves generally pleasant & dash in & out of the windows. Fortunately for them our cats have lost themselves somewhere, which I the less regret as they sat and glared at the poor little birdies in a very dreadful manner.

General Order No. 1 'The embarkation of all the stores of the Army, & the Railway is to be completed by the 7th. July '&c. Such was the order that came down to us a few minutes ago, I don't myself think it possible to be carried out, but if it is we shall start homewards then of course.

Letter 135

Balaklava, 10 July

I really think that at last, we are on the point of starting for home. We have got a ship, a fine one, the *Argo* who, by the way, was nearly drowned on her last trip by being run into by a French Man-of-War. And we embark our horses tomorrow, ourselves, they say, the next day – Saturday. I think probably Sunday. As far as Company goes, we shall be happy enough, but considerably crowded. We shall probably be the very last to leave this beloved shore. Only one of my *Harbinger* Shipmates goes with me, our Adjutant General Smith. We came out together and landed the first day of the Campaign in the Crimea, and shall go away the last, having not been away for a day. Sir W. Codrington is here and goes away on Saturday in his brother's Ship, the *Algiers*. We shall land, I suppose, at Spithead and I will write to you by any opportunity that may occur of your getting a letter before I arrive.

Letter 136

Malta, 22 July

We start from here today at 4 P.M. (in half an hour), and with ordinary good fortune, expect to be in England about the 5th. of next month. You must excuse this absurd little epistle, but the truth is I am only writing on the chance of your getting this before my own arrival. We have had as yet a goodish passage, but are rather crowded, 3 in a tiny cabin, the thermometer generally over 90. I will tell you all about our adventure &c I trust in a day or two after you get this. I shall have on my arrival to go to town for a day or two on business, (report my arrival &c.), & if you are not there will come down to you the moment I can get away.

Letter 137

The Dreary Ship '*Argo*', 5 August

I am writing these few lines to tell you that we are getting close to Portsmouth where we shall probably disembark some time tomorrow, and I purpose going as soon as I can straight up to town to put my horses in some stable and report myself at Head Quarters &c. I conclude you are not at No. 17, but will have left word about your present address, for tho' you told me whereabouts you were going, you didn't tell me the name of your house. Of course I shall come to you as soon as possible, probably Wednesday evening or Thursday. The only thing that prevents my at once coming down to you is the reporting myself to the Adjutant General, and the horses. We have had a fair slow passage & are all well. I hope to catch the eve mail at Portsmouth with this. Hoping in not many hours to find you both quite well and to kiss you many times.

Afterword

Fred Dallas arrived back in England on Monday 5 August 1856, almost two years to the day from the date he left. He left England an unblooded Lieutenant, he returned a veteran, a Brevet-Major and a General's ADC. Despite his cogently-expressed feelings about other officers obtaining decorations and rapid promotion through influence and high birth, he himself did not do too badly out of the war. In addition to his position on the staff as ADC to 'General Chaos' (the universal nickname for Garrett, which the loyal Dallas at no time even mentions), his Captaincy and Brevet-Majority, he was awarded not only the Crimea Medal with four clasps, and the Turkish Crimea Medal, but was also created a Knight of the Legion of Honour and a member of the Turkish Order of Mejedie.

Within a month of returning to England, he was once again back on foreign service as Garrett's ADC; this time in peaceful, luxurious Gibraltar. The contrast between Gibraltar in the winter of 1856–7 and the Crimea during the previous two winters must have been extreme.

But then came the Second China War, and the Indian Mutiny.

The Second China War, sometimes known as the Arrow War, after the *causus belli,* a nominally British *lorcha* subjected to Chinese harassment, would perhaps be better named the Oriental War of British Prestige. Effectively, Britain went to war with China on a point of supposed principle; the principle being that no foreigner had the right to interfere with the activities of a subject of Her Majesty, or indeed of anyone who claimed the right to British protection. The China of 1857 was very little different from the China of a thousand years before; in fact the rulers of the country saw no change worth noticing. The difference was there, however. Since the China War of 1842, British merchants and traders had been granted certain rights by treaty – and Britain, in the shape of Lord Elgin, was about to explain this, backed up by two brigades and a naval flotilla.

Garrett was appointed to command the First Brigade, and sailed for China, with his staff, in April of 1857, stopping at Malta where they met up temporarily with General Ashburnham, and reviewed 7,000 troops of the garrison. Passing India a few days before the

Mutiny broke out, they arrived in Hong Kong per the *Aden* on 24 May. Within the week Fred was in the thick of the fighting; the *London Gazette* records that he took part in the battle of Fatshan Creek, a naval engagement, as a volunteer on the gunboat *Haughty*.

The troops which Garrett was to command never got as far as China, Elgin having been requested on 3 June whilst at Singapore to divert them to India.

> Elgin does not seem to have hesitated. The 5th and 90th regiments, totalling about 1,700 men, had already reached Singapore and were despatched to Calcutta. Messages were sent to divert the further three regiments which were on the way from England. This last step proved unnecessary; in the event the Governor of the Cape Colony, Sir George Grey, diverted the troopships to India on his own responsibility. (Douglas Hurd, *The Arrow War*)

In fact the 5th Regiment did not arrive at Singapore until the 19th June, but was then immediately despatched to India.

The situation in India was desperate, and every officer and man was required there as soon as possible. It was clear that Garrett and his staff had no function in China, with no troops to command, nor any likelihood of any, and consequently Garrett was ordered to India, with the local rank of Major General, dated August 1857. Assuming six weeks for this order to reach him, he must have reacted almost instantaneously; he and his staff sailed for Calcutta on the steamer *Lancefield* on 19 September.

The exact date of arrival in India of Garrett and his party is not known, but it would have been sometime during late September 1857 (Dallas' Service Record states September 1858, which is clearly an error). At this time Sir Colin Campbell had been in Calcutta for the best part of two months, preparing his campaign against the Sepoys.

As one of the highest-ranking soldiers in India, it would have been expected that Garrett should have been given the command of a brigade at the very least, more likely a division. What he got was a garrison, Umballah, hundreds of miles from the fighting, and even this command was granted grudgingly, and after a great deal of time. It is not until February of 1858 that he and Fred Dallas are reported as heading for this station in the foothills of the Himalayas!

Garrett was not the only senior officer to be passed over for high command in India. Sir Colin Campbell explained in a letter to the Duke of Cambridge (Commander-in-Chief of the Army) that he had:

> selected the officers to command divisions with the greatest possible care, having found that an officer inexperienced in war in this country cannot act for himself, but must for a time be at the mercy of staff officers or gentlemen of the civil service who may be associated with him. Until a man has passed some time in India, it is quite impossible for him to be able to weigh the value of intelligence. In like manner he cannot judge what are the resources of the country, and he is totally unable to make an estimate for himself of the resistance the enemy opposed to him is likely to offer... I do not wish to undervalue the merits of general and other officers lately arrived ... but merely to indicate to your Royal Highness the difficulties against which they have to contend.

Campbell, it should be remembered, had soldiered extensively in India, most recently in 1852.

Clearly, Campbell had gained a particularly uncomplimentary opinion of Garrett in the Crimea, and wanted him out of the way. Windham, 'Redan' Windham, also a Major General, but a Crimean success, was given by Campbell what passed for a division in India at that time and ordered to defend Cawnpore, the lynch-pin of the entire district. Hindsight shows us that even the worst officer in the army could hardly have made greater errors than Windham at Cawnpore; Garrett, not an officer noted for his *élan*, would have been a much safer pair of hands than the vainglorious Windham.

An acquaintance of Fred's in the Crimea, the future Field Marshal Lord Wolseley, then a subaltern in the 90th Light Infantry, often observed that the way for a young officer to get on was to try to get himself killed. Fred showed his inclination to follow this maxim on at least two occasions; at Inkermann and again in Fatshan Creek, but being on the staff of a General who was posted as far away from the fighting as possible meant that he was unable to further his career in India. The qualification for the award of the Indian Mutiny medal was merely to have been under fire or to have borne arms against the rebel sepoys. Neither Garrett nor Dallas received the medal.

Fred remained on Garrett's staff in India after the end of the Mutiny — Garrett was not given a command in China for the finale of that war in 1860. In June of 1856 Fred had been promoted to the rank of Brevet-Major. Five years later he was still a Brevet-Major, had been on active service in a further two wars, and saw no signs of being promoted any further. For an active soldier like Fred, service in India in the shocked peace that followed the Mutiny must have been enervating in the extreme. In November of 1861 he returned to England, and took advantage of the Royal Warrant which allowed Brevet-Majors to exchange to a substantive Majority on half-pay. He also met and married the beautiful Maria Louisa Taylor, of the Taylors of Strensham Court.

Fred remained on half-pay for fourteen years, was promoted Lieutenant Colonel (Unattached) in 1868, and finally retired from the army by the sale of his commission in 1876, aged 49.

Fred's marriage prospered; he had three daughters and a son. (See Appendix for his descendants.) He died on 1 February 1888, aged 58.

Appendix – Known Descendants of George Frederick Dallas

Lt. Col. George Frederick Dallas, JP (1827–1888) m. Maria Louisa Taylor, da. of James Arthur Taylor, Esq., MP, of Strensham Court, Worcs. (she m. 2ndly Sir Herbert Edmund Frankland Lewis, Bart.), and had issue:

Fredericka Dallas who m. John Bertram Askew (1869–1930), and had issue:

    Felicity Katherine Sarah Askew (1899–19– –) who m. — Kourmoiaroff and had issue:

        Joan Kourmoiaroff-Askew (1933–)

        Robert Askew, who m. Helen – – –

Lucy Clara Dallas (1872–1955) who m. (1stly) Maj. Charles Edward Every-Clayton, JP, The King's Own (Royal Lancaster Regiment), (1857–1935) (who subsequently adopted the surname of Every-Halsted) and (2ndly) Thomas Fitzroy Phillipps Fenwick (1873–1956) and had issue by her first marriage:

    Evelyn Stella Every-Halsted (1893–1969), who m. Col. Arthur George Pardoe, RE (TF) (1885–1951) and had issue:

        Lt. Arthur Anthony Pardoe, RN (1916–1940, kia)

        Charles Evelyn Pardoe (1919–1919)

        Sarah Stella Pardoe (1920–) who m. Lt. Col. Edward Robert Guy Ripley, KSLI (1911–1944, kia) and has issue:

            Patience Anna Ripley (1944–) who m. Richard Michael Tudor Morgan (1935–) and has issue:

                David Paul Edward Morgan (1964–) who m. Anna Maureen Hodgson (196– –) and has issue:

                    Jessica Chelsea Morgan (1993–)

                    Imogen Rose (1995–)

                Charlotte Sarah Morgan (1965–) who m. Kevin Thomas Ingram (1962–) and has issue:

                    Rebecca Sarah Ingram (1988–)

                    Rachel Elizabeth Ingram (1990–)

                    Abigail Jayne Ingram (1993–)

                Timothy Michael Julian Morgan (1969–)

        Elizabeth Jane Pardoe (1921–) who m. Stanley Matthew Grafton Sprague (1923–1978) and has issue:

Susan Elizabeth Grafton Sprague (1954–)

Jonathan Charles Grafton Sprague (1957–1979)

Mary Ruth Every-Halsted (1898–1991) who m. (1stly) Capt. Gerald Hargreave Mawson, MC, RE, (TF) (1890–1964) (m. diss.) and (2ndly) Rev. Henry William Lancelot-Reed Haywood (1896–1957) and had issue by her first marriage:

Mary Patricia Hargreave Mawson (1920–1963) who m. James Surtees Phillpotts, MD (1912–1994) and had issue:

Ruth Phillpotts (1947–) who m. (1stly) James McEwan (m. diss) and (2ndly) John Burke (m. diss), and has issue by her first marriage:

    Gregor McEwan (1977–)

and by her second marriage:

    Claire Burke (1985–)

Midshipman Michael Gerald Hargreave Mawson, RN (1921–1941, kia)

John Arthur Hargreave Mawson, sometime Capt., Royal Signals, (1923–) who married (1stly) Wenona Brown (1924–) (m. diss.) and (2ndly) Lois Pinson (1921–), and has issue by his first marriage:

Simon Hargreave Mawson (1952–) who m. Ann Walker (1953–) and has an adopted son:

    Douglas John Hargreave Mawson (1996–)

Maj. Charles Edward Hargreave Mawson, R. Sigs., (1926–1994), who m. (1stly) Ann Mary Eastick (1928–) (m. diss.) and (2ndly) Iris May Duthie (1928–), sometime Flight Officer, PMRAFNS, and had issue by his first marriage:

Angela Mary Hargreave Mawson (1952–1952)

Susan Mary Hargreave Mawson (1953–) who m. Rory Anthony Rank Askew (1949–) and has issue:

    Henrietta Charlotte Askew (1980–)

    Georgina Anne Askew (1982–)

Rosemary Ann Hargreave Mawson (1954–) who m. (1stly) John Langley-Smith (m. diss) and (2ndly) Peter Jenkins and has issue by her first marriage:

    Elizabeth Langley-Smith (1982–)

    Peter Langley-Smith (1983–)

and by her second marriage:

    James Jenkins (1991–)

Phillipa Mary Jenkins (1992–)

and by his second marriage:

Michael Charles Hargreave Mawson (1967–) who m. Rachel Caroline Young (1962–) and has issue:

Charles Henry Frederick Hargreave Mawson (1996–)

Elizabeth Margaret Hargreave Mawson (1969–) who married David Charles Harrison (1962–)

Richard James Hargreave Mawson (1928–1936)

Alice Muriel Dallas, JP, (18– –1950) who m. Lt. Col. Percy Archer Clive, DSO, MP, JP, DL, Gren Gds (1873–1918, kia) and had issue:

Judith Clive (1905–1993) who m. Col. the Hon. Richard Glynne Lyttelton (1893–1977) and had issue:

Spencer Clive Lyttelton (1939–1996)

Thomas Glynne Lyttelton (1940–)

Maj. Meysey George Dallas Clive, Gren Gds (1907–1943, kia) who m. Lady Mary Katherine Pakenham (1907–) and had issue:

George Meysey Clive (1940–1999)

Alice Mary Clive, JP, DL (1942–) who m. Hon. Simon Donald Rupert Neville Lennox-Boyd, later 2nd Viscount Boyd of Merton (1939–) and has issue:

Hon. Charlotte Mary Lennox-Boyd (1963–), who m. Charles C.J. Mitchell, and has issue:

Gwendolen Charlotte Julia Mitchell (1994–)

Albert James Edward Mitchell (1996–)

Reginald Alexander Philip Mitchell (1998–)

Hon. Benjamin Alan Lennox-Boyd (1964–) who m. Sheila Mary Margaret Carroll (née Williams), and has issue:

Alan George Simon Lennox-Boyd (1993–)

Mary Alice Lennox-Boyd (1994–)

Henry Simon Lennox-Boyd (1997–)

Hon. Edward George Lennox-Boyd (1968–) (who subsequently adopted the surname of Clive) who m. Tamsin S. Hichens, and has issue:

Jago George Antony Clive (formerly Lennox-Boyd) (1997–)

William Enys Clive (formerly Lennox-Boyd) (1998–)

Hon. Philippa Patricia Lennox-Boyd (1970–) who m. Hon. Patrick Nathaniel George Spens (1968–), and has issue:

Patrick Lathallan Spens (2000–)

Lewis Clive (1910–1938, kia)

Virginia Clive (1913–1995), sometime Section Officer, WAAF, who m. Lt. Col. Henry Philip Hunloke, TD, JP, as his 2nd wife, and had issue:

Clare Hunloke (1947–1964)

Sarah Hunloke (1949–) who married Antonio Correa de Sa (1950–) and has issue:

Marta Correa de Sa (1978–)

Inez Correa de Sa (1979–)

Sophie Correa de Sa (1985–)

Caroline Henrietta Clive (1916–1996) who m. Maj. John Campbell Walker, TD, JP, Rifle Brigade (1914–), and has issue:

Amanda Christine Walker (1951–) who m. Robert James Willis (1950–) (m. diss), and subsequently had issue by Peregrine Michael Hungerford Pollen (1931–):

Joshua Michael Hungerford Pollen (1982–)

Alice Matilda Hungerford Pollen (1986–)

Alexander Lewis Walker (1952–) who m. Rosalind Anna Hayne (19– –) and has issue:

Jake John Walker (1993–)

Lily Caroline Walker (1995–)

Alexander Guy Walker (1999–)

Veryan Mary Walker (1954–) who m. John Stewart (19– –) (m. diss)

Simon Francis Clive Walker (1956–) who m. Elizabeth Susanna Purdey (19– –)

Herbert George Dallas (18– –1940) who m. Maud – – – and had issue:

Herbert Frederick Dallas, LCpl, 2/19th Battalion, Australian Imperial Force, (1910–1943, d. a POW)

Kenneth Dallas (1914–) who m. Phyllis – – – (1919–) and has issue:

Ivan Dallas (1935–)

Glossary

1st Lieutenant	Commissioned officer in the Royal Artillery, Royal Engineers or Royal Marines, senior to a *2nd Lieutenant*: the equivalent of a *Lieutenant* in the Infantry or Cavalry.
2nd Captain	Commissioned officer in the Royal Artillery or Royal Engineers, junior to a *Captain*, but senior to a *1st Lieutenant*; the equivalent of a *Captain* in the Cavalry or Infantry.
2nd Lieutenant	Most junior commissioned officer in the Royal Artillery, Royal Marines or Royal Engineers; equivalent to an *Ensign*.
Acting Assistant Surgeon	A junior medical officer holding a temporary commission for the duration of the war.
Adjutant	Appointment held by a junior commissioned officer in a regiment who was responsible for regimental discipline and administration. Frequently, but by no means invariably, Adjutants had been commissioned from the ranks.
Adjutant General (AG)	Staff appointment held by a senior commissioned officer, responsible for discipline and administration of an army.
Almacks	A famous, and extremely exclusive, gambling club in London in the Regency period.
Araba	A bullock cart.
Armament	A force equipped for war.
Armourer Sergeant	Non-commissioned officer responsible for the weapons of a regiment.
Assistant Adjutant General (AAG)	Staff appointment held by a commissioned officer in the Adjutant General's Department, junior to a *Deputy Adjutant General*, but senior to a *Deputy Assistant Adjutant General*.
Assistant Commissary General (AGC)	Commissioned rank in the Commissariat, equivalent to *Captain*.
Assistant Quartermaster General (AQG)	Staff appointment held by a commissioned officer in the Quartermaster General's Department, junior to a *Deputy Quartermaster General*, but senior to a *Deputy Assistant Quartermaster General*.
Assistant Surgeon	A junior medical officer holding a permanent commission.
Ball	Solid ammunition used in muskets, rifles and guns, not necessarily spherical.

Battalion	A unit of approximately 900 men. Actual strength could vary from as few as 700 in peacetime to as many as 1100 at full war strength.
Battery	A unit of artillery comprising two or more guns.
Bombardier	The most junior non-commissioned rank in the Artillery.
Brevet	Rank awarded for distinguished or meritorious service, increasing the recipient's seniority in the Army, but not in his regiment. cf. *Substantive Rank.*
Brigade	Sub-unit of a *Division*, typically comprised four or more *battalions*.
Brigade-Major/Major of Brigade	Staff appointment held by a commissioned officer, responsible for the administration of a *brigade*.
Brigadier General	Appointment held by an officer (usually a substantive *Colonel*) in command of a *Brigade*.
Brougham	A closed carriage pulled by a single horse.
Canister	A form of artillery shell made up of a thin case containing numerous steel balls which dispersed as the shell left the muzzle, giving a deadly, spreading fire similar to a modern shotgun but with much larger balls.
Captain	Rank of a commissioned officer junior to *Major*; *company*, troop or *battery* commander.
Case(-shot)	Equivalent to *canister*.
Clerk	Most junior commissioned rank in the Commissariat, equivalent to *Ensign*.
Colonel	Rank of a commissioned officer, junior to a *Major General*.
Colonel of a Regiment	Appointment held by senior *general officers*, of mainly ceremonial significance. Occasionally used, erroneously, to mean the *Lieutenant Colonel* commanding a regiment.
Colour Sergeant	A non-commissioned officer senior to a *Sergeant*, but junior to a *Sergeant Major*.
Commissary General (CG)	Most senior commissioned rank in the Commissariat, equivalent to a *Brigadier General*.
Company	A body of around 80–100 men under the command of a *Captain*. To 'get one's company' meant to be promoted from *Lieutenant* to *Captain*.
Cornet	Most junior commissioned rank in a Cavalry regiment, equivalent to *Ensign* and *2nd Lieutenant*.
Corporal	Non-commissioned officer, junior to a *Sergeant*.
Corps d'Armée	A unit of two or more *Divisions*.

Deputy Assistant Adjutant General (DAAG)	Staff appointment held by a commissioned officer in the Adjutant General's Department, junior to an *Assistant Adjutant General*.
Deputy Assistant Commissary General (DACG)	Commissioned rank in the Commissariat, equivalent to *Lieutenant*.
Deputy Assistant Quartermaster General (DAQG)	Staff appointment held by a commissioned officer in the Quartermaster General's Department, junior to an *Assistant Quartermaster General*.
Deputy Adjutant General (DAG)	Staff appointment held by a commissioned officer in the Adjutant General's Department, junior to an *Adjutant General*, and senior to an *Assistant Adjutant General*.
Deputy Commissary General (DCG)	Senior commissioned rank in the Commissariat, junior to a *Commissary General*, but senior to an *Assistant Commissary General*. Equivalent to *Major* (after three years' service in the rank, to a *Lieutenant Colonel*).
Deputy Quartermaster General (DQG)	Staff appointment held by a commissioned officer in the Quartermaster General's Department, junior to a *Quartermaster General*, and senior to an *Assistant Quartermaster General*.
Division	A unit of two (or, occasionally, three) *Brigades*.
Enfield	The British 1853-pattern rifle musket.
Ensign	Most junior commissioned rank in a guards or line infantry regiment.
Extinguisher	Conical device for snuffing candles.
Field Marshal	Most senior commissioned rank in the British Army.
General	A commissioned officer junior to a Field Marshal, but senior to a Lieutenant General; an army commander.
General officer	A commissioned officer with the rank of *Brigadier General* or higher.
Grape(-shot)	An artillery shell composed of steel balls held together by an internal frame. In flight the balls flew loose and thus dispersed with deadly effect.
Gunner	Private soldier in the artillery.
Gunner and Driver	Private soldier in the Artillery qualified to drive the horses pulling the guns.
Hospital Sergeant	A non-commissioned officer of a regiment, responsible, under the regimental *Surgeon*, for the regimental hospital.
Lancaster Gun	An experimental gun with an oval, twisting bore, designed to fire shells of oval cross-section which were thus spun, increasing range and accuracy.

Lieutenant	Commissioned rank junior to a *Captain* and senior to an *Ensign*.
Lieutenant Colonel	Commissioned rank junior to a *Colonel* and senior to a *Major*; commanding officer of a *regiment*.
Lieutenant General	Commissioned rank junior to a *General*, but senior to a *Major General*.
Local Rank	See *Temporary/Local Rank*.
Major	Commissioned rank junior to a *Lieutenant Colonel* and senior to a *Captain*.
Major General	Commissioned rank junior to a *Lieutenant General*, but senior to a *Colonel* holding the appointment of *Brigadier General*. A *general officer* commanding a *division*.
Marshal/Maréchal	Most senior commissioned rank in the French Army.
Minié	Any *rifle musket*, particularly those which worked on the Minié principle; the British 1851-pattern rifle musket.
Musket/musquet	Shoulder-arm with a smooth bore, inferior in performance to a *rifle/rifle musket*.
Orderly Room Clerk	Non-commissioned officer (usually a *Sergeant*) responsible, under the regimental *Adjutant*, for regimental administration.
Paymaster	Appointment held by a commissioned officer in a *regiment*, responsible for the administration of the pay of the *regiment*.
Paymaster Sergeant	Non-commissioned officer (usually, but not necessarily, a *Sergeant*) responsible, under the regimental *Paymaster*, for the administration of the pay of the *regiment*.
Picket/picquet	Small group of men standing sentry in advance of the front line. Their job was to raise the alarm in the case of an attack, by firing on the attackers. Whilst a picket was expected to delay an enemy attack, it was not expected to hold its ground, or drive the attack off.
Private	Most junior rank in the army.
Quartermaster	Appointment held by a junior commissioned officer in a *regiment*, responsible for regimental supplies. Frequently, Quartermasters had been commissioned from the ranks.
Quartermaster General (QMG)	Appointment held by a senior commissioned officer, responsible for the supplies of an army.
Recruit	Newly-enlisted *Private*.
Redoubt	Defensive work, usually made of heaped earth, specifically, one of a number of such works placed along the Causeway Heights by the British.

Regiment	In the British and French armies, a unit of one or two *battalions*; in the Russian and Turkish armies, a unit of three or four *battalions*.
Regimental Sergeant Major	Senior non-commissioned officer in an Infantry regiment.
Rifle/Rifle Musket	Shoulder-arm with a grooved ('rifled') barrel, superior in range and accuracy to a smoothbore *musket*.
Rifleman	*Private* soldier in a Rifle regiment.
Rococo	Old-fashioned and quaint.
Sapper	*Private* soldier in the Royal Sappers and Miners.
Sergeant	Non-commissioned officer junior to a *Colour Sergeant* and senior to a *Corporal*.
Shell	Hollow ammunition, containing an explosive charge.
Shot	Solid spherical ammunition used in artillery-pieces; a cannon-ball.
Spahi	A French Algerian cavalryman.
Subaltern	Commissioned officer junior to a *Captain*. Sometimes abbreviated to 'sub'.
Substantive Rank	Rank in the regiment.
Surgeon	Commissioned medical officer. Each regiment had a Surgeon (who may or may not have had any medical qualifications), and there were also Surgeons on the Medical Staff (outside of the regimental system).
Temporary/Local Rank	Rank applicable only in certain circumstances, for example 'whilst commanding a *brigade* in the Crimea'.
Troop Sergeant Major	Senior non-commissioned officer in a Cavalry regiment.
Trooper	*Private* soldier in a Cavalry regiment.
Vedette	A mounted sentry stationed to watch the enemy.
Welsh wig	Covering for the head made of wool.
Wing	Half a *battalion*.
Zouave	Soldier in a French light infantry regiment, originally recruited in Algeria, but by this time composed largely of Europeans.
Zumarra	A heavy overcoat.

Chronology*

1854

Mar	28	England and France declared war.
	30	Baltic fleet left Kiel.
Apr	14	Russians commenced Siege of Silistria.
	15	Convention between England, France and Turkey.
	18	Omar Pacha defeated Lüders near Rassova.
	20	Austria and Prussia, Convention of Neutrality.
	21	Odessa bombarded.
May	1	Allied armies advanced to Bosphorus.
	4	Turkish Fleet entered Black Sea.
	12	Loss of the *Tiger* off Odessa.
	28	Allies advanced to Varna.
	29	Desperate *sortie* at Silistria.
Jun	9	Russians advanced towards Kars.
	13	Allied fleets joined in the Baltic.
	22	Russians raised Siege of Silistria.
Jul	7	Turks gained Battle of Giurgevo.
	21	Fleets advanced to reconnoitre Crimea.
	28	Russians evacuated Wallachia.
	30	French army joined Baltic Fleet.
Aug	13–16	Siege of Bomarsund.
	20	Austrians entered Principalities.
	25	Expedition to Crimea announced.
Sep	4	Allies defeated at Pètropaulovsk.
	5	Allied armament began to leave Varna.
	14	Allies landed at Old Fort.
	15	Russians evacuated Moldavia.
	19	Cavalry skirmish at Bulganak.
	20	Battle of the Alma.
	23	Allies commenced flank march.
	23	Menchikoff sank Russian fleet.
	24	Menchikoff's flank march to Baktchèserai.
	24	British wounded began to reach Scutari.
	24	General Williams arrived at Kars.
	26	British took possession of Balaclava.
	29	Death of Marshal St. Arnand.
	30	Todleben began to fortify Sebastopol.
Oct	2	Siege army encamped before Sebastopol.
	12	*Times'* Sick and Wounded Fund established.
	13	Patriotic Fund established.
	17	First bombardment of Sebastopol commenced.

	23	Miss Nightingale departed to the East.
	25	Battle of Balaclava.
	26	First Battle of Inkermann.
Nov	5	Second (or Great) Battle of Inkermann.
	14	Destructive hurricane at Crimea.
	20	Contests at the 'Ovens', near Sebastopol.
Dec	2	Tripartite treaty against Russia.
	22	Sir E. Lyons succeded Admiral Dundas.
	24	Admiral Bruat succeded Admiral Hamelin.
	28	Memorandum on the 'Four Points'.

1855

Jan	26	Sardinia entered the Alliance.
	29	Sebastopol Committees appointed.
	31	Aberdeen Ministry resigned.
Feb	5	Palmerston Ministry formed.
	6	Warrant giving Commissions to Sergeants and Corporals.
	20	Night march in snow to Tchernaya.
	22	White Works constructed by Russians.
	24	French defeated at the White Works.
Mar	2	Tsar Nicholas died.
	15	Vienna Conferences commenced.
	22	Great *sortie* from Sebastopol.
Apr	4	Baltic fleet left Spithead.
	9	Second bombardment at Sebastopol.
	16	Black Sea telegraph completed.
	19	Rifle pits taken by Colonel Egerton.
	24	Sardinian army embarked at Genoa.
	26	Vienna Conferences closed.
May	1,2	French captured rifle pits.
	16	Pellissier succeeded Canrobert.
	22,23	Fierce contests near cemetery at Sebastopol.
	23	Expedition to Sea of Azof.
	25	Allies took Kertch and Yenikalé.
	25	Russian ships escaped from De Castries Bay.
	26	Allies entered Sea of Azof.
Jun	1	Allied fleets joined in Baltic.
	6	Third bombardment of Sebastopol.
	8	Mamelon, Quarries and White Works taken.
	17	Fourth bombardment of Sebastopol.
	18	Alies defeated at Malakoff and Redan.
	18	Sebastopol Committee issued report.
	28	Death of Lord Raglan.
Jul	26	Funeral of Lord Raglan.

Aug	9–11	Bombardment of Sweaborg.
	16	Battle of the Tchernaya.
	17	Fifth bombardment of Sebastopol.
Sep	5	Final bombardment commenced.
	9	Allies entered Sebastopol.
	29	Cavalry action near Eupatoria.
	29	General Williams defeated Mouravieff at Kars.
Oct	3	Omar Pacha landed at Soucoum-Kalé.
	17	Bombardment and capture of Kinburn.
Nov	6	Omar Pacha forced passage of the Ingour.
	10	Tsar Alexander visited Sebastopol.
	15	Terrible explosion of French magazine.
	21	Treaty of Sweaborg with Western Powers.
	25	Surrender of Kars.
	29	Nightingale Fund established.
Dec	8	Omar Pacha ended Mingrelian expedition.

1856

Jan	16	Russia accepted Bases of Negotiation.
	29	Sultan issued new Hatti-humayoon.
Feb	25	Plenipotentiaries meet at Paris.
	29	Armistice commenced in Crimea.
Mar	30	Treaty of Peace signed in Paris.
Apr	8	Discussion in Congress on state of Europe.
	15	Separate tripartite treaty signed.
	16	Paris Congress closed.
	16	Sardinian memorandum on Affairs of Italy.
	27	Treaty of Peace ratified in Paris.

---

*This Chronological Table has been adapted from Dodd's 'Chronological Table of the Chief Events During the War' (Dodd, 1856).

Bibliography

Books

Adkin, M., *The Charge*, Leo Cooper, 1996

Airlie, M., Countess of, *With the Guards We Shall Go*, Hodder and Stoughton, 1933

Adye, Lt. Col. J., *A Review of the Crimean War*, Hurst and Blackett, 1860

Adye, Gen. Sir J., *Recollections of a Military Life*, Smith, Elder and Co., 1895

Anderson, O., *A Liberal State at War*, Macmillan, 1967

Anglesey, Marquis of, *Little Hodge*, Leo Cooper, 1971

Anon., *A Month in the Camp Before Sebastopol by a non-combatant*, Longman, Brown and Green, 1855

Anon., *Memorials of Captain Hedley Vicars*, James Nisbet & Co., 1858

Anon., *Eminent Persons: Biographies Reprinted from the Times 1870–79*, The Times, 1880

Anon., *The Times Past Present and Future*, The Times, 1985

Archer, T., *William Ewart Gladstone and his Contemporaries,* (4 Vols), New Edition, Blackie and Son, 1885

Ball, T. F., *Queen Victoria, Her Life and Reign*, S.W. Partridge & Co., 1886

Barker, A.J., *The Vainglorious War*, Weidenfeld and Nicolson, 1970

Barnes, Maj. R.M., *A History of the Regiments & Uniforms of the British Army*, Sphere Books, 1972

Barthorp, Maj. M., *Heroes of the Crimea*, Blandford, 1991

Baumgart, W., *The Crimean War 1853–56*, Arnold, 1999

Bazancourt, The Baron de, (trans. R. Howe Gould), *The Crimean Expedition*, (2 Vols), Sampson, Low, Son & Co., 1856

Beauchamp Walker, General Sir. C.P., *Days of a Soldier's Life*, Chapman and Hall Ltd., 1894

Belfield, E., *The Queen's Dragoon Guards*, Leo Cooper, 1978

Benson, A.C. and Esher, Viscount, *The Letters of Queen Victoria, First Series 1837–1861* (3 Vols), John Murray, 1908

Bilcliffe, J., *Well Done the 68th*, Picton Publishing, 1995

Bonham-Carter, V. (ed.), *Surgeon in the Crimea, The Experiences of George Lawson Recorded in Letters to His Family, 1854–1855*, Constable, 1968

Boulger, D.C., *The Life of Gordon*, T. Fisher Unwin, 1896

Bowen, J., *The History and Battlefields of the Civil War*, Wellfleet Press, 1991

Brackenbury, G., *The Campaign in the Crimea*, (2 Vols), P& D Colnaghi, 1856

Burke, B., *Peerage and Baronetage*, various

Burke, B., *Landed Gentry*, various

Caldwell, G., and Cooper, R., *Rifle Green in the Crimea*, Bugle Horn Publications, 1994

Calthorpe, S.J.G., *Letters from Headquarters*, (2 Vols), John Murray, 1857

Campbell, C., *Letters from Camp to His Relatives During the Siege of Sebastopol*, Richard Bentley and Son, 1894

Cannon, R., *Historical Record of the Forty-Sixth, or The South Devonshire, Regiment of Foot*, Parker, Furnival and Parker, 1851

Carew, T., *The Royal Norfolk Regiment*, Leo Cooper, 1970

Carew, T., *How the Regiments got their Nicknames*, Leo Cooper, 1974

Chesney, K., *Crimean War Reader*, Frederick Muller, 1960

Clifford, Maj. H.H., VC, *Henry Clifford VC, His Letters and Sketches from the Crimea*, Michael Joseph, 1956

Clowes, Sir W. Laird, *The Royal Navy, A History*, (Vol VI), Sampson, Low, Marston and Company, 1901

Cockayne, G.E., *The Complete Peerage*, (12 Vols), 1910–59

Colborne, Capt. the Hon. J. and Brine, Capt. F., *Memorials of the Brave*, Second Edition, Ackermann and Co., 1858

Compton, P., *Colonel's Lady and Camp-Follower*, Robert Hale, 1970

Cooke, B., *The Grand Crimean Central Railway*, Second Edition, Cavalier House, 1997

Cope, Z., *Florence Nightingale and the Doctors*, Museum Press, 1958

Cox, M. and Lenton, J., *Crimean War Basics*, (2 Vols), Raider Books, 1988

Dallas, J., *A History of the Family of Dallas*, T. and A. Constable, 1921

Dallas, K., *The Cruel Wars – 100 Soldier's Songs from Agincourt to Ulster*, Wolfe, 1972

Dasent, A.I., *John Thadeus Delane*, (2 Vols), John Murray, 1908

Debrett, J., *Peerage*, various

Delafield, Maj. R., Mordecai, Major A. and McClellan, Capt. G.B., *Report of the Secretary of War*, (3 Vols), U.S. Senate, 1857, 1858, 1860

Dodd, G., *Pictorial History of the Russian War 1854–56*, Chambers, 1856

Douglas, G. and Ramsey, G.D. (eds), *The Panmure Papers*, (2 Vols), Hodder and Stoughton, 1928

Evelyn, G.P., *Diary of the Crimea*, Duckworth, 1954

Ewald, A.C., *The Rt. Hon. Benjamin Disraeli, Earl of Beaconsfield, KG, and His Times* (5 Vols), William Mackenzie, 1884

Falls, C. (ed.), *Great Military Battles*, Weidenfeld and Nicolson, 1964

Farwell, B., *For Queen and Country*, Allen Lane, 1981

Featherstone, D., *Weapons and Equipment of the Victorian Soldier*, Blandford, 1978

Fenwick, K. (ed.), *Voice from the Ranks*, Folio Society, 1954

Ffrench Blake, R.L.V., *The Crimean War*, Leo Cooper, 1971

Fitzgerald, Rear-Admiral C.C. P., *Life of Vice Admiral Sir George Tryon, KCB*, Blackwood, 1897

Forbes, A., *Camps, Quarters and Casual Places*, Macmillan, 1896

Fortescue, J.W., *History of the British Army* (Vol XIII), Macmillan, 1930

Fortescue, J.W., *The Royal Army Service Corps, A History of Transport and Supply in the British Army* (Vol I), Cambridge University Press, 1930

Gibbs, P., *Crimean Blunder*, Muller, 1960

Gibbs, P., *The Battle of the Alma*, Weidenfeld & Nicholson, 1963

Gibson, J., *Memoirs of the Brave*, London Stamp Exchange, 1989

Godman, R.T., (ed. P. Warner), *The Fields of War*, John Murray, 1977

Gordon, Maj. L.L., *British Orders and Awards*, W.H. Smith and Son, 1959

Grey, E., *The Noise of Drums and Trumpets*, Longman, 1971

Hake, A. Egmont, *The Story of Chinese Gordon*, Remington and Co., 1884

Hall, Capt. J., (ed. E. Tyson), *Letters from the Crimea*, Second Edition, King's Own Royal Regimental Museum Lancaster, 1993

Hallows, I.S., *Regiments and Corps of the British Army*, New Orchard Editions, 1994

Hamley, Lt. Col. E. Bruce, *The Story of the Campaign of Sebastopol*, Blackwood, 1855

Hamley, Gen. Sir E., *The War in the Crimea*, Seeley and Co., 1910

Harris, J., *The Gallant Six Hundred,* Hutchinson, 1973

Harris, S.M. *British Military Intelligence in the Crimean War*, Cass, 1999

Hart, Lt. Col. H.G., *Annual Army Lists*, various

Hayward, J.B. (ed.), *Casualty Roll for the Crimea*, J. B. Hayward & Son, 1976

Hibbert, C., *The Destruction of Lord Raglan,* Penguin, 1963

Hibbert, C., *The Great Mutiny India 1857*, The Viking Press, 1978

Hibbert, C., *The Illustrated London News Social History of Victorian Britain*, Angus and Robertson, 1975

Higginson, Gen. Sir G., *Seventy-One Years of a Guardsman's Life*, Smith, Elder and Co., 1916

Hume, D. and Cooke Stafford, W., *The History of England* (Vol IV), London Printing and Publishing Company, c. 1869

Hurd, D., *The Arrow War*, Macmillan, 1967

James, L., *Crimea, 1854–56,* Hayes Kennedy, 1981

Joslin, E.C., Litherland, A.R. and Simpkin, B.T., *British Battles and Medals,* Sixth Edition, Spink and Sons, 1988

Kelly, *Handbook to the titled, landed and official classes*, Kelly's Directories, various

Kelly, Mrs. T., *From the Fleet in the Fifties*, Hurst and Blackett, 1902

Kerr, P., et al., *The Crimean War,* Boxtree, 1997

Kinglake, A.W., *The Invasion of the Crimea*, (8 Vols), Blackwood, 1863–87

Lalumia, M.P., *Realism and Politics in Victorian Art of the Crimean War*, UMI Research Press, 1984

Lambert, A. and Badsey, S., *The War Correspondents: The Crimean War*, Alan Sutton, 1994

Lodge, E., *The Peerage of the British Empire,* Seventh Edition, Saunders and Otley, 1838

Loizillon, H., *La Campagne de Crimée*, Ernest Flammarion, c. 1891

Longford, Lady E., *Wellington, The Years of the Sword,* Weidenfeld and Nicholson, 1969

Lorne, Marquis of, *V.R.I. Her Life and Empire*, Harper and Brothers, 1901

Loy Smith, G., *A Victorian RSM*, Costello, 1987

Lummis, W.M. and Wynn, K.G., *Honour the Light Brigade*, Hayward, 1973

Lysons, Gen. Sir D., *The Crimean War from First to Last*, John Murray, 1895

MacMunn, Lt. Gen. Sir G., *The Crimea in Perspective*, G. Bell and Sons, 1935

Malleson, Col. G.B., *The Indian Mutiny of 1857*, Seeley and Co., 1892

Maurice, Maj. Gen. Sir F. and Arthur, Sir G., *The Life of Lord Wolseley*, William Heinemann, 1924

Maxwell, Sir H., *The Life of Wellington, The Restoration of the Martial Power of Great Britain* (2 Vols), Third Edition, Sampson, Low, Marston and Company, 1900

McCormick, R.C., *A Visit to the Camp before Sebastopol*, D. Appleton and Co., New York, 1855

Mercer, P., *Inkermann, 1854*, Osprey, 1998

Mercer, P., *'Give them a Volley and Charge!'*, Spellmount, 1998

Montgomery, J., *Florence Nightingale*, Heron Books, 1970

Mullen, A.L.T., *The Military General Service Roll 1793–1814*, The London Stamp Exchange, 1990

Myatt, F., *The Soldier's Trade*, Macdonald and Jane's, 1974

Napier, Gen. Sir W., *History of the War in the Peninsula* (6 Vols), various, 1828–40

Newman, Sgt. G., (ed. D. Inglesant), *The Prisoners of Voronesh*, Unwin, 1977

North, R., *Military Uniforms*, Hamlyn, c. 1975

Ouchterlony, J., *The Chinese War*, Saunders and Otley, 1844

Pack, Col. R., *Sebastopol Trenches*, Kerby and Endean, 1878

Paget, G.A.F., *The Light Cavalry Brigade in the Crimea, Letters and Journals of Lord George Paget*, 1881

Palmer, A., *The Banner of Battle*, Weidenfeld and Nicolson, 1987

Patrick, D. and Groome, F.H. (eds), *Biographical Dictionary*, Chamber's, 1897

Pearse, Maj. H. (ed.), *'Redan Windham': The Crimean Diary and Letters of Lt. Gen. Sir Charles Ash Windham, KCB*, Kegan Paul, Trench, Trubner and Co., 1897

Pemberton, W.B., *Battles of the Crimean War*, Batsford, 1962

Pownall, Mrs. F. (ed.), *At Home and on the Battlefield, Letters from the Crimea, China and Egypt 1854–1888 by Sir Frederick Charles Arthur Stephenson GCB*, John Murray, 1915

Ramsay, B.D.W., *Rough Recollections of Military Service and Society* (2 Vols), Blackwood, 1882

Rich, N., *The Age of Nationalism and Reform, 1850–1890,* Second Edition, W.W. Norton and Company Inc., 1977

Ridley, J., *Lord Palmerston*, Constable, 1970

Roads, C.H., *The British Soldier's Firearm, 1850–1864*, Herbert Jenkins Ltd., 1964

Robins, Maj. C. (ed.), *The Murder of a Regiment*, Withycut House, 1994

Royle, T., *War Report*, Mainstream, 1987

Royle, T., *Crimea*, Little Brown, 1999

Russell, W.H., *The War*, (2 Vols), George Routledge and Co., 1855, 1856

Russell, W.H., *My Diary in India*, Routledge, Warne and Routledge, 1860

Ryan, G., *Our Heroes of the Crimea*, Routledge, 1855

Seaton, A., *The Crimean War: A Russian Chronicle*, Batsford, 1977

Selby, J., *The Thin Red Line of Balaklava*, Hamish Hamilton, 1970

Sewell, A., *Medals for the Crimea Campaign of 1854–56 awarded to the 46th (South Devon) Foot*, privately published, 1995

Sewell A. and McGuigan, R., *Senior Commanders in the Crimea*, privately published, 1995

Shadwell, Lt. Gen. L., *Life of Colin Campbell, Lord Clyde*, Blackwood, 1881

Slade, Admiral Sir A., *Turkey and the Crimean War*, Smith, Elder and Co., 1858

Small, E. Milton, *Told From the Ranks*, Andrew Melrose, 1897

Smith, K.W., *Constantin Guys*, Cleveland Museum of Art (US), 1978

Smyth, Lt. B., *History of the XX Regiment 1688–1888*, Simpkin, Marshall & Co., 1889

Soyer, A., *A Culinary Campaign*, Southover Press, 1995

Stephenson, Sir F.C.A., *At Home and on the Battlefield*, John Murray, 1915

Sterling, Lt. Col. A., *The Highland Brigade in the Crimea,* Absinthe Press (US), 1995

Stuart, B. (ed.), *Soldier's Glory*, G. Bell & Sons Ltd, 1956

Sweetman, J., *War and Administration,* Scottish Academic Press, 1984

Sweetman, J., *Raglan, From the Peninsula to the Crimea*, Arms and Armour Press, 1993

Temperley, H.W.V., *England and the Near East, The Crimea*, Longman, Green and Co., 1936

Thomas, D., *Charge! Hurrah! Hurrah! A Life of Cardigan of Balaklava*, Routledge and Kegan Paul, 1974

Thorburn, W.A., *French Army Regiments and Uniforms*, Arms and Armour Press, 1969

Thorne, J.O. and Collocott, T.C. (eds), *Biographical Dictionary*, Chambers, 1984

Tisdall, E.E.P., *Mrs. Duberly's Campaigns*, Jarrolds, 1963

Todleben, Gen. F. E. I., *Défense de Sébastopol*, 1863–70 (believed to be an official Russian Government publication.)

Tooley, S., *The Life of Florence Nightingale*, S.H. Bousfield & Co., 1904

Tyrrell, H., *The History of the War with Russia* (6 Vols), London Printing and Publishing Company, c. 1856

Vieth, F.H., *Recollections of the Crimean Campaign*, privately published in Montreal, 1907

Vulliamy, C.E., *Crimea, The Campaign of 1854–56*, Jonathan Cape, 1939

Walford, E., *County Families of the United Kingdom*, Spottiswoode, Ballantyne & Co., various

Ward, S.G.P. (ed.), *The Hawley Letters*, SAHR, 1970

Warner, P., *The Crimean War: A Reappraisal*, Barker, 1972

Welch, R.C., *The Harrow School Register, 1801–1893*, Longmans, Green and Co., 1894

Whitwell Wilson, P. (ed.), *The Greville Diary*, (2 Vols), Heinemann, 1927

Whyte, F. and Atteridge, A.H., *A History of the Queen's Bays (2nd Dragoon Guards) 1685–1929*, Cape, 1930

Wilkinson, F., *Small Arms*, Ward Lock, 1965

Wood, Gen. Sir E., *The Crimea in 1854 and 1894*, Chapman and Hall, Ltd., 1895

Wood, Field Marshal Sir E., *From Midshipman to Field Marshal,* (2 Vols), Methuen, 1906

Woodham Smith, C., *Florence Nightingale*, Constable & Co., 1950

Woodham Smith, C., *The Reason Why*, Constable & Co., 1953

Woodham Smith, C., *Queen Victoria, Her Life and Times*, Hamish Hamilton, 1972

Woodward, Sir L., *The Age of Reform 1815–1870,* Second Edition, Oxford University Press, 1962

Periodicals

Bedford Times
Cassell's Illustrated Family Paper
Illustrated London News
Illustrated Times
London Gazette
New Calcutta Directory
Punch
The Times
War Correspondent (Journal of the Crimean War Research Society)

Unpublished Manuscript Sources

Anon., *Historical Records of the Queen's Bays*, 1st Queen's Dragoon Guards Regimental Museum, 1834–58
Curtis, Lt. F., *Letters,* National Army Museum (NAM) 8307-48, 1854–55
Dunscombe, Capt., *Private Journal*, DoCLI Museum, 1854–56
Earle, Capt. A.M., *Letters*, NAM 9403-153, 1854–57
Long, Adj. Gen., *Papers*, NAM 6807-219-1, 1809

Papers at the Oriental and India Office Collection

British General Orders by the Commander in Chief 1857, L/MIL/17/2/306
British General Orders by the Commander in Chief 1858 (2 Vols), L/MIL/17/2/307
British General Orders by the Commander in Chief 1859, L/MIL/17/2/308
Officers of British Army Regiments in India 1857-65, L/MIL/15/3

Papers at the Public Record Office, Kew

Various documents in the WO12, WO25, WO76, WO97 and WO100 series.

Selected Internet Resources

British Regiments Mailing list – BritRegiments@egroups.com
Crimean War Mailing list – CrimeanWar@egroups.com
Crimean War Research Society Web site – *http://www.crimeanwar.org*

Index of those Mentioned in the Letters

The numbers **in bold** at the end of each entry refer to the numbers of the Letters. An 'f' suffix denotes that the reference is to be found in a footnote.

Guide to Post-nominals
CB = Commander of the Most Honourable Order of the Bath; **CIE** = Commander of the Most Eminent Order of the Indian Empire; **CSI** = Commander of the Most Exalted Order of the Star of India; **DCL** = Doctor of Civil Law; **FRS** = Fellow of the Royal Society; **FSA** = Fellow of the Society of Antiquaries; **GCB** = Knight Grand Cross of the Most Honourable Order of the Bath; **GCMG** = Knight Grand Cross of the Most Distinguished Order of St. Michael and St. George; **GCSI** = Knight Grand Commander of the Most Exalted Order of the Star of India; **KB** = Knight Bachelor; **KCB** = Knight Commander of the Most Honourable Order of the Bath; **KCH** = Knight Commander of the Royal Guelphic Order; **KCMG** = Knight Commander of the Most Distinguished Order of St. Michael and St. George; **KCSI** = Knight Commander of the Most Exalted Order of the Star of India; **KG** = Knight of the Most Noble Order of the Garter; **KH** = Knight of the Royal Guelphic Order; **KP** = Knight of the Most Illustrious Order of St. Patrick; **KT** = Knight of the Most Ancient and Most Noble Order of the Thistle; **LLD** = Doctor of Law; **MA** = Master of Arts; **MD** = Doctor of Medicine; **MGS** (medal) = Military General Service (medal); **OM** = Order of Merit; **PC** = Privy Councillor; **RA** = Royal Artillery; **RE** = Royal Engineers; **RN** = Royal Navy; **VC** = Victoria Cross

Aberdare, Lord [Mr Bruce in the Letters]
Henry Austin Bruce, P.C., G.C.B., D.C.L., 1st Baron Aberdare; born at Duffryn, Glamorganshire on the 16th Apr. 1815; Home Secretary 1868–73, Lord President of the Council 1873–74. A close friend of both the Dallas and Napier families, he married one of Sir William's daughters. He died 25th Feb. 1895. **125**

Aberdeen, Earl of
George Hamilton Gordon, K.G., K.T., M.A., F.R.S., F.H.S., F.S.A., 4th Earl of Aberdeen, Viscount Formartine; Lord Haddo, Methlic, Tarves and Kellie, Viscount Gordon of Aberdeen; born on the 28th Jan. 1784, succeeded his grandfather as 4th Earl, 13th Aug. 1801. Ambassador to Vienna, 1813–14; Foreign Secretary 1828–30 and 1841–46. Prime Minister, 1852–55. He died in London, on the 13th Dec. 1860. **35f**

Agar, Capt. The Hon. C. W. Herbert, 44th Regiment
Ens, 30th Mar. 1844; Lt., 27th Feb. 1846; Capt., 25th Mar. 1853. Killed in the assault on the Redan, 18th Jun. 1855. **59**

Airey, Gen. Sir Richard, K.C.B.
Ens., 15th Mar. 1821; Lt., 4th Dec. 1823; Capt., 22nd Oct. 1825; Maj., 9th May,

1834; Lt. Col., 10th Feb. 1838; Col., 11th Nov. 1851; Maj. Gen., 12th Dec. 1854. Served throughout the Crimean War, as Quarter Master General of the Army of the East. He was present at the battles of Alma, Balaklava and Inkermann, and at the Siege and Fall of Sebastopol (Medal and clasps, K.C.B., Commander of the Legion of Honour, Commander 1st Class of the Military Order of Savoy and 2nd Class of the Mejedie). **70, 84, 89, 91, 115**

Alexander II, Czar of All the Russias
Born 29th Apr. 1818; succeeded to the throne 2nd Mar. 1855, and continued vigorously to prosecute the war. In 1856 he agreed to a negotiated peace, which virtually returned Russia to the *status quo ante*, and did nothing to protect Turkey. Despite his passion for all things military, his greatest achievement was the emancipation of the serfs in 1861. He was assassinated 13th Mar. 1881. **91, 99f, 107**

Allonville, Armand Octave Marie d', General of Division
General of Brigade, *Chasseurs d'Afrique*, Mar. 1854; General of Division, May, 1855. Elements of his Brigade were in action at Balaklava, and were responsible for considerably reducing the casualties suffered by the British Light Brigade. In Sep. 1855 he was transferred to Eupatoria with three of his regiments where he remained to the end of the war in command of the French, Turkish and (briefly) British troops. **81f, 82**

Autemarre d'Erville, Charles Francois Xavier d', General of Division
General D'Autemarre d'Erville was appointed General of Brigade, 3rd Jan., 1852. He was assigned to command the 1st Brigade of the 2nd Division of the Army of the Orient in Mar. 1854. Promoted in Mar. 1855, he was assigned to command the 1st Division of the 1st Corps of the army during the remainder of the Siege of Sebastopol. Served at Alma and Inkermann, and at the siege and fall of Sebastopol. **81, 82**

Baillie, Maj. Gen. Duncan James, Royal Horse Guards
Cornet, 28th Feb. 1845; Lt., 28th Sep. 1847; Capt., 21st Apr. 1854; Maj. and Bt. Lt. Col., 5th Jun. 1866; Lt. Col. Commanding the Regiment, 7th Dec. 1866; Col., 5th Jun. 1871; Maj. Gen., 9th Mar. 1882. Baillie never saw any active service; his visit to the Crimea in 1856 was the closest he came. **132**

Barker, Lt. Frederick Grote, 68th Regiment
Born 1834; Ens., 12th Dec. 1851; Lt., 17th Mar. 1854; killed in action at Inkermann, 5th Nov. 1854. **12**

Barlow, Lt. Gen. Maurice, C.B.
Ens., 21st Jul. 1814; Lt., 23rd Mar. 1815; Capt., 20th Dec. 1821; Maj., 12th Jun. 1828; Brevet Lt. Col., 23rd Nov. 1841; Lt. Col., 24th Dec. 1847; Col., 20th Jun. 1854; Brig. Gen., 30th Jul. 1855; Maj. Gen., 26th Oct. 1858; Lt. Gen., 24th Apr. 1866; Col., 14th Regiment of Foot, 9th Aug. 1870. Served as a general in the trenches during the Siege of Sebastopol, and commanded a brigade in the 4th Division at its fall. He was awarded the C.B.; the Crimea medal with clasp for

Sebastopol; the Sardinian *Al Valore Militare*; the Legion of Honour (5th Class); the Turkish Order of the Mejedie (3rd Class) and the Turkish medal. 69

Barnard, Lt. Gen. Henry William, C.B.
Ens., 9th Jun. 1814; Capt., 15th Aug. 1822; Lt. Col., 17th May, 1831; Col., 9th Nov. 1846; Maj. Gen., 20th Jun. 1854; Local Lt. Gen., 30th Jul. 1855. Served in the Crimea initially as a Brigade commander, and then as commander of the Second Division. He was awarded the C.B.; the Crimea medal with one clasp and the Turkish Crimea Medal. 26, 29, 70, 73, 84, 91, 97, 98, 101, 104, 127, 128, 130

Bell, Maj. Gen. Edward William Deddington, V.C., C.B.
Born, 18th May, 1824; 2nd Lt., 15th Apr. 1842; Lt., 17th Nov. 1843; Capt., 18th Dec. 1848; Bt. Maj., 12th Dec. 1854; Maj., 23rd Mar. 1855; Brevet Lt. Col., 26th Dec. 1856; Lt. Col., 8th Jan. 1858; Col., 17th May, 1862; later Maj. Gen.. Bell served in the Crimea from the first landing, including the battles of Alma and Inkermann, and the siege of Sebastopol. He was awarded the Victoria Cross for his actions at Alma. He also received the C.B., the Crimea medal with three clasps, the Legion of Honour (5th Class); the Order of the Mejedie (5th Class) and the Turkish Medal. He later served in India during the mutiny, receiving the Mutiny Medal with clasp for Lucknow. Bell died in Belfast on 10 November 1879. 7

Bentinck, General Sir Henry John William, K.C.B.
Ens., 25th Mar. 1813; Lt. & Capt., 18th Jan. 1820; Capt. & Lt. Col., 16th May, 1829; Col., 23rd Nov. 1841; Maj. Gen., 20th Jun. 1854; Col., 28th Regiment, 11th Oct. 1854; Lt. Gen., 24th Apr. 1860; General, 8th Dec. 1867. Commanded the Guards Brigade during the Crimean War, until 8th Nov. 1854, including the battles of Alma, Balaklava and Inkermann (wounded in the arm), siege of Sebastopol; commanded Fourth Division Jun.–Oct. 1855. Sir Henry was awarded the K.C.B.; the Crimea medal with four clasps; the Legion of Honour (3rd Class); the *Al Valore Militare*; the Order of the Mejedie (2nd Class), and the Turkish medal. 47, 54, 58, 63, 71

Blackwood, Capt. Sir Francis, RN, 4th Bart.
Born 11th Nov. 1838, entered the Royal Navy in 1850; succeeded to the title on the death of his brother in 1854; became Commander 1869; Capt. (retired), 1886. Sir Francis served in the Crimea, and was awarded the Crimea medal with two clasps, and the Turkish medal. He died in 1924. 10

Blakeney, Brevet Maj. Robert, 48th Regiment
Ens., 3rd Nov. 1846; Lt., 10th Sep. 1847; Capt., 2nd Apr. 1852; Bt. Maj. 6th Jun. 1856; Maj., 24th Sep. 1858. Maj. Blakeney served in the Crimea from 2nd Jun. 1855, at the siege and fall of Sebastopol, and on detached duty in the Dockyard from 14th Jan. to 14th Mar. 1856. He was awarded the Crimea medal with clasp for Sebastopol and the Turkish medal. 134

Blake, Col. Frederick Rodolph, C.B., 33rd Regiment
Ens., 30th Jun. 1825; Lt., 14th Aug. 1827; Capt., 23rd Aug. 1831; Maj., 14th Apr.

1843; Lt. Col., 3rd Oct. 1848; Col., 28th Nov. 1854. Col. Blake commanded the 33rd in the Crimea from the landing until being wounded in the assault on the Redan on the 18th Jun. 1855. He was invalided home and died of his wounds the following August. 10

Blane, Col. Robert, C.B., Unattached
Ens., 1st Nov. 1831; Lt., 25th Mar. 1836; Capt., 8th Jun. 1838; Maj., 11th Nov. 1851; Lt. Col., 12th Dec. 1854; Col., 11th Apr. 1860. Col. Blane served in the Crimea as Assistant Adjutant-General, and subsequently as Military Secretary, including the battles of Alma, Balaklava and Inkermann, and the siege and fall of Sebastopol. He was awarded the C.B.; the Crimea medal with four clasps; the Legion of Honour (5th Class); the Order of St. Maurice and St. Lazarus (Commander 2nd Class); the Order of the Mejedie (5th Class) and the Turkish medal. 112, 118

Bosquet, Maréchal Pierre Joseph François
Born 10th Nov. 1810, Bosquet saw service in Algeria from 1834, rising rapidly to the rank of General of Division, 10th Aug. 1853. With the outbreak of war Bosquet was assigned to command the 2nd Division of the Army of the Orient, and gave valuable service at the battle of the Alma. In October he was placed in command of the Corps of Observation, which he commanded until the cessation of hostilities, including at the battle of Inkermann. He was wounded in the assault of the 8th Sep. and left the Crimea on Oct. 17, 1855. His Crimean services were rewarded by Napoleon III with the baton of a Maréchal of France. He died on the 4th Feb. 1861. 26, 29, 32, 47

Brooks, 1901 Cpl. William, 46th Regiment
William Brooks, a labourer, enlisted in the 46th Regiment on 13th Jan. 1844. He sailed for the Crimea with the main body of the regiment, and landed at Balaklava on the 8th Nov. 1854. He died of cholera on 25th Nov. 1854, and was posthumously awarded the Crimea medal with clasp for Sebastopol. 24

Brown, Gen. Sir George, G.C.B., K.H.
Born, 1790; Ens., 23rd Jan. 1806; Lt., 18th Sep. 1806; Capt., 20th Jun. 1811; Maj., 26th May, 1814; Lt. Col., 29th Sep. 1814; Col., 6th May, 1831; Maj. Gen., 23rd Nov. 1841; Lt. Gen., 11th Nov. 1851; Col. Commandant, Rifle Brigade, 18th Jan. 1855; General, 7th Sep. 1855. Sir George served at the siege and capture of Copenhagen in 1807, in the Peninsula from Aug. 1808 to Jul. 1811; and again from Jul. 1813, to May, 1814 (twice wounded). Served afterwards in the American War (twice wounded). He commanded the Light Division during the Crimean War, including the battles of the Alma (horse shot under him) Balaklava and Inkermann (severely wounded – shot through the arm), and siege of Sebastopol. He received the G.C.B., the MGS Medal with seven clasps; the Crimea medal with four clasps, the Grand Cross of the Legion of Honour, the Order of the Mejedie (1st Class), the *Al Valore Militare* and the Turkish medal for these services. Sir George was a famous martinet, with a deep hatred of informal dress. He died in 1865. 37, 41, 59, 60, 61

Crimea medal. He was appointed Commander in Chief of the British Army in 1856, oversaw the radical 'Cardwell' reforms of the 1870s and 1880s, relinquished the position in 1895 and died in 1904. 40

Cameron, Gen. Duncan Alexander, G.C.B.
Ens., 8th Apr. 1825; Lt., 15th Aug. 1826; Capt., 21st Jun. 1833; Maj., 23rd Aug. 1839; Lt. Col., 5th Sep. 1843; Col., 20th Jun. 1854; Maj. Gen., 25th Mar. 1859; Col., 42nd Regiment, 9th Sep. 1863; Lt. Gen., 1st Jan. 1868; General, 5th Dec. 1874. Sir Duncan commanded the 42nd Regiment at the battle of the Alma, and the Highland Brigade at the battle of Balaklava, on the expedition to Kertch, siege and fall of Sebastopol and the assault on the 18th June; he commanded the forces in New Zealand during the War of 1863–65 and was governor of the Royal Military College from 1868 to 1875. He was awarded the Crimea medal with three clasps, the New Zealand Medal, the Legion of Honour (4th Class), the Order of the Mejedie (3rd Class); the *Al Valore Militare* and the Turkish Crimea medal. 115

Campbell, Brevet Col. Colin Frederick, 46th Regiment
Born 3rd Mar. 1824; Ens., 1st May 1840; Lt., 10th Mar. 1842; Adjutant, 46th Regiment, 22nd Feb. 1847 to 12th Aug. 1847; Capt., 13th Aug. 1847; Maj, 11th May 1855; Acting Assistant-Engineer, May 1855 to 24th Sep. 1855; Brevet Lt. Col., 2nd Nov. 1855; Brevet Col., 23rd Jan. 1863. Col. Campbell landed in the Crimea with the main body of the 46th Regiment on 8th Nov. 1854; was wounded slightly in 1855 whilst serving as Acting Assistant-Engineer in the trenches. He was awarded the Crimea Medal with clasp for Sebastopol; the Legion of Honour (5th Class); the Order of the Mejedie (5th Class); the *Al Valore Militare* and the Turkish Crimea medal. He died in India on 14th Sep. 1868. 12f, 17, 20, 26, 57, 68, 75, 77, 79, 81, 82, 92, 97

Campbell, Sir Colin – see Clyde, Lord

Campbell, Maj. Gen. Sir John, Bt.
Born, 8th Apr. 1807, succeeded as 2nd Baronet in 1843 and died leading the assault on the Redan, 18th Jun. 1855. Ens., 25th Nov. 1821; Lt., 1st Jul. 1824; Capt., 11th Jul. 1826; Maj., 29th Dec. 1837; Lt. Col., 7th Aug. 1840; Col., 11th Nov. 1851; Maj. Gen., 12th Dec. 1854. He commanded a brigade of the 3rd Division in the Crimea until being appointed to the command of the Fourth Division in Nov. 1854, a command which he was forced to relinquish in Jun. 1855, on the arrival of Lt. Gen. Bentinck. After commanding a brigade in the expedition to Kertch, he was appointed to the command of a brigade in what had been his Division for seven months. Sir John Campbell was awarded the Army of India Medal with clasp for Ava and, posthumously, the Crimea medal with clasps for Alma, Inkermann and Sebastopol. 14, 37, 41, 47, 52, 58, 59, 64, 93, 94, 125

Canrobert, Maréchal François Antoine Certain
Born 27th Jun. 1809; served in Algeria 1835-39 and 1841-51. His promotions came rapidly, and his support of Napoleon III's coup led to him being promoted General of Division. He commanded the French 1st Division at the battle of the

Alma, and succeeded to the command of the Army on the march to Sebastopol, which position he resigned on 16th May, 1855. He was awarded a Maréchal's baton for his Crimean services, and commanded the Third Corps in Italy in 1859, including the Battles of Magenta, and Solferino. He commanded the Sixth Corps in the Franco-Prussian War. He died at Paris on 28th Jan. 1895. 14, 26, 51, 69, 99f

Cardigan, James Thomas Brudenell, K.C.B., Earl of
Born 16th Oct. 1797; succeeded his father, as 7th Earl, in 1837. He was commissioned Cornet, 6th May, 1824; Lt., 13th Jan. 1825; Capt., 9th Jun. 1826; Maj., 3rd Aug. 1830; Lt. Col., 3rd Dec. 1830; Col., 9th Nov. 1846; Maj. Gen., 20th Jun. 1854; Col., 5th Dragoon Guards, 14th Aug. 1859. Commanded the Light Cavalry Brigade in the Crimea in 1854, including the battles of the Alma, Balaklava, Inkermann and siege of Sebastopol. He was awarded the K.C.B.; the Crimea medal with four clasps, the Legion of Honour (3rd Class) and the Order of the Mejedie (2nd Class), and was appointed Inspecting General of Cavalry on his return to England. 10, 40, 68

Carter, Lt. John Henry Stockman, Royal Engineers
2nd Lt., 22nd Dec. 1852; Lt., 17th Feb. 1854; killed in the trenches before Sebastopol, 2nd May, 1855. 48f

Cathcart, Lady Georgiana
Born 17th Jul. 1798, the daughter of Louisa, Countess of Mansfield (née Cathcart) and her second husband, the Hon. Robert Greville, Lady Georgiana Greville married Sir George Cathcart on 12th May, 1824. She died in 1871. 57

Cathcart, Lt. Gen. Hon. Sir George, K.C.B.
Born 12th May, 1794; Cornet, 10th May, 1810; Lt., 1st Jul. 1811; Capt., 24th Dec. 1818; Maj., 8th Apr. 1826; Lt. Col., 13th May, 1826; Col., 23rd Nov. 1841; Maj. Gen., 11th Nov. 1851; Local Lt. Gen., 30th Jan. 1852. Sir George served in the campaigns of 1813 and 1814 in Germany, and in the campaign of 1815, as Aide de Camp to the Duke of Wellington, and was present at the battles of Quatre Bras and Waterloo. He achieved major success in the prosecution of the Kaffir War of 1853, and was the holder of the 'Dormant Commission' (making him Commander in Chief of the Army of the East should anything happen to Raglan). He served at the battles of Alma, Balaklava and Inkermann, where he lost his life. He was awarded the K.C.B., the Waterloo Medal, the Kaffir War Medal and, posthumously, the Crimea Medal with four clasps and the Turkish Crimea Medal. 1, 1f, 2, 5, 10f, 11, 11f, 12, 12f, 13, 14, 47, 57

Caulfield, Capt. Francis William Thomas, 44th Regiment
Ens., 17th Jan. 1845; Lt., 10th Apr. 1849; Capt., 29th Dec. 1854; killed in the assault on the Redan, 18th Jun. 1855. 59

Charles X, King of France
Born 9th Oct. 1757, came to the throne in 1824, and abdicated in 1830. Much of his life was spent in England as an exile. He died on 6th Nov. 1836. 15

Chekib Effendi, Interpreter. 2

Clapham, 1628 Sgt. Thomas, 46th Regiment
Thomas Clapham, a labourer, enlisted in the 46th Regiment on 30th Oct. 1841. He sailed for the Crimea with the main body of the regiment, landing at Balaklava on 8th Nov. 1854. He died of dysentery on 10th Mar. 1855. He was posthumously awarded the Crimea medal with clasp for Sebastopol. 29, 35, 36, 37

Clyde, Colin Campbell, Field Marshal Lord, G.C.B.
Born Colin Macliver, 20th Oct. 1792; Ens., 26th May, 1808; Lt., 28th Jun. 1809; Capt., 9th Nov. 1813; Maj., 26th Nov. 1825; Lt. Col., 26th Oct. 1832; Col., 23rd Dec. 1842; Maj. Gen., 20th Jun. 1854; Lt. Gen., 4th Jun. 1856; Col., 93rd Highlanders, 15th Jan. 1858; General, 14th May, 1858; Field Marshal, 1860. Served in the 9th Regiment at Walcheren and in the Peninsula, and in America in 1814–15 in the 60th Rifles. Was Bde. Maj. of the troops engaged in quelling the insurrection in Demerara in 1823. Commanded the 98th Regiment in the expedition to China in 1842. Commanded the Third Division of the army of the Punjab campaign of 1848–9. Saw further arduous service in India in 1851–52. Commanded the Highland Brigade and later the Highland Division during the Crimean War, including the battles of the Alma and Balaklava, and the siege of Sebastopol. Commanded the British Forces in India during the Indian Mutiny with great success, for which service he was awarded a Barony. His awards also included the G.C.B., the MGS Medal with five clasps, the First China War Medal, the Punjab Medal with two clasps, the Crimea medal with three clasps, the Indian Mutiny Medal with two clasps, the Grand Officer of the Legion of Honour; the Grand Cross of the Order of St. Maurice and St. Lazarus, the Order of the Mejedie (1st Class) and the Turkish Crimea medal. Lord Clyde died on 14th Aug. 1863. 10, 10f, 13, 29, 31, 32, 41, 50, 61, 70, 73, 81, 85, 90, 91, 95, 96, 99, 100, 103, 113, 114, 115, 119, 121

Codrington, Gen. Sir William John, G.C.B.
Born 1804; Ens., 22nd Feb. 1821; Ens. & Lt., 24th Apr. 1823; Lt. & Capt., 20th Jul. 1826; Capt. & Lt. Col., 8th Jul. 1836; Col., 9th Nov. 1846; Maj. Gen., 20th Jun. 1854; Lt. Gen., 6th Jun. 1856; Col. of the 23rd Royal Welch Fusiliers, 27th Dec. 1860; General, 27th Jul. 1863; Col. of the Coldstream Guards, 16th Mar. 1875. Commanded a brigade of the Light Division, and afterwards a Division, during the Crimean War, including the battles of Alma and Inkermann, the siege and fall of Sebastopol. From October 1855 until the evacuation of the Crimea, he was Commander in Chief of the Eastern Army. He was awarded the G.C.B., the Crimea medal with three clasps, the Commander of the Legion of Honour, the Grand Cross of the Military Order of Savoy, the Order of the Mejedie (1st Class) and the Turkish Crimea Medal. He also received the French *Médaille Militaire*, an award restricted to other ranks and to officers commanding armies in alliance with France. Sir William died in 1884. 59, 60, 61, 90, 90f, 91, 93, 94, 95, 98, 100, 101, 103, 106, 107, 112, 113, 114, 115, 118, 120, 123, 124, 125, 130, 133, 135

Constantine Nikolaievitch, Grand Duke
Born in 1827, the second son of Tsar Nicholas I and brother of Alexander II. He commanded the Russian Fleet in the Baltic during the Crimean War, including the defence of Cronstadt. He became the Viceroy of Poland in 1862, and was made President of the Council of the Empire in 1865. In 1882 he was stripped of his dignities due to his revolutionary sympathies, and his eldest son was banished to Tashkent. Constantine died in 1892. 99f

Coppinger, Acting Deputy-Assistant-Commissary-General William P.
Born 1826, a Sub-Inspector of the Irish Constabulary, serving as a volunteer with the Commissariat. He died of disease, 11th Aug. 1855. 2, 47

Cornat, Capt. Auguste Victor Cassiodore, 2e Chasseurs d'Afrique. 119f

Craigie, Capt. Anthony David, Royal Engineers
2nd Lt., 19th Mar. 1839; Lt., 23rd Nov. 1841; Capt., 9th Apr. 1848. Killed in action, 13th Mar. 1855. 36

Curtis, Lt. Frank John, 46th Regiment
Born 27th Feb. 1832, the fourth son of Charles Berwick Curtis, the third son of the first baronet Curtis of Cullands Grove; educated at Winchester College; Ens., 22nd Nov. 1850; Lt., 16th Dec. 1853; Acting Adjutant, 29th Dec. 1854 to 1st Mar. 1855. Frank Curtis landed in the Crimea with the main body of the regiment, on 8th Nov. 1854, and was killed by a roundshot in the Greenhill Trenches, 2nd May, 1855. He is buried in the cemetery on Cathcart's Hill. 14f, 48, 49, 50

Dalhousie, Lord [Lord Panmure in the letters]
Fox Maule, eleventh Earl of Dalhousie and second Baron Panmure, born 1801, succeeded to the Barony, 1852, and to the Earldom, 1860. He was Secretary of State at War, 1848–52 and Secretary of State for War, 1855–58; he died in 1874. 97, 113

Dallas-Yorke, Capt. Thomas Yorke 'Jack', 11th Hussars
Cornet, 29th Dec. 1843; Lt., 21st Apr. 1846; Capt., 14th Jun. 1850. Saw no active service in the Crimea due to illness, and retired on the 24th Feb. 1857. A fourth cousin (once removed, by marriage) of Fred Dallas, he adopted the additional surname of Yorke in 1856. 4, 6

Dallas, Lt. Henry, 98th Regiment
One of Fred Dallas' three elder brothers, born Sep. 1822, died in Hong Kong, 25th Jul. 1844. Fought in the First China War, including the assault on Chinkiangfoo. 41

Dalzell, Lt. Col. the Hon. Robert Alexander George, C.B., 63rd Regiment
Born 19th Aug. 1816; Ens., 21st Mar. 1834; Lt., 11th Sep. 1835; Capt. 30th Jul. 1844; Maj., 7th Mar. 1851; Lt. Col., 6th Nov. 1854. Served in the Crimea with the 63rd Regiment, succeeding to its command on the death of Col. Swyny. Resigned

his command of the 63rd in favour of the command of the Provisional Depot Battalion at Malta on 7th Apr. 1855, and retired from the Army due to ill-health on 1st Oct. 1856. Was awarded the C.B., the Crimea medal with four clasps, the Order of the Mejedie (5th Class), the *Al Valore Militare* and the Turkish Crimea Medal. Col. Dalzell died on the 19th Oct. 1878. 68f

Davidson, Capt. Duncan, RN
Another of Fred Dallas' cousins. Mate, 25th Feb. 1852; Lt., 20th Apr. 1855; Capt., 29th May, 1872, retired from the navy in 1880 and died in 1882. Served in the Baltic campaign of 1854 and in the Black Sea, on HMS Prince Regent (from 7th Mar. 1854) and HMS Royal Albert (from 14th Nov. 1854). 23

Delafield, Brevet Maj. Gen. Richard, U.S. Army
Born 1st Sep. 1798, in New York City, Richard Delafield was the first graduate of the Military Academy to receive a merit class standing, ranking first in his class (1818). He superintended the construction of coast defences for New York Harbour (1846–55), was a military observer at the siege of Sebastopol, where he was allowed to make observations first hand from the British (but not the French) lines (1855); wrote *Report on the Art of War in Europe*. He was in charge of New York Harbour defences (1861–64) and Chief Engineer from Apr. 1864 until his retirement in August. He died on the 5th Nov. 1873. 87f

Delane, John Thaddeus
Born 11th Oct. 1817; Editor of the *Times* from May 1841, resigning from this position in 1877. He died on 22nd Nov. 1879. 95

Derby, Edward Geoffrey Smith Stanley, 14th Earl of
Born 29th Mar. 1799, a prominent Conservative politician and statesman, Prime Minister 1852, 1858–9, 1866–68, died 23rd Oct. 1869. A severe critic of the mishandling of the Crimean War, he however declined to form a ministry on the fall of Lord Aberdeen in 1855. 18f

Doucherty, 1027 CSgt. Charles, 46th Regiment
Charles Doucherty enlisted in the 46th Regiment in the autumn of 1835, and sailed for the Crimea with the main body of the regiment, landing at Balaklava on 8th Nov. 1854. Like so many others he succumbed to disease, and he spent months at Scutari before being sent home to England on 23rd Mar. 1855. He was awarded the Crimea medal with clasp for Sebastopol. 48

Dowbiggin, Maj. Montagu Hamilton, 4th and 99th Regiments
Ens., 30th Jun. 1848; Lt., 16th Sep. 1851; Capt., 29th Dec. 1854; Bt. Maj., 17th Jul. 1855; exchanged to 99th Regiment as Maj., 1st Feb. 1856. Served on the Staff in the Crimea, including the battle of the Alma, siege of Sebastopol and capture of Kinburn. Was awarded the Crimea medal with two clasps, Legion of Honour (5th Class); Order of the Mejedie (5th Class) and the Turkish Crimea Medal. 113, 119

Duberly, Mrs. Henry ('Fanny')
The wife of the Paymaster of the 8th Hussars, Mrs. Duberly became famous for her

exploits in the Crimea, and in India during the Mutiny. Her journals were published at the time, to a mixed reaction. **26, 30, 116**

Dundas, Admiral Sir James Whitley Deans, G.C.B., R.N.
Commander in Chief in the Mediterranean and Black Sea until 22nd Dec. 1854. Born, 4th Dec. 1785; Lt., 25th May, 1805; Com., 8th Oct. 1806; Capt., 13th Oct. 1807; Rear-Adm., 23rd Nov. 1841; Vice-Adm., 17th Dec. 1852; Admiral, 8th Dec. 1857. He died on 7th Oct. 1862. **30, 68**

Dunkellin, Ullick Canning De Burgh Canning, Lt. Col. Lord, Coldstream Guards
The eldest son of the Marquess and Earl of Clanricade, born 12 Jul. 1827; Ens. & Lt., 27th Mar. 1846; Lt. & Capt., 27th Apr. 1849; Capt. & Lt. Col., 3rd Nov. 1854. Served in the Crimea at the battle of the Alma, and the siege of Sebastopol, was taken prisoner before dawn of the 22nd Oct. 1854. Was awarded the Crimea medal with two clasps, the Order of the Mejedie (5th Class) and the Turkish Crimea Medal. Lord Dunkellin died in 1867. **13, 89**

Dunscombe, Capt. Nicholas, 46th Regiment
Born 18th Jan. 1835; Ens., 23rd Nov. 1852; Lt., 3rd Feb. 1854; Capt., 2nd Oct. 1855; to half pay, on reduction, 10th Nov. 1856; Capt., 2nd Regiment, by appointment, Aug. 1857. Retired by the sale of his commission, 3rd Feb. 1869. Capt. Dunscombe landed in the Crimea on 8th Nov. 1854, and was awarded the Crimea medal with clasp for Sebastopol, the *Al Valore Militare* and the Turkish Crimea medal. **1f**

Earle, Brevet Maj. Arthur Maxwell, 57th Regiment
Ens., 18th Jan. 1850; Lt., 15th Feb. 1853; Capt., 29th Dec. 1854; Bt. Maj., 6th Jun. 1856. Maxwell Earle landed in the Crimea with his regiment on 23rd Sep. 1854, and did duty as Aide de Camp to Brig. Gen. Goldie until the death of the latter at the battle of Inkermann; he was appointed Bde. Maj. in the 4th Division on 17th Nov. 1854, and was present at the assaults of 18th Jun. and 8th Sep. 1855, and at the capture of Kinburn. He was three times mentioned in despatches, and was awarded the Crimea Medal with clasps for Balaklava, Inkermann and Sebastopol, the Legion of Honour (5th Class), the Order of the Mejedie (5th Class) and the Turkish Crimea medal. Maxwell's sister, Emily Florence Earle, had married Fred's brother, Robert William Dallas, and so the two friends were also effectively brothers-in-law. **10, 11, 12f, 23f, 38, 40f, 41, 82, 84, 90, 91, 104, 112, 130, 133, 134**

Earle, Maj. Gen. William, C.B., C.S.I.
Born 1833, Ens., 49th Regiment, 17th Oct. 1851; Lt., 6th Jun. 1854; Capt., 16th Feb. 1855; exchanged to the Grenadier Guards as Lt. & Capt., Mar. 1857; Capt. & Lt. Col., 28th Apr. 1863; Col., 20th May, 1870; Maj., 21st Aug. 1878; Maj. Gen., 1880. Served with the 49th Regiment in the Crimea, including the battles of Alma and Inkermann, siege of Sebastopol, sortie of 26th Oct. 1854, and assault on the Redan of 18th Jun. 1855. He was awarded the C.S.I. (1880), the C.B. (1884), the

Crimea medal with three clasps, the *Al Valore Militare* the Order of the Mejedie (5th Class), and the Turkish Crimea Medal. 85

Edward, Prince – see Saxe-Weimar

Edwardes, Capt. Richard Lloyd, 68th Regiment
Born 6th Aug. 1832; Ens., 23rd Jan. 1852; Lt., 6th Jun. 1854; Capt., 13th Apr. 1855. Capt. Edwardes served in the Crimea with his regiment, including the battles of the Alma, Balaklava and Inkermann, and the siege of Sebastopol; he was killed in action in the trenches before Sebastopol, 11th May, 1855. He was posthumously awarded the Crimea medal with four clasps. 50

Egerton, Col. Thomas Graham, 77th Regiment
Ens., 24th Dec. 1829; Lt., 9th Mar. 1832; Capt., 23rd Jan. 1835; Maj., 7th Feb. 1845; Lt. Col., 27th Dec. 1850; Bt. Col, 28th Nov. 1854; killed in action, 20th Apr. 1855. Commanded the 77th Regiment in the Crimea. 45

England, Lt. Gen. Sir Richard, G.C.B., K.H.
Ens., 25th Feb. 1808; Lt., 1st Jun. 1809; Capt., 11th Jun. 1811; Maj., 4th Sep. 1823; Lt. Col., 29th Oct. 1825; Col., 28th Jun. 1838; Maj. Gen., 11th Nov. 1851; Col., 50th Regiment, 20th Sep. 1854; Lt. Gen., 4th Jun. 1856; Col., 41st Regiment, 20th Apr. 1861; General, 6th Jul. 1863. Served in the attack on Flushing in 1809, and in the operations in Sicily in 1810–11. Joined the Army in Paris in 1815. Commandant of Kaffraria, and employed throughout the Kaffir War of 1836–37. Commanded the Bombay Division in the Afghan War of 1842. Commanded the Third Division in the Crimean War in 1854–55, including the battles of Alma and Inkermann, the assault of the 18th June and the siege of Sebastopol. Sir Richard was awarded the G.C.B., the K.H., the South Africa Medal, the First Afghan War Medal, the Crimea medal with three clasps, the Order of the Mejedie (1st Class), the Legion of Honour (2nd Class), the *Al Valore Militare* and the Turkish Crimea Medal. 69

Ennismore, Capt. the Viscount – see Listowel, Capt. the Earl of

Estcourt, Maj. Gen. James Bucknall
Ens., 13th Jul. 1820; Lt., 9th Dec. 1824; Capt., 4th Nov. 1825; Maj., 21st Oct. 1836; Lt. Col., 29th Mar. 1839; went on half-pay, 25th Aug. 1843; Col., 11th Nov. 1851; Maj. Gen., 12th Dec. 1854. Served in the expedition to the River Euphrates from Jan. 1835 to Jun. 1837 and as Adjutant-General in the Crimea until his death on 24th Jun. 1855, including the battles of Alma, Balaklava and Inkermann, and the siege of Sebastopol. He was posthumously awarded the Crimea medal with four clasps. 60, 61f

Eugénie, Empress of France
Eugénie, Comtesse de Teba, Empress of France, née Eugénia Maria de Montuo de Guzmán, was born on 5th May, 1826. She married Napoleon III in 1853, and came to be a significant influence on his rule. She gave birth to the Prince Imperial (who

was killed in action in the British service, 1st Jun. 1879) on 16th Mar. 1856; served as Regent in the absence of her husband in 1859, 1865 and 1870 and died on the 11th Jul. 1920. 115

Evans, Lt. Gen. Sir de Lacy, G.C.B.
Ens., 1st Feb. 1807; Lt., 1st Dec. 1808; Capt., 12th Jan. 1815; Maj., 11th May, 1815; Lt. Col., 18th Jun. 1815; Col., 10th Jan. 1837; Maj. Gen., 9th Nov. 1846; Col., 21st Fusiliers, 29th Aug. 1853; Lt. Gen., 20th Jun. 1854; General, 10th Mar. 1861. Served in India in 1807–10, in the Peninsula in 1812–14, in America 1814–15, Belgium and France 1815–18, Spain in 1835-37 and in the Crimea 1854–56, as commander of the Second Division. He was five times wounded in action, and had six horses killed under him during his years of active service. He received the G.C.B., the MGS Medal with clasps for Vittoria, Pyrenees and Toulouse; the Crimea Medal with four clasps, the Grand Cross of St. Ferdinand, the Grand Cross of Charles III, the Order of the Mejedie (1st Class), the Legion of Honour (2nd Class) and the Turkish Crimea Medal. 16, 119

Eyre, Maj. Gen. Sir William, K.C.B.
Ens., 17th Apr. 1823; Lt., 5th Nov. 1825; Capt., 20th Mar. 1827; Maj., 19th Jul. 1839; Lt. Col., 12th Nov. 1847; Col., 28th May, 1853; Maj. Gen., 12th Dec. 1854. Served in the Kaffir War of 1853; commanded a brigade of the Third Division, and afterwards the Division throughout the Crimea War, and was present at the battle of Alma, and the siege and fall of Sebastopol. During the battle of Inkermann he held command of the troops in the trenches. He was awarded the K.C.B., the South Africa Medal, the Crimea Medal with two clasps, the Legion of Honour (3rd Class), the Order of the Mejedie (2nd Class), the *Al Valore Militare* and the Turkish Crimea Medal. 58, 59, 69, 73, 89, 90, 103

Fane, Capt. John Augustus, 46th Regiment
Born 23rd Sep. 1830; Ens., 19th Oct. 1849; Lt., 31st Dec. 1852; Capt., 29th Dec. 1854. Landed in the Crimea on 8th Nov. 1854, and returned home on 6th Feb. 1855. He resigned from the Army by the sale of his commission 29th May, 1857, and subsequently served in the Oxfordshire Rifle Volunteers. He died in 1908. 25f, 27

Fenwick, Capt. Bowes, 44th Regiment
Ens., 29th Jan. 1842; Lt., 12th Jul. 1844; Capt., 24th Nov. 1848. Killed in the assault on the Redan, 18th Jun. 1855. 59f

Filder, Commissary-General William, C.B.
Assistant Commissary-General, 10th Aug. 1811; Deputy Commissary-General, 26th Oct. 1816; Commissary-General, 1st Jul. 1840. Served in the Peninsula and in France; commanded the Commissariat of the Crimean Army until the end of Jul. 1855, including the battles of Alma, Balaklava, Inkermann and the siege of Sebastopol. Was awarded the C.B., MGS Medal with nine clasps, the Crimea medal with four clasps, the Order of the Mejedie (4th Class) and the Turkish Crimea Medal. 70

Forde, Maj. Thomas, 46th Regiment
Born 19th Dec. 1830; Ens., 15th Oct. 1852; Lt., 20th Jan. 1854; Capt., 5th June 1855; Capt., half pay, by reduction, 10th Nov. 1856; Capt., 46th Regiment, 31st Mar. 1857; Maj., 10th Feb. 1869; Maj., half pay, 23rd Mar. 1872. Landed in the Crimea on 8th Nov. 1854, subsequently appointed ADC to Maj. Gen. Garrett. Maj. Forde received the Crimea Medal with clasp for Sebastopol, the Order of the Mejedie (5th Class) and the Turkish Crimea Medal; he died in 1897. **69, 70, 71, 94, 97, 104, 128**

Forey, Gen. Elie F.
Born 1804, served in Algeria, 1830, the expedition of Medeah, the expedition of the Portes de Fer, again in Algeria (1841–4, as Maj., and subsequently Lt. Col., Commanding 6th Regiment of *Chasseurs à Pied*). He was promoted Col., 4th Nov. 1844, and General of Brigade in 1848; General of Division, 22nd Dec. 1852, and appointed to the command of the Siege Corps before Sebastopol, 20th Oct. 1854. **33**

Forrest, Gen. William Charles, C.B.
Cornet, 11th Mar. 1836; Lt., 5th Jan. 1839; Capt., 7th Sep. 1841; Maj., 3rd Oct. 1848; Bt. Lt. Col., 12th Dec. 1854; Lt. Col., 5th Aug. 1859; Col., 8th Mar. 1860; Brig. Gen. commanding Cawnpore Brigade, Bengal, 19th Apr. 1866; Maj. Gen., 6th Mar. 1868; Lt. Gen., 1st Oct. 1877; General, 1st Jul. 1881; Col., 11th Hussars, 8th Feb. 1886. Served in the Crimea with the 4th Dragoon Guards, including the battles of Balaklava and Inkermann and the siege of Sebastopol, the night attack on the Russian outposts on 19th Feb. 1855, and the battle of the Chernaya. Gen. Forrest was awarded the C.B., the Crimea medal with three clasps, the *Al Valore Militare*; the Order of the Mejedie (5th Class) and the Turkish Crimea Medal. **26**

Foster, Maj. William John, 46th Regiment and 19th Regiment
Born 27th Jan. 1835; Ens., 21st Feb. 1855; Lt., 2nd October 1855; Lt., 2nd Battalion, 19th Regiment, by appointment, 14th April 1858; Capt., 8th Jul. 1859; Maj., 5th Jul. 1872. Landed in the Crimea with a draft of reinforcements, 18th Aug. 1855. Was awarded the Crimea medal with clasp for Sebastopol, and the Turkish Crimea Medal. **73f**

Garrett, Lt. Col. Algernon Robert, 46th Regiment and 16th Regiment
Born 21st Jul. 1823, the son of Sir Robert Garrett; Ens., 46th Regiment, 1st Jun. 1841; Lt., 27th Sep. 1842; Capt., 28th Apr. 1848; Bt. Maj., 2nd Nov. 1855; Maj., 31st Aug. 1858; Maj., 16th Regiment, by exchange, 2nd Dec. 1859; Lt. Col., half-pay, unattached, 28th Jun. 1864. Sailed for the Crimea with the main body of the 46th regiment, landing at Balaklava on 8th Nov. 1854. Appointed Bde. Maj., 2nd Brigade, 4th Division in the Crimea; Bde. Maj. at Gibraltar after the Crimean War; Bde. Maj., 1st Brigade, 1st Division in China, 1857. Lt. Col. Garrett was awarded the Crimea medal with clasp for Sebastopol, the *Al Valore Militare*, the Order of the Mejedie (5th Class) and the Turkish Crimea medal. **92f**

Inspector General of Hospitals, 28th Mar. 1854. Served in the campaign of 1815 in Flanders, served in the Kaffir War of 1847–8 (Mentioned in General Orders, Mentioned in Despatches), and as Principal Medical Officer in the campaign of 1851 (Mentioned in General Orders). Principal Medical Officer in the Crimean War. He was awarded the K.C.B., the Crimea medal, the Legion of Honour (4th Class); the Order of the Mejedie (4th Class) and the Turkish Crimea medal. **70, 130**

Hampson, 1060 Sgt. James, 46th Regiment
Formerly of the 18th Regiment, James Hampson transferred to the 46th at the beginning of 1836; he sailed for the Crimea as part of the two advance companies of the regiment, and landed on 14th Sep. 1854. He was present at the battle of the Alma, but fell sick on 23rd Sep. 1854, being sent to Scutari, where he remained for the greater part of the war. He was awarded the Crimea medal with clasp for Alma, and the Turkish Crimea medal. **6, 17, 29, 35, 37, 46, 48**

Harding, Col. Francis Pym, C.B., 22nd Regiment
En.s, 16th Mar. 1838; Lt., 18th Dec. 1840; Capt., 29th Jan. 1847; Maj., 27th Oct. 1854; Bt. Lt. Col., 12th Dec. 1854; Lt. Col., 25th Dec. 1857; Col., 9th Sep. 1858. Served in the defence of the residency at Hyderabad, and at the battle of Meeanee (wounded, mentioned in despatches) during the Conquest of Scinde. Served as Persian interpreter to Sir Charles Napier with the expedition against the Afridis in forcing the Kohat Pass in 1850. Served in the Crimean War as Aide de Camp to General Pennefather, including the battles of Alma (horse shot under him), Balaklava, Inkermann (severely wounded, horse killed under him), the sortie of 26th Oct. and the siege of Sebastopol. Was commandant at Balaklava from Jan. 1855 until the evacuation of the Crimea. Col. Harding was awarded the C.B., the Scinde Medal for Meeanee, the Crimea Medal with four clasps, the Legion of Honour (5th Class), the Order of the Mejedie (5th Class) and the Turkish Crimea Medal. **66**

Hardinge, Field Marshal Viscount, G.C.B.
Born 30th Mar. 1785, Henry Hardinge, First Viscount Hardinge of Lahore and King's Newton, entered the army as an Ens., 8th Oct. 1798; Lt., 25th Mar. 1802; Capt., 7th Apr. 1804; Maj., 13th Apr. 1809; Lt. Col., 30th May, 1811; Col., 19th Jul. 1821; Maj. Gen., 22nd Jul. 1830; Lt. Gen., 23rd Nov. 1841; Col. of the 57th Regiment, 31st May, 1843; Commanding in Chief the Forces, 28th Sep. 1852; General, 20th Jun. 1854; Field Marshal, 2nd Oct. 1855. Lord Hardinge served throughout the Peninsular War, nearly the whole of the time as Deputy Quarter Master General of the Portuguese army, (twice wounded); served in the Campaign of 1815, and was severely wounded at Ligny (left hand amputated). As Governor-General of India he was engaged at the battles of Moodkee, Ferozeshah and Sobraon. He was awarded the G.C.B., the Peninsula Gold Cross and five clasps, the Waterloo medal and the Sutlej Medal with two clasps; he also received four foreign orders of knighthood. He died 24th Sep. 1856. **84**

Hardy, Lt. Gen. William, C.B.
Born 11th Mar. 1822; Ens., 46th Regiment, 27th Sep. 1842; Lt., 8th May, 1846;

Capt., 12th Oct. 1852; Bt. Maj., 12th Dec. 1854; Maj., unattached, half-pay, 2nd Oct. 1855; Maj., Depot Battalion, 1st Oct. 1856; Lt. Col., 16th Sep. 1861; Col., 16th Sep. 1866; Maj. Gen., 1st Oct. 1877; Lt. Gen., 21st Sep. 1882. Landed in the Crimea on 14th Sep. 1854; served at the battle of the Alma; commanded the advance party of two companies 46th Regiment, at the Battles of Balaklava and Inkermann (wounded severely), and in the Siege of Sebastopol. He was awarded the C.B., the Crimea Medal with bars for Alma, Balaklava, Inkermann and Sebastopol, the Order of the Mejedie (5th Class) and the Turkish Crimea Medal. 11f, 12, 18, 36

Hawley, Capt. Robert B., 89th Regiment. **68f**

Hay, Lt. Col. Alexander Sebastian Leith, 93rd Regiment. 119

Helyar, Lt. Col. Edward Hawker
Born, 1st Jul. 1834; Ens., 46th Regiment, 4th Feb. 1854; Lt., 8th Dec. 1854; Capt., 24th Jan. 1860; Capt., 2nd Battalion, 2nd Regiment, by exchange, 2nd Dec. 1862; Bt. Maj., 5th Jul. 1872; Maj., 7th Jul. 1875; Hon. Lt. Col., 23rd Jan. 1878, on which date he left the army by the sale of his commission. He landed in the Crimea on 15th Oct. 1854, and served at the Battles of Balaklava and Inkermann (wounded slightly) and at the siege of Sebastopol. Helyar was awarded the Crimea Medal with three clasps and the Turkish Crimea Medal. He left the Crimea 12th Mar. 1855 commanding the escort for Russian prisoners of war who were being shipped to England. 11f

Herbert, Maj. Gen. the Hon. Percy Egerton, C.B.
Ens., 17th Jan. 1840; Lt., 7th Sep. 1841; Capt., 19th Jun. 1846; Maj., 27th May, 1853; Lt. Col., 28th May, 1853; Col., 28th Nov. 1854; Maj. Gen., 28th Jan. 1868. Served in the Kaffir War of 1851–53; Assistant Quarter Master General of the 2nd Division in the Crimea until Nov. 1855, and subsequently as Quarter Master General of the Army of the East until Jun. 1856. Present at the battle of Alma (wounded); the affair of 26th Oct. (the Battle of Little Inkermann), the battle of Inkermann and the siege and fall of Sebastopol. Served with the 82nd Regiment in Rohilcund in 1858, and in command of the districts at Cawnpore and Futtehpore until the Spring of 1859. He commanded a force in pursuit of Ferozeshah and a rebel force to the banks of the Jumna. He was awarded the C.B., the Kaffir War Medal, the Crimea medal with three clasps, the Indian Mutiny Medal, the Legion of Honour (4th Class), the Order of St. Maurice and St. Lazarus (Commander, 2nd Class), the Order of the Mejedie (3rd Class), and the Turkish Crimea Medal, and was appointed a Queen's ADC for his Crimean service. 63, 68, 86, 91, 128

Herbert, Sidney, Lord Herbert of Lea
Born 16th Oct. 1810, Secretary at War 1845–46 and December 1852–Feb. 1855; Secretary of State for the Colonies for a few weeks in Feb. 1855; Secretary of War, 1859; died, 2nd Aug. 1861. Florence Nightingale's main political ally. 121f

Hesketh, Capt. William Reginald, 46th Regiment
Born 5th Feb. 1830; Ens., 21st Jul. 1848; Lt., 23rd Apr. 1852; Capt., 29th Dec.

1854; retired from the army by the sale of his commission, 25th Oct. 1855. He landed in the Crimea on 8th Nov. 1854, served in the siege of Sebastopol, and left for England on sick leave, 30th May, 1855. He was awarded the Crimea Medal with clasp for Sebastopol and the Turkish Crimea Medal. 53

Higgins, Matthew James, a.k.a. Jacob Omnium
Born, 4th Dec. 1810; died 14th Aug. 1868. Radical essayist and pamphleteer. 95

du Holbec, Commandant, *Garde Imperiale*. 61

Horn, Gen. Sir Frederick, K.C.B., 20th Regiment
Ens., 26th Jan. 1826; Lt., 17th Apr. 1828; Capt., 16th Jun. 1837; Maj., 7th Sep. 1841; Lt. Col., 14th Apr. 1846; Col., 20th Jun. 1854; Maj. Gen., 13th Oct. 1860; Col., 45th Regiment, 21st Apr. 1868; Lt. Gen., 18th Jan. 1870; Col., 20th Regiment, 17th Mar. 1876; General, 2nd Jun. 1877. He commanded a Brigade of the 4th Division at the battle of the Alma, and the 20th Regiment at the battles of Balaklava and Inkermann (twice wounded, and horse shot under him), succeeding to the command of the Fourth Division, and in the siege and fall of Sebastopol. Col. Horn was awarded the K.C.B., the Crimea Medal with four clasps, the Legion of Honour (4th Class), the *Al Valore Militare*, the Order of the Mejedie (3rd Class) and the Turkish Crimea Medal. 17

Inglis, Capt. William, 57th Regiment. 18

James, Lt. Edward Renouard, Royal Engineers. 64, 67

Johnson, 3128 Pte. Elijah, 46th Regiment
Elijah Johnson (or Johnsons) from Siddington, a labourer, enlisted in the 46th Regiment on the 20th Oct. 1852. He sailed for the Crimea with the main body of the regiment, and landed at Balaklava on 8th Nov. 1854. He died of diarrhoea, 28th Mar. 1855, and was posthumously awarded the Crimea Medal with clasp for Sebastopol. He was probably the brother of Corporal Jacob Johnson. 24, 43

Johnson, 2575 Cpl. Jacob, 46th Regiment
Jacob Johnson from Siddington, a labourer, enlisted in the 46th Regiment on the 8th Oct. 1850; he sailed for the Crimea with the main body of the regiment, and landed at Balaklava on 8th Nov. 1854. He died of dysentery, 1st Jan. 1855 , and was posthumously awarded the Crimea Medal with clasp for Sebastopol. He was probably the brother of Private Elijah Johnson. 24

Jones, Maj. Gen. Sir Harry David, K.C.B.
2nd Lt., Royal Engineers, 17th Sep. 1808; Lt., 24th Jun. 1809; Capt., 12th Nov. 1813; Bt. Maj., 10th Jan. 1837; Lt. Col., 7th Sep. 1840; Bt. Col., 11th Nov. 1851; Col., 7th Jul. 1853; Maj. Gen., 12th Dec. 1854. Served in the expedition to Walcheren in 1809, and the campaigns of 1810–14 in the Peninsula. Appointed Brig. Gen. for particular service in the Baltic in 1854, and commanded the British forces at the siege operations against Bomarsund. Appointed Commanding Royal Engineer in the Crimea, 10th Feb. 1855, and served at the siege and fall of

Sebastopol. Appointed one of the members of the Council of War in Paris in 1856. Sir Harry received the K.C.B., the MGS Medal with five clasps, the Baltic Medal, the Crimea Medal with clasp for Sebastopol, the Legion of Honour (3rd Class), the Military Order of Savoy (Commander, 1st Class), the Order of the Mejedie (2nd Class) and the Turkish Crimea Medal. **30, 52, 66, 83, 85**

Kelson, Ens. Thomas Mortimer, 46th Regiment and 6th Regiment
Born 13th Jan. 1835; Ens., 46th Regiment, 15th Mar. 1855; Lt., 16th Jan. 1856; Lt., 6th Regiment, 23rd Oct. 1857; Capt., 1st Dec. 1862; retired by the sale of his commission, 31st May, 1864. Kelson landed in the Crimea, 17th Aug. 1855, and received the Crimea Medal with clasp for Sebastopol, and the Turkish Crimea Medal. **73f**

Kerr, Lt. Col. Lord Mark, 13th Regiment. **112**

Lacy, Ens. Gilbert de Lacy, 63rd Regiment. **104**

Lawrenson, Gen. John
Cornet, 12th Nov. 1818; Lt., 6th Dec. 1821; Capt., 27th Aug. 1825; Bt. Maj., 28th Jun. 1838; Maj., 31st Dec. 1839; Lt. Col., 27th Jun. 1845; Col., 20th Jun. 1854; to half-pay, 30th Sep. 1856; Maj. Gen., 6th Apr. 1860; Lt. Gen., 25th Aug. 1868; Col., 13th Hussars, 10th Dec. 1868; General, 2nd Nov. 1875. Commanded the 17th Lancers during the early part of the Crimean War, including the battle of Alma, being appointed to the command of the Heavy Brigade with the Local rank of Brig. Gen., 30th Jul. 1855, and subsequently succeeding to the command of the Cavalry Division, in Dec. 1855. He was awarded the Crimea Medal with two clasps, the *Al Valore Militare*, the Order of the Mejedie (4th Class) and the Turkish Crimea Medal. **96**

Lempriere, Capt. A., 77th Regiment. **45**

Liprandi, Gen. Pavel Petrovitch
Born in 1796. Served against the French in 1813–14, in the Russo-Turkish War of 1828–9 and commanded a regiment in the Polish uprising of 1831. Led a special detachment in Wallachia 1853-4 before transferring to the Crimea, where he distinguished himself at Balaklava. He died in 1864. **73**

Listowel, Capt. the Earl of, Scots Fusilier Guards
William Hare, K.P., 3rd Earl of Listowel, Viscount Ennismore and Listowel, Baron Ennismore and Baron Hare, born 29th May, 1833; Ens. & Lt., 14th May, 1852; Lt. & Capt., 26th Dec. 1854, succeeded to the Earldom, 3rd Feb. 1856. Served throughout the Crimean War with the Scots Fusilier Guards, including the battles of the Alma, Balaklava and Inkermann, and the siege and fall of Sebastopol. The Earl was awarded the Crimea Medal with four clasps and the Turkish Crimea Medal. **109**

Lluellyn, Capt. Richard, 46th Regiment
Born, 18th May, 1832; Ens., 15th Dec. 1849; Lt., 28th Oct. 1853; Capt., 2nd Feb.

1855; retired from the army by the sale of his commission, 24th Aug. 1858. He arrived in the Crimea on 8th Nov. 1854, and served at the siege of Sebastopol before returning to the Depot Companies, 6th Feb. 1855. He was awarded the Crimea Medal with clasp for Sebastopol (presented by the Queen), and the Turkish Crimea Medal. 13f

Lucan, Earl of, G.C.B.
General George Charles Bingham, third Earl of Lucan, and Baron Lucan of Castlebar was born 16th Apr. 1800; Ens., 29th Aug. 1816; Lt., 24th Dec. 1818; Capt., 16th May, 1822; Maj., 23rd Jun. 1825; Lt. Col., 9th Nov. 1826; Col., 23rd Nov. 1841; Maj. Gen., 11th Nov. 1851; Lt. Gen., 24th Dec. 1858; Col., 1st Life Guards, 22nd Feb. 1865; General, 28th Aug. 1865. Served in the campaign of 1828 on the staff of the Russian Army in Bulgaria, commanded the Cavalry Division in the Crimea in 1854, including the battles of the Alma, Balaklava (wounded) and Inkermann, and in the siege of Sebastopol. Lord Lucan was awarded the G.C.B., the Crimea Medal with four clasps, the Order of St. Anne of Russia (3rd Class), the Legion of Honour (3rd Class), the Order of the Mejedie (1st Class), the Russian War Medal of 1828 and the Turkish Crimea Medal. 10

Luders, Gen. Count Alexander Nikolaievich
Born 1790; enrolled in the Bryansk Musketeer Regiment in 1805, fought at Austerlitz, commissioned in 1807. Took part in the Turkish campaign of 1810; the 1812 campaign and 1813 campaign (wounded in the leg at Kulm) and in the Turkish War of 1828–29 (wounded). As a major general and commander of the 1st Brigade of the 3rd Infantry Division, he was in the Polish campaign of 1831. In 1840 his 1st Infantry Division made a landing on the eastern shore of the Black Sea in connection with the Caucasus wars. In 1848 he was made commander of the forces in the Danubian Principalities. In 1849 his force (5th Infantry Corps) crossed into Hapsburg Transylvania to help out the Austrians with their own Hungarian revolt. Served in the Danubian Principalities in 1853–4, and in 1855 was made commander of the Southern Army and the Crimean Army. In 1856 he was released due to illness and until 1861 lived a private life in Odessa. Recalled to serve as viceroy in Poland and commander-in-chief of the 1st Army. He died in 1874. 119, 123, 124

Lyons, Admiral Lord, G.C.B., K.C.H.
Admiral Sir Edmund Lyons, First Baron Lyons, was born in 1790; he commanded in the Dutch West Indies in 1810–11, and in the Black Sea in 1854–55. He was awarded the G.C.B., the K.C.H., the Crimea Medal with clasp for Sebastopol, the Order of St. Louis and the Redeemer (Knight), the Order of the Mejedie (1st Class). He died in 1858. 98

Lysons, Gen. Sir Daniel, G.C.B.
Ens., 26th Dec. 1834; Lt., 23rd Aug. 1837; Capt., 29th Dec. 1843; Maj., 3rd Aug. 1849; Lt. Col., 21st Sep. 1854; Col., 17th Jul. 1855; Maj. Gen., 6th Mar. 1868; Lt. Gen., 2nd Jun. 1877; Col., 45th Regiment, 25th Aug. 1878; General, 14th Jul.

1879. Served in Canada during the rebellion of 1838–39 (Mentioned in Despatches); served in the Crimea, including the battles of the Alma (Mentioned in Despatches) and Inkermann, and the siege and fall of Sebastopol. He led the main column in the assault on the Redan of the 18th Jun. and commanded a brigade in the later part of the action (slightly wounded, Mentioned in Despatches), and took part in the final assault of 8th Sep. (severely wounded, Mentioned in Despatches), and commanded the 2nd Brigade of the Light Division from October 1855 until the evacuation of the Crimea. He was awarded the G.C.B., the Crimea Medal with three clasps, the Legion of Honour (4th Class), the Al Valore Militare, the Order of the Mejedie (3rd Class) and the Turkish Crimea Medal. 113

Maitland, Gen. Charles Lennox Brownlow, C.B.
Ens. & Lt., 9th Apr. 1841; Lt. & Capt., 27th Mar. 1846; Bt. Maj., 15th Sep. 1848; Capt. & Lt. Col., 28th Sep. 1854; Col., 15th Jan. 1860; to half-pay 14th Apr. 1863; Maj. Gen., 6th Mar. 1868; Lt. Gen., 1st Oct. 1877; Col., 1st Battalion, Wiltshire Regiment, 1st Mar. 1884; General, 1st Dec. 1884. Served in the Kaffir War of 1846–7, and in the Crimea War as Deputy Assistant Adjutant General of the Fourth Division, including the battles of the Alma, Balaklava and Inkermann (dangerously wounded), and the siege of Sebastopol. He received the C.B., the Crimea Medal with four clasps, the Legion of Honour (5th Class), the Order of the Mejedie (5th Class) and the Turkish Medal. 1f, 12, 13, 14

de Mallet, Col. Baron Molesworth
Born in England, 2nd Sep. 1808, commissioned into the French army, 10th Jul. 1826. He served in the *Légion Étrangère* and later the *3e Bataillon d'Infanterie Légère d'Afrique*, rising to the rank of Captain on 1st Nov. 1837. He transferred to the *12e de Ligne* (23rd Mar. 1840), and the *7e de Ligne* (30th May, 1842), then to the *14e de Ligne* with promotion to the rank of *Chef de Bataillon* (27th Apr. 1846). He transferred in this rank to the *21re de Ligne* 22nd Nov. 1852 and it was in this regiment that he served in the Crimea in the Fifth Division, part of the Siege Corps. The division was left at Varna in September but crossed to Sebastopol in Oct. 1854. On 24th Jan. 1855, he was promoted Lt. Col., and appointed to the *42e de Ligne* and on 22nd Sep. 1855, he was promoted and transferred as Col. of the *49e de Ligne*. He became General of Brigade 12th Aug. 1866, and remained with the Army till the Franco-Prussian War. His war services included extensive campaigns in North Africa, 1832–39; the Crimean War (siege and fall of Sebastopol); and in Italy in 1859. He was awarded the Legion of Honour (3rd Class), the *Al Valore Militare* and the Crimea medal with clasp for Sebastopol. He died in Edinburgh on 4th Oct., 1886. 86, 112

Markham, Maj. Gen. Frederick, C.B.
Ens., 13th May, 1834; Lt., 22nd Oct. 1825; Capt., 16th Apr. 1829; Maj., 28th Sep. 1839; Lt. Col., 22nd Jul. 1842; Col., 2nd Aug. 1850; Maj. Gen., 28th Nov. 1854. Served in Canada during the rebellion of 1837 (wounded severely); in the Punjab Campaign of 1848–9, commanding 2nd Infantry Brigade at the first and second

siege operations at Mooltan (wounded) and the Division at the action of Soorjkoond, and the Bengal Column at the storming and capture of Mooltan on 2nd Jan. 1849, commanded the Brigade at the battle of Goojerat; commanded the Second Division in the Crimea from 18th Jul. 1855 until 29th Sep. 1855, when he left for England on Medical Certificate: he was to die before the year was out. He was awarded the C.B., the Punjab Medal with two clasps and the Crimea Medal with clasp for Sebastopol. 66, 69, 81, 82, 91, 92, 94

de la Marmora, Gen. Alfonso Ferrero, Sardinian Army
Born 18th Nov. 1804; entered Sardinian army, 1832; distinguished himself at the siege of Peschiera del Garda in May 1848, commanded the Sardinian Army in the Crimea, including the battle of the Chernaya and the siege and fall of Sebastopol. Prime Minister, 1859–60 and 1864–66; resigned to take command of an Army Corps during the war of 1866, which force was heavily defeated by the Austrians at Custozza. He died on 5th Jan. 1878. 63, 91, 96, 98

Marsack, Capt. Henry Charles, 46th Regiment and 2/24th Regiment
Born 7th Aug. 1822; Ens., 46th Regiment, 1st May, 1855; Lt., 2nd Battalion, 24th Regiment, by promotion, 13th Jul. 1858; Capt., 7th Jan. 1862; retired by the sale of his commission the following year. He landed in the Crimea on 18th Aug. 1855, and served at the siege and fall of Sebastopol. He received the Crimea Medal with clasp for Sebastopol, and the Turkish Crimea Medal. 73f

de Martimprey, Gen. Edmond Charles
Born on the 16th Jun. 1808. Entered St.-Cyr, 16th Nov. 1826 and commissioned 1st Oct. 1828. He campaigned each year in Algeria between 1835 and 1852 and participated in no less than twenty-two expeditions, sieges, combats, etc. He was sent to the Crimea in 1854 in the rank of General of Brigade as Chief of the General Staff of the Army of the Orient, a position he held through the war under Marshal de Saint-Arnaud, and Generals Canrobert and Pélissier. He served at the battles of Alma and Inkermann and in the siege and fall of Sebastopol. He was promoted General of Division 11th Jun. 1855. After the end of the Crimean War he saw service in North Africa (1857–59), Italy (1859, including the battles of Magenta and Solferino) and again in Algeria (1859–64). He became a Senator in 1864, and saw service for the last time during the Franco-Prussian War of 1870–71. He died in Paris on 24th Feb. 1883. 115

Maude, Lt. Col. George Ashley, Royal Artillery
2nd Lt., 19th Dec. 1834; Lt., 27th Mar. 1837; Capt., 1st Apr. 1846; Bt. Maj., 12th Dec. 1854; Lt. Col., 23rd Feb. 1856. Served in the campaign in the Crimea of 1854 in command of a Troop of Horse Artillery, including the battles of Alma and Balaklava (dangerously wounded, and horse shot under him), and the siege of Sebastopol. He was awarded the C.B., the Crimea Medal with three clasps, the Order of the Mejedie (5th Class) and the Turkish Crimea Medal. 10

Maunsell, Capt. Edward Beauchamp, 39th Regiment. 64

Maxse, Commander Frederick Augustus. 68

McClellan, Gen. George Brinton, U.S. Army
The most controversial figure of the American Civil War, relieved of his command
of the Army of the Potomac in 1862 for his failure to prosecute the war aggressively,
he nevertheless achieved the rank of General-in-Chief of the Armies of the United
States in 1864. He was Democratic Nominee for President of the United States in
1864, Chief Engineer of the New York City Department of Docks 1868–72,
President of the Atlantic and Great Western Railroad 1872–78 and Governor of
New Jersey from 1878–81. He visited the Crimea as an observer, and his observations were published in 1857. He died in 1885. 87f

McDougall, Gen. Sir Patrick Leonard, K.C.M.G.
Born, 1819; 2nd Lt., 13th Feb. 1836; Lt., 11th May, 1839; Capt., 7th Jun. 1844;
Maj., 9th Feb. 1849; Bt. Lt. Col., 17th Jul. 1855; Col., 17th Jul. 1858; Maj. Gen.,
6th Mar. 1868; Lt. Gen., 1st Oct. 1877; Local rank of General Commanding the
Forces in Canada, 1878; Col., 2nd West India Regiment, 21st Dec. 1881; General,
1st Oct. 1883; Col., Leinster Regiment, 26th Aug. 1891. Commandant of the Staff
College, 1854–1861; employed 'on particular service' in the Crimea, acting on the
Quarter Master General's Staff to the Kertch Expedition, for which he received the
Crimea Medal with clasp for Sebastopol, and the Turkish Crimea Medal. Sir Patrick
married one of Sir William Napier's daughters, hence Fred Dallas' acquaintance
with him. 61, 70, 75

MacMahon, General of Division Marie Edme Patrice Maurice, Duc de Magenta
Born 13th Jul. 1808; commissioned in the French Army, 1827; served extensively in Algeria, and achieved the rank of General of Division by 1852; arrived
in the Crimea, 18th Aug. 1855, and assumed the command of Canrobert's former division, the First of the Second Corps, two days later. During the assault of
8th Sep. 1855, his division was tasked to assault the Malakoff. It was his division's success in taking and holding the Malakoff despite repeated Russian
attempts during the remainder of the day to recapture it that led to the evacuation of Sebastopol the following day. Further distinguished himself in the Italian
Campaign of 1859 as the victor of Magenta. Appointed Governor-General of
Algeria, 1864; commanded the I Army Corps during the Franco-Prussian War of
1870–71; wounded and defeated at the Battle of Wörth. Appointed to the command of the Versailles Army, which defeated the Communards in May 1871.
Elected President of the Republic on 24th May, 1873, and resigned on 28th Jan.
1879. He died on 17th Oct. 1893. 88, 98

McMurdo, Col. William Montagu Scott, C.B.
Ens., 1st Jul. 1837; Lt., 5th Jan. 1841; Capt., 7th Jul. 1843; Bt. Maj., 18th Feb.
1848; Bt. Lt. Col., 21st Oct. 1853; local rank of Col., 28th Nov. 1854; Maj., 12th
Oct. 1855; Col. Commandant, Military Train, 1st Apr. 1857. Served as Assistant
Quarter Master General of the Army under Sir Charles Napier during the campaign

Mordecai, Maj. Alfred, U. S. Army
Graduated first in his class at the U.S. Military Academy, West Point, 1819; commissioned 2nd Lt., U.S. Army Corps of Engineers, 1819; served in the Mexican War, 1846–48; and as an observer in the Crimean War, 1855–56. His report was published in 1860. Mordecai was indeed an 'Old Clo'' in Dallas' terms, and was the subject of a motivational book for young Jews, *The Uncommon Soldier*, published in America in 1959. **87**

Morris, Louis Michel, General of Division
General of Division, 22nd Dec. 1851. Assigned to command the Cavalry Division of the Army of the Orient in March 1854, and remained in command of a reorganised cavalry division which was constituted in May 1855, assigned to the First Corps. Served at the battles of Balaklava, Inkermann and the Chernaya, and in the siege and fall of Sebastopol. **88**

La Motte de la Motte Rouge, Joseph Edouard, General of Division
Born 1804; entered St.-Cyr, 1815; commissioned, 1822; promoted General of Brigade as a result of his support for the coup of 1851. Commanded a Brigade of the Siege Corps at the siege of Sebastopol from Oct. 1854 until 26th May, 1855, when he was promoted and assigned to command the 5th Division of the Second Corps. His division was charged with responsibility for the defence of the Mamelon Vert and during the assault of 8th Sep. 1855, it was tasked to assault the curtain wall between the Malakoff and the Small Redan. Motte Rouge and his two brigade commanders, General Charles Bourbaki, and Col Joseph Picard of the 91st of the Line, were all wounded in this effort. Motte Rouge remained in the Crimea until May 13, 1856 when he embarked for France with his staff. Commanded a Division in Italy in 1859 (wounded at Magenta), and a Corps in the Franco-Prussian War of 1870–71. He died on 29th Jan. 1883. **112**

Munro, Lt. Col. William, 39th Regiment. **89**

Napier, Lt. Gen. Sir William Francis Patrick, K.C.B.
1785–1860; author of the definitive *History of the War in the Peninsula* and friend of the Dallas family. **10, 13, 39, 57, 66**

Napoleon III, Emperor of the French
Born 20th Apr. 1808; spent the majority of his adult life in prison or in exile; was elected President of the Republic in 1848, dissolved the Constitution in 1851, and assumed the title of Emperor in 1852. His enthusiasm for the Crimean War was based in part on his desire to emulate his uncle, the first Napoleon, and it was with difficulty that he was persuaded not to meddle in the affairs of his commanders in the Crimea. He oversaw the French involvement in the Second China War (1857–60) and the Austrian war of 1859, and declared war on Prussia in 1870, taking personal command of the French Army in the field. France lost the war of 1870–71, and Napoleon III returned to exile, dying at Chiselhurst in Kent, on 9th Jan. 1873. **69, 74, 115**

and in the Danubian Principalities in 1853–4. He landed in the Crimea in Feb. 1855, and took command at Eupatoria, with mostly Turkish troops, where he was highly successful in its defence against superior Russian forces. In 1861 he again pacified Bosnia and Herzegovina, and overran Montenegro in 1862. He died on 18th Apr. 1871. **43, 44, 46, 47, 63, 97, 101, 103**

Omnium, Jacob – see Higgins

Orloff, Prince Count Alexei Theodorovich
Born in 1786; commissioned 1804, served at Austerlitz, in Prussia, and in the rest of the campaigns of the Napoleonic Wars (wounded seven times at Borodino). Accompanied Nicholas I in the field during the Russo-Turkish War of 1828–29. Head of the Corps of Gendarmes and the 3rd Section of His Imperial Majesty's Own Chancellery (i.e., the secret police) from 1844. Was received by Napoleon III in Paris in 1856 in connection with the conclusion of the Crimean War. He died in 1861. **99f**

Osten-Sacken, Gen. Count Dmitri Yerofeyevitch
Born 1789; fought against the French in the Napoleonic War and with distinction in the wars with Persia (1826–7) and Turkey (1828–9); also in the suppression of the uprisings in Poland (1831) and Vienna (1848). Organised the defence of Odessa against allied bombardment in April 1854 and took command of Sebastopol in February 1855, temporarily succeeding Prince Mentschikov until Gorschakov assumed overall command of the Crimean army. Made Count after his retirement in 1856. He died in 1881. **64, 67**

Oxenden, Brevet Maj. Charles Vernon, 1st Rifle Brigade. **134**

Paget, Gen. Lord George Augustus Frederick
Born, 16th Mar. 1818; Cornet, 25th Jul. 1834; Lt., 1st Dec. 1837; Capt., 17th Aug. 1841; Maj., 30th Jan. 1846; Lt. Col., 29th Dec. 1846; Col., 20th Jun. 1854; Maj. Gen., 11th Nov. 1861; Col. 7th Dragoon Guards, 28th Jan. 1868; Lt. Gen., 28th Feb. 1871; Col., 4th Hussars, 1874; General, 1 Oct. 1877. Commanded 4th Light Dragoons at Alma and Balaklava; Light Cavalry Brigade at Inkermann, and the Cavalry Division for part of 1855. Was awarded the K.C.B., the Crimea medal with four clasps, the Legion of Honour (4th Class), the *Al Valore Militare*, the Order of the Mejedie (3rd Class) and the Turkish Crimea Medal. He died 30th Jun. 1880 **40, 63, 64, 104f**

Palmerston, Lord
Henry John Temple, third Viscount Palmerston, born 20th Oct. 1784; Secretary at War, 1809–28; Foreign Secretary, 1830–1841, 1846–1851; Home Secretary, 1852–55; Prime Minister, 1855–57; 1857–58, 1859–65. Died 18th Oct. 1865. One of the great statesmen of the Victorian era, famous for his bullish approach to foreign policy issues, and his general good humour. **35f**

Panmure, Lord – see Dalhousie, Lord

awarded the G.C.B., the Scinde Medal for Meeanee, the Crimea Medal with four clasps, the Legion of Honour (2nd Class), the Order of St. Maurice and St. Lazarus (Commander, 1st Class), the Order of the Mejedie (2nd Class) and the Turkish Crimea Medal. 18, 29, 59, 60, 64, 116

Piper, Capt. Robert William, 46th Regiment
Born 6th Dec. 1824; Ens., 28th May, 1842; Lt., 11th Jul. 1845; Capt., 23rd Apr. 1852; resigned by the sale of his commission, 25th Jan. 1860. Served in the Crimea from 8th Nov. 1854, including the siege and fall of Sebastopol. Was awarded the Crimea medal with one clasp, the Order of the Mejedie (5th Class) and the Turkish Crimea Medal. 116, 125

Ponsonby, Lt. Col. Henry Frederick, Grenadier Guards. 112

Raglan, Field Marshal Lord, G.C.B.
Fitzroy James Henry Somerset, first Baron Raglan; born 30th Sep. 1788; Cornet, 9th Jun. 1804; Lt., 30th May, 1805; Capt., 5th May, 1808; Maj., 9th Jun. 1811; Lt. Col., 27th Apr. 1812; Col., 28th Aug. 1815; Maj. Gen., 27th May, 1825; Col., 53rd Regiment, 19th Nov. 1830; Lt. Gen., 28th Jun. 1838; General, 20th Jun. 1854; Field Marshal, 5th Nov. 1854. Lord Raglan was for many years Aide de Camp and Military Secretary to the Duke of Wellington, and served throughout the campaigns in Spain, Portugal, France and Belgium (wounded at Busaco and at Waterloo). He served as Master-General of the Ordnance from Sep. 1852 until May, 1855, and was Colonel-in-Chief of the Royal Artillery and the Royal Engineers. He commanded the British Forces in the Invasion of the Crimea, including the battles of the Alma, Balaklava and Inkermann, and the siege of Sebastopol. His awards included the G.C.B., the Peninsular Gold Cross with five clasps, the MGS Medal with five clasps, the Waterloo Medal, and, posthumously, the Crimea Medal with four clasps, and the Turkish Crimea Medal. He died 28th Jun. 1855. 13, 14, 16, 18, 19, 20, 22, 23, 24, 27, 28, 29, 30, 32, 35, 36, 37, 38f, 49, 55, 56, 61, 62, 63, 64, 66, 68, 69, 85, 125

Ramsbottom, Lt. H. B., 97th Regiment. 22f

Read, Gen., [Wrede in the letters] Russian Army Commander of the Russian 3rd Infantry Corps, killed at the battle of the Chernaya, 18th Aug. 1855. 73

Rokeby, Gen. Lord, G.C.B.
Henry Montagu, 6th Baron Rokeby, and a Baronet, was born 2nd Feb. 1798; Ens., 21st Apr. 1814; Lt. & Capt., 12th Jun. 1823; Capt. & Lt. Col., 21st Sep. 1832; Col., 9th Nov. 1846; Maj., 28th Jun. 1850; Lt. Col., 17th Feb. 1854; Maj. Gen., 20th Jun. 1854; Col., 77th Regiment, 13th Feb. 1861; Lt. Gen., 20th Sep. 1861; General, 8th Mar. 1869; Col., Scots Guards, 13th May, 1875. Served in the campaign of 1815 with the 3rd Guards, and was present at Quatre Bras and Waterloo; served in the Crimean War commanding the 1st Division, including the siege and fall of Sebastopol. He was awarded the K.C.B., the Waterloo Medal, the Crimea Medal with one clasp, the Legion of Honour (3rd Class), the *Al Valore*

Scarlett, Lt. Gen. Hon. Sir James Yorke, K.C.B.
Cornet, 26th Mar. 1818; Lt., 24th Oct. 1821; Capt., 9th Jun. 1825; Maj., 11th Jun. 1830; Lt. Col., 3rd Jul. 1840; Col., 11th Nov. 1851; Maj. Gen., 12th Dec. 1854; Col., 5th Dragoon Guards, 3rd Aug. 1860; Lt. Gen., 9th Nov. 1862. Commanded the Heavy Cavalry Brigade, and later the Cavalry Division, in the Crimea, including the battles of Balaklava, Inkermann and the Chernaya and the siege and fall of Sebastopol. He was awarded the K.C.B., the Crimea Medal with three clasps, the Legion of Honour (3rd Class), the *Al Valore Militare*, the Order of the Mejedie (2nd Class) and the Turkish Crimea Medal. 10f, 88

Sefton, Lt. William P., Earl of, Grenadier Guards. 129

Seymour, Lt. Col. Charles Francis, Scots Fusilier Guards
Ens. & Lt., 5th Jun. 1835; Lt. & Capt., 23rd Nov. 1838; Capt. & Lt. Col., 1st Aug. 1848. He served on Sir George Cathcart's staff in the Kaffir Wars of 1842–3 and 1846–7, and in the Crimean War, including the battles of the Alma, Balaklava and Inkermann, where he met his end. 1f, 11, 12, 13, 14

Shadforth, Lt. Col. Thomas, 57th Regiment. 58

Shervinton, Capt. Charles Robert, 46th Regiment, Land Transport Corps, Military Train and Commissariat & Transport Corps
Born, 26th Sep. 1823; Ens., 46th Regiment, 20th May, 1842; Lt., 6th Jul. 1845; Capt., 22nd Sep. 1854; Bt. Maj., 6th Jun. 1856; Bde. Maj., Military Train, 3rd Mar. 1857; Bt. Lt. Col., 1st Jan. 1868; Assistant Commissary General, 1st Jan. 1870. He sailed for the Crimea with the advance party, landing on 14th Sep. 1854 at Calamita Bay, and served throughout the Crimean War, including the battles of the Alma, Balaklava and Inkermann, and the siege and fall of Sebastopol. He was appointed to the command of the 1st Battalion, the Land Transport Corps in 1856. He was awarded the Crimea Medal with four clasps, the Order of the Mejedie (5th Class) and the Turkish Crimea Medal. 25, 116, 125

Simpson, Gen. Sir James, G.C.B.
Ens., 3rd Apr. 1811; Lt. & Capt., 25th Dec. 1813; Capt. & Lt. Col., 28th Apr. 1825; Col., 28th Jun. 1838; Maj. Gen., 11th Nov. 1851; Lt. Gen., 29th Jun. 1855; Col., 87th Regiment, 29th Jun. 1855; General, 8th Sep. 1855. Served in the Peninsula from May 1812 to May 1813, and in the campaign of 1815, being severely wounded at Quatre Bras. He was second-in-command to Sir Charles Napier in his campaign of 1845, served in the Crimea, 1855-56, as Chief of the Staff, and subsequently Commander-in-Chief, including the siege and fall of Sebastopol. He was awarded the G.C.B., the Waterloo Medal, the Crimea Medal with clasp for Sebastopol, the Legion of Honour (1st Class), the Military Order of Savoy (1st Class), the Order of the Mejedie (1st Class) and the Turkish Crimea Medal. 38, 61, 62, 63, 66, 75, 81, 82, 84, 85, 89, 90, 91, 93, 113, 119

Smith, Brevet Lt. Col. Hugh, 3rd Regiment. 1f, 47, 135

Swire, Capt. Roger, 17th Regiment. 86

Swyny, Lt. Col. Exham Schomberg Turner, 63rd Regiment
Ens., 1st Oct. 1829; Lt., 17th Oct. 1833; Capt., 8th Aug. 1838; Maj., 22nd Oct. 1847; Lt. Col., 23rd Dec. 1853. Commanded the 63rd Regiment at the battles of Alma, Balaklava and Inkermann, where he fell in action. He was posthumously awarded the Crimea medal with four clasps and the Turkish Crimea Medal. 11, 12

Talon, Vicomte. 119f, 122, 123

Thesiger, Brevet Maj. Frederick Augustus, Grenadier Guards. 92

Todleben, Gen. Francis Edward
Born 1818; Russian general and military engineer; distinguished himself in the Danubian Principalities, 1853–54, and devised and conducted the defence of Sebastopol, 1854–55. Commanded the besieging forces at Plevna, 1877–78, and captured that city. He died in Germany in 1884, and was buried in Sebastopol. 64, 95

Torrens, Maj. Gen. Sir Arthur Wellesley; K.C.B.
Lt., 14th Apr. 1825; Capt., 12th Jun. 1830; Lt. Col., 11th Sep. 1840; Col., 11th Nov. 1851; Maj. Gen., 12th Dec. 1854. Appointed to the command of the 2nd Brigade of the Fourth Division in the Crimean War, served at the battles of Alma, Balaklava and Inkermann, and in the siege of Sebastopol. He was severely wounded at Inkermann, and died in Paris, where he had been sent as Military Commissioner, in Aug. 1855. He was awarded the K.C.B., the Crimea Medal with four clasps, and the Turkish Crimea Medal. 1f, 7f, 11, 12, 13, 14

Trollope, Gen. Sir Charles, K.C.B.
Ens., 19th Nov. 1825; Lt., 10th Oct. 1826; Capt., 23rd Aug. 1831; Maj., 16th Jun. 1843; Lt. Col., 20th Nov. 1846; Col., 20th Jun. 1854; Brig. Gen., 31st Jul. 1855; Maj. Gen., 20th Sep. 1861; Col., 53rd Regiment, 27th Dec. 1868. Lt. Gen., 24th Feb. 1871; General, 1st Oct. 1877. Served in the Crimea from 10th Nov. 1854, firstly as commander of 1st Brigade, Second Division, and subsequently as commander (with local rank of Brig. Gen.) of 2nd Brigade, Third Division. He received the K.C.B., the Crimea medal with one clasp, the Legion of Honour (4th Class), the *Al Valore Militare*, the Order of the Mejedie (3rd Class) and the Turkish Crimea Medal. 69

Tryon, Lt. Henry, Rifle Brigade
2nd Lt., 2nd Jul. 1847; Lt., 12th Oct. 1852; killed in action in the Crimea, 20th Nov. 1854. 14, 36

Vesey, Maj. Arthur George, 46th Regiment
Born, Nov. 1819; Ens., 29th May, 1835; Lt., 25th Aug. 1837; Capt., 22nd Jul. 1842; Bt. Maj., 20th Jun. 1854; Maj., 29th Dec. 1854; Lt. Col., 31st Aug. 1858; Col., 31st Aug. 1863. Landed in the Crimea on 8th Nov. 1854, and served at the siege and fall of Sebastopol. He was awarded the Crimea Medal with one clasp, the Order of the Mejedie (5th Class) and the Turkish Crimea Medal. He died in 1868. 25, 27

Veselitskii [Vassilefsky and other variations also used], Gen. Sergei Gavrilovich, Russian Army
Born 1804; commissioned, 1822; Maj. Gen., 1850. As a brigade commander (1st Brigade, 5th Infantry Division), he was distinguished by his strict sense of duty and was energetic in investigating malfeasance in commissariat matters. Veselitskii's zeal in uncovering the practice of adding ashes to the flour for soldiers' bread supposedly led to his retirement by General Field-Marshal Paskevich, but Gorchakov recognised his qualities and recalled him to serve as a divisional commander. He was wounded in early 1854 during the crossing of the Danube at Brailov, for which he was awarded a gold sword for bravery. He was awarded the Order of St. Stanislas 1st Class for his actions at the siege of Silistria in May of 1854, when his position was to carry out special assignments for the commander-in-chief of the 3rd, 4th and 5th Infantry Corps (Gortchakoff). He held the same position later in 1854 under Gorchakov when that general assumed command of the Southern Army. In 1855, Veselitskii was acting commander of the 17th Infantry Division. After the war, he commanded the 6th Infantry Division; he died in 1866. **99f, 124, 125, 127**

Victoria, Her Majesty Queen
Born 24th May, 1819; Queen, 20th Jun. 1837; Empress of India, 1876; died 22nd Jan. 1901. Arguably the greatest Monarch in British history, her name came to symbolise the era of empire, of industrial growth, and of Britain's pre-eminent position in the world. **74, 104, 116**

Vinoy, Joseph Baptiste, General of Division
Commanded the 2nd Brigade of the French First Division in the Crimea, including the battles of the Alma and Balaklava, and the assault on the Malakhov of 8th Sep. 1855. Vinoy was appointed to the command of a Division on 10th Oct. 1855. **121**

Vivian, Gen. Sir Robert John Hussey, G.C.B.
Born 1802; Ens., 12th Jun. 1819; Lt., 13th Jun. 1819; Capt., 1st Aug. 1825; Maj., 9th Dec. 1836; Lt. Col., 15th Oct. 1841; Col., 15th Sep. 1851; Maj. Gen., 28th Nov. 1854; Col., 102nd Regiment, 30th Sep. 1862; Lt. Gen., 24th Oct. 1862; General, 22nd Nov. 1870; retired from the service, 1877. Served throughout the Burma War of 1824–26, including the assault and capture of Rangoon. In 1855 he became a director of the Honourable East India Company, and on 25th May he was appointed Local Lt. Gen. commanding the Turkish Contingent. The Contingent served in the Crimean War, 1855–56, including the occupation of Kertch. Sir Robert was awarded the G.C.B., the Army of India Medal with clasp for Ava, the Order of the Mejedie (1st Class) and the Turkish Crimea Medal. He died on 3rd May 1887. **101**

Waldy, Capt. Alfred Henry, 46th Regiment
Born, 28th Jan. 1827; Ens., 14th Dec. 1849; Lt., 1st Apr. 1853; Capt., 29th Dec. 1854; Instructor of Musketry, 15th Depot Battalion, 25th Nov. 1861; retired from the service by the sale of his commission, 15th Nov. 1864. Landed in the Crimea on 8th Nov. 1854, served at the siege and fall of Sebastopol. Capt. Waldy was awarded the Crimea Medal with clasp for Sebastopol and the Turkish Crimea Medal. **25f, 27**

Warre, Gen. Sir Henry James, K.C.B., 57th Regiment
Ens., 3rd Feb. 1837; Lt., 1st Jun. 1841; Capt., 8th Jan. 1847; Maj., 7th Nov. 1854;
Lt. Col., 9th Mar. 1855; Col., 9th Mar. 1858; Maj. Gen., 6th Mar. 1868; Lt. Gen.,
1st Oct. 1877; Col., 90th Regiment, 9th Oct. 1880; General, 26th Dec. 1880.
Served at the siege of Sebastopol from Mar. 1855, commanding the 57th Regiment
after the death of Col. Shadforth, including the assaults of 18th Jun. and 8th Sep.
and the expedition to Kinburn; commanded the 57th in the Indian Mutiny; also in
the Maori Wars of 1861-66 (Mentioned in Despatches; pension for distinguished
conduct). General Warre was a noted artist, and his sketches of the Crimea were
published shortly after the end of the war. He received the K.C.B., the Crimea
medal with one clasp, the New Zealand Medal, the Order of the Mejedie (5th Class)
and the Turkish Crimea Medal. 113

Webb, Capt. Augustus Frederick Cavendish, 17th Lancers. 10

Westmorland, Earl of, C.B. [Lord Burghersh in the Letters]
Francis William Henry Fane, 12th Earl of Westmorland, was born 19th Nov. 1825,
the third son of the 11th Earl. He became Lord Burghersh on the deaths of his elder
brothers. Ens., 24th Feb. 1843; Lt., 26th Jul. 1844; Capt., 1st Aug. 1848; Bt. Maj.,
7th Jun. 1849; Maj., 22nd Apr. 1853; Brevet Lt. Col., 20th Jun. 1854; Capt. & Lt.
Col., 12th Dec. 1854; Col., 11th Jan. 1860. Lord Burghersh served in the Punjab
Campaign of 1848-9 and as ADC to Lord Raglan, both during the latter's time as
Master-General of the Ordnance and in the Crimea, conveying the despatches after
the battle of the Alma to England. He returned to the Crimea before the fall of
Sebastopol and was awarded the C.B., the Punjab Medal with clasp for Goojerat, the
Crimea medal with clasps for Alma and Sebastopol, the Legion of Honour (5th Class),
the Order of the Mejedie (5th Class) and the Turkish medal. He succeeded to the title
of Earl of Westmorland on the death of his father in 1857, and died in 1891. 36

Wetherall, Col. Sir Edward Robert, C.B., K.C.S.I.
Ens., 27th Jun. 1834; Lt., 22nd Aug. 1837; Capt., 19th Dec. 1845; Maj., 12th Dec.
1854; Lt. Col., 17th Jul. 1855; Col., 11th Dec. 1855. Served in Canada during the
disturbances of 1837-39, and in the Crimea, as Assistant Quarter Master General,
including the battles of Alma, Balaklava and Inkermann, and the siege and fall of
Sebastopol; served at Kertch as Deputy Quarter Master General of the Turkish
Contingent, was subsequently Director-General of the Land Transport Corps in the
Crimea; Deputy Quarter Master General to the Forces in China in 1857; Chief of
Staff to the Central India Field Force during the Mutiny (Mentioned in Despatches,
horse shot under him); commander of the South Oudh Field Force, 1858. He was
awarded the C.B., the K.C.S.I., the Crimea Medal with four clasps, the Indian
Mutiny Medal with one clasp, the Legion of Honour (5th Class), the Order of the
Mejedie (3rd Class) and the Turkish Crimea Medal. 32, 91, 100, 101, 105

Whyte-Melville, Maj. George John
Born 1821; Ens., 93rd Regiment, 19th Jul. 1839; Ens. & Lt., Coldstream Guards,
11th Sep. 1840; Lt. & Cap.t, 29th Dec. 1846; retired from the Army in 1849, but

joined the Turkish Contingent in 1855. Well known as the author of such popular songs as *Drink Puppy Drink* and *The Tarpaulin Jacket* and of a number of novels. He died in 1878. 26

Wilbraham, Col. R., C.B. 86

Windham, Lt. Gen. Sir Charles Ash, K.C.B.
Ens. & Lt., 30th Dec. 1826; Lt. & Capt., 31st May, 1833; Bt. Maj., 9th Nov. 1846; Capt. & Lt. Col., 29th Dec. 1846; Col., 20th Jun. 1854; Maj. Gen., 8th Sep. 1855; Col., 46th Regiment, 17th Jun. 1861; Lt. Gen., 5th Feb. 1863. Served in the Canadian Rebellion from 1838–42; in the Crimea as Assistant Quarter Master General to the 4th Division, subsequently as Brig. Gen. commanding the 2nd Brigade, Second Division, as Maj. Gen. commanding Fourth Division, and latterly as Chief of the Staff of the Army. He was present at the battles of Alma, Balaklava and Inkermann, and at the siege and fall of Sebastopol, distinguishing himself on 8th Sep. 1855 in command of the storming party of the Second Division. He served in the Indian Mutiny of 1857–8 as a Divisional commander, but with limited success. He was awarded the K.C.B., the Crimea Medal with four clasps, the Indian Mutiny Medal, the Legion of Honour (3rd Class), the Military Order of Savoy (Commander, 1st Class), the Order of the Mejedie (2nd Class) and the Turkish Crimea Medal. He died on the 3rd Feb. 1870. 1f, 2, 10f, 20, 23f, 36, 47, 57, 68, 78, 84, 85, 86, 89, 91, 94, 97, 100, 101, 103, 104, 105, 106, 109, 111, 113, 115, 125, 128, 129f, 133

Wolseley, Rt. Hon. Field Marshal Viscount, P.C., K.P., G.C.B., G.C.M.G., O.M., D.C.L., LL.D.
Garnet Joseph Wolseley, First Viscount Wolseley and First Baron Wolseley of Cairo and Wolseley, born 4th Jun. 1833; Ens., 80th Regiment, 12th Mar. 1852; Lt., 90th Regiment, 16th May, 1853; Capt., 26th Jan. 1855; Maj., 24th Mar. 1858; Lt. Col., 26th Apr. 1859; Col., 5th Jun. 1865; Maj. Gen., 6th Mar. 1868; Lt. Gen., 25th Mar. 1878; General, 18th Nov. 1882; Field Marshal, 26th May, 1894; Colonel in Chief, Royal Irish Regiment, 20th Jul. 1898. He saw service all over the globe, from Burma in 1852 to the Sudan in 1885, and was Commander in Chief of the British Army from 1895–1900 – he is remembered as much for his reforms of the British Army as for his many successful battles. He died in 1913. 75

Wombwell, Lt. Gen. Arthur
Born 17th May, 1822; Ens., 46th Regiment, 5th Apr. 1839; Lt., 29th Oct. 1841; Capt., 8th May, 1846; Bt. Maj., 2nd Nov. 1855; Maj., 24th Feb. 1857; Lt. Col., 22nd Jun. 1864; Col., 1st Aug. 1870; Maj. Gen., 1st Oct. 1881; Lt. Gen., 1st Oct. 1881. He landed in the Crimea with the main body of the regiment, on 8th Nov. 1854, and served at the siege and fall of Sebastopol. He was awarded the Crimea Medal with clasp for Sebastopol, the Order of the Mejedie (5th Class) and the Turkish Crimea Medal. He was Fred Dallas's closest friend and 'constant pardner' in the Crimea. 13, 14, 15, 17, 20, 23, 24, 26, 30, 32, 33, 38, 40, 41, 49, 53, 54, 57, 61, 65, 69f, 73, 81, 82, 92, 97